MAN UP

Boys, Men and Breaking the Male Rules

Rebecca Asher

Harvill Secker
LONDON

1 3 5 7 9 10 8 6 4 2

Harvill Secker, an imprint of Vintage,
20 Vauxhall Bridge Road,
London SW1V 2SA

Harvill Secker is part of the Penguin Random House group of companies whose
addresses can be found at global.penguinrandomhouse.com

This book is a work of non-fiction. In some cases names of people and places
and the detail of events have been changed solely to protect the privacy of others.

 Penguin
Random House
UK

Rebecca Asher has asserted her right to be identified as the author of this Work
in accordance with the Copyright, Designs and Patents Act 1988

First published by Harvill Secker in 2016

penguin.co.uk/vintage

A CIP catalogue record for this book is available from the British Library

ISBN 9781910701065

Typeset in India by Thomson Digital Pvt Ltd, Noida, Delhi
Printed and bound in Great Britain by Clays Ltd, St Ives PLC

Penguin Random House is committed to a sustainable future for our business,
our readers and our planet. This book is made from Forest Stewardship
Council® certified paper.

To Hal and Erica
brother, sister, equals

CONTENTS

Introduction: About the Boys   1

1. TOUGH START: Early Boyhood

You can't tell a book by its cover (or a child by its sex)   15
'Gender equality' is an oxymoron   17
Hard-wiring and other hocus-pocus   18
'I was amazed at how quickly he became a boy'   25
Let's focus on what we can change   26
Boys and their toys   28
An emotional education   34
'Busy, filthy, sweaty boys'   37
Screen time   42
Seizing the initiative   45

2. FROM INDULGENT SMILE TO CURLED LIP: Schooldays

Playground politics   49
Sports scores   56
What should parents do?   58
'A man should look like a boss'   60
That's so gay   62
'Looking good is pretty key'   67
Is there a 'boy crisis' in the classroom?   71
Are boys born with a dislike of books?   72
Are boys born badly behaved?   75
'Unconditional positive regard'   81

3. OPPOSITES ATTACK: Boys vs. Girls

A show of strength   89
Violence and control   90
The porn panic   95
'The pussy of the gang'   107
One of the lads   109

'How do I want my kids to find out about sex?' 114
Get real 117
Making change happen 119

4. **HERE COMES TROUBLE: Angry Young Men**

Falling from favour 125
'You are The Man' 127
'If you are not a bad boy … you are a victim' 129
Male role models – a miracle cure? 136
Boys behind bars 139
Crime – a male problem 144
Intimate terrorism 148
The fight to be free 155

5. **GREATER GAINS: Family Men**

In the lead 165
'I want to live a full life for my kids' 167
Involved fatherhood – why care? 171
'Parental Leave Dad!' 173
Mystical motherhood 185
Missing men 188
'Daddy duty' 193
The new pioneers 195

6. **LONE MALES: Friends, Love and Later Life**

What do men want from friendship? 201
Looming loneliness 203
'As a bloke, I need clubs' 205
Family are the new friends 207
Low-income loneliness 210
Lonely old men 211
The strong man myth 213
The man killer 215
'It brings us all together' 222

Conclusion: Save the Male 227

Notes 243
Acknowledgements 279
Index 281

INTRODUCTION
About the Boys

'Boys are like dogs.' The first time I heard this said I was taken aback. Another mother had made the comment, as we watched our sons run around in the park. 'Both have boundless energy and bottomless appetites,' she explained. At the time I wondered how anyone could compare our complex, enchanting little boys to dogs. But since then I have heard the same remark made on many more occasions. It's a cliché but it's true, I'm told. Boys are exhausting but their needs are simple. A run outside and a hearty meal and you'll have them eating out of your hands.

This one-dimensional, one-size-fits-all view of boys crops up frequently. Dropping in to a local community centre recently, I spotted a display of photos from a day trip. It included an image of a toddler careering towards the camera, delightedly showing off his mud-covered hands. 'Jayden is a typical boy and loves running around and getting mucky!' ran the description below. Like the dog analogy, this is a celebration of a child's spirit and energy. But both also capture something more about society's attitude towards boys: there is a 'typical boy' and he is boisterous, messy and easily pleased. His feelings do not run deep. His interests are basic and superficial.

This view of male nature does not change as boys age. In fact, it becomes more embedded. Scan most card or gift selections 'for men' in a shop and certain themes crop up repeatedly: beer, football, cars, DIY, farting. Apparently, these are men's favoured pastimes. The more chichi retailers may extend the choice to wine paraphernalia or cuff-links. Why does our society hold this shallow and colourless image of men? Why do men and women buy this stuff for their brothers, fathers, partners, friends and sons? Yet 'boys are like dogs' is said with a hint of self-congratulation and pride by parents: 'Look at the fine specimen of manhood I have produced!' Boys are best. And so the more demonstratively boyish they can be, the better. Noise, action and thick-skinned swagger are encouraged. Boys are top dog.

As I watch the boys around me grow up, I see them turn from impetuous, full-feeling sprites into more wary, self-conscious little men. Some of this is simply socialisation. They are finding their place in the world. But it goes beyond that. They are beginning to adopt the characteristics they have learned are needed to get along as a boy: stoicism, one-upmanship and superiority over girls. Boys become aware of the male rules from a very young age, and so they change, adapting their behaviour to fit the mould. Among many adult men, you can see the full-blown version, with its brittle defensiveness, awkwardness and anxiety over status.

In the 1970s, American social scientists came up with four rules that define Western masculinity: 'No Sissy Stuff', be a 'Big Wheel', be a 'Sturdy Oak' and 'Give 'Em Hell'.[1] Five decades later, these requirements remain instantly recognisable markers of manliness. Men still, on the whole, avoid shows of emotion and femininity; they want to be powerful, tough and to call the shots. Nowadays it is boiled down to one simple phrase: 'man up'. In this book, I set out to investigate why the norms of male behaviour are so restrictive and what can be done to liberate boys and men from them.

When I talk to men about what being a man means to them, the response is grimly familiar. 'Emotional distance, machismo, work, offices, pecking orders,' says Ian, a father-of-two I interviewed as part of my research. I quiz a teenage visitor to our house: 'Having a six-pack, drinking loads of beer, wooing lots of women,' he tells me, framing the latter delicately so as not to offend his middle-aged inquisitor. 'The only time I feel like a proper bloke is when I'm at a football match,' remarks Lee, another interviewee. He laughs as he says it, but it is interesting that for him a 'proper bloke' is distinct from other men and that qualifying as one hangs on such a stereotypically male pastime. Despite some loosening up of social norms in recent decades, we are not as unbuttoned as we like to think. As a society we still largely expect boys and men to behave in particular ways and to adhere to rigid codes. Some men will reject these outright and others will quibble about the details, yet time and again men will say they feel under pressure to comply. Even those who reject the pressure to 'man up' define their identities in opposition to its imperatives. The stereotypes encapsulated in the male rules continue to dominate our social horizons: they have remarkable sticking power. This is the 'masculine mystique' identified by the feminist writer Betty Friedan in an epilogue to the tenth anniversary edition of *The Feminine Mystique*, and it still exists for men today.[2]

The pervasive power of the 'masculine mystique' feeds into every aspect of life and all its stages, and there is clear evidence of its harmful effect. Boys are four times more likely than girls to have behavioural, emotional or social difficulties[3] and they are three times as likely to be temporarily excluded from school.[4] Ninety-five per cent of prisoners are male,[5] as are three-quarters of suicides.[6] These are mercifully minority outcomes for boys and men but, while every case is different and some lives are far more difficult than others, they are each nonetheless symptoms of a deeper malaise.

Our beliefs about manhood shape the way in which we treat young boys from the very start of their lives, encouraging (often unconsciously) what we imagine to be natural and appropriate masculine behaviour, just as we encourage supposedly feminine behaviour in girls. The post-hippy equality sensibility that promoted a gender-neutral childhood in the 1970s and 1980s – all unisex dungarees and primary-colour building blocks – has given way to the grip of biological determinism. Despite the lack of good evidence, many in the world of science, the media and business now cast boys as naturally rowdy and unfeeling. Giving 'em hell and avoiding sissy stuff is simply the way they are: it's not sexism, it's science. In just the same way that we box girls into the ornamental, compliant and nurturing corner, we trammel boys into particular ways of being too.

While writing this book, I have become more aware of the ways I stereotype my own son and daughter, such as the underlying assumptions I make about their friendship groups and the activities they will be interested in. In the majority of families this stereotyping takes place in a domestic environment where mothers do the bulk of the childcare and fathers do the bulk of the earning. Attitudes to roles within families are stubbornly conservative and the different treatment of the sexes is constantly reinforced at home. Yet, whereas the life-long effects of stereotyping on girls are apparent and are actively monitored – eating disorders, sexual harassment, domestic inequalities, the motherhood earnings penalty, lack of career progression, and so on – the future effect on boys is less well understood. It manifests itself in a lack of close friendships, sexist attitudes towards women and family life, workplace stress, experience of violence and poorer health. It is these themes and the expectations that we set down for boys and men that I will explore in the following chapters.

Yet despite all that flows from notions of what it is to be a man, explorations of the issue have been curiously thin on the ground. Men hide in plain sight. They are regarded as neutral, the default. There have been occasional eruptions of self-analysis since the 1970s. 1990 saw the publication in the USA of Robert Bly's *Iron John*, the bible of the mythopoetic men's movement, in which he encouraged men to leave behind corporate workplaces and feminised domestic spaces and head to the woods for a dose of physical labour, storytelling and male bonding. His call for men to release their 'Zeus energy' (which Bly defined as 'male authority accepted for the sake of the community') remained on the *New York Times* bestseller list for over a year.[7] Other books exploring what it is to be a man were published around the same time: Martin Amis reviewed a clutch of them in the *London Review of Books*.[8] Many came out of the US but the UK produced its share too, along with the 'anti-sexist' men's magazine *Achilles Heel*, 'a forum for discussion of men and masculinity' produced by the Changing Men Publishing Collective. Much of this writing looked at what was next for men at a time when women's roles were shifting. But the flurry passed and the self-examination stalled, and it is only in the past few years that there have been signs of renewed interest in the need to address the pressures that men face. A great deal of this recent debate has focused on a supposed 'crisis in masculinity'. Cries of a masculinity crisis have rung out at various points throughout history, whether prompted by concern about the undernourished cannon-fodder fighting for Britain in the Boer War or present-day gang-related deaths. It paints a picture of all men, as a homogeneous mass, racked by self-doubt or causing havoc when the reality is far more varied and nuanced than that. Often these theoretical crisis-ridden males are posited in relation to equally theoretical self-assured females, creating the impression that if one sex is up the other must be down. Of course, it is not credible to argue that men as a group are worse off than women: on measures of earnings, power and authority within our society men have the advantage over women. But men are still restricted by the straitjacket of the male stereotype. It is detrimental to their emotional well-being, their friendships and relationships with girls and women, and their ability to express their full humanity. And those men who are socially excluded, unqualified and uncared for fare much worse than their female counterparts.

I am aware that I am entering choppy waters, as a woman commenting on the state of men. Some men are adamant that their sex is fine as it is. It is astonishing that any man can look at the male-dominated statistics on educational exclusion, high alcohol consumption, dangerous driving, criminality, preventable diseases and suicide and think that the guys are all right. For others, it is not men who are the problem but women, specifically feminists who – according to men's rights activists – have been so successful at standing up for their own rights that they now call the shots, leaving men in neutered limbo. For this movement of militant, anti-feminist men, equality between the sexes would entail a rebalancing in their favour. Men's rights activists are marginal but they make quite a noise. They are active online and, in the UK, formed a political party ahead of the 2015 General Election, Justice for Men and Boys. It stood in two seats and gained 216 votes in total. Undeterred, the party intends to stand candidates again in 2020.[9]

Likewise, some feminists are wary of acknowledging the problems boys and men experience, feeling that it detracts from the task of female emancipation. But it is not a zero-sum game. Showing understanding and compassion towards the opposite sex does not reduce the likelihood of making life better for women. In fact, the very opposite is true: enabling boys and men to be more rounded and fulfilled human beings is likely to improve girls' and women's lives, as they would be surrounded by better fathers, brothers, school mates, colleagues, partners and fellow citizens. After all, the male obsession with hierarchy and domination is the bedrock of patriarchy and its oppression of women. Patriarchy is an unfashionable word, yet it is an invaluable one, describing a system that sustains men as inherently superior to women and so able to dominate them, from the mocking of all things girlish in boyhood to routine discrimination against the female workforce in adulthood. It is precisely the inter-related nature of our existence and fortunes as men and women that motivates my analysis of the male world.

As a parent who, like thousands of others in the UK, is attempting to raise my children to be decent, independent and thoughtful human beings, I am concerned about the stereotypes that my son might feel under pressure to live up to, just as I am about those that might influence my daughter. The early differentiation and opposition between the sexes is bad for everyone, with both boys and girls cut off from realising their full selves. Just as I am preoccupied by the significant cultural and economic penalties faced by girls and women, I worry about boys suppressing their emotions, switching off from school, being disrespectful towards girls, indulging in risky behaviour, and then in adult life failing to prioritise friends and family over material success and status. And I would like to live in a world that was safer because men weren't violent and antisocial. We all stand to gain if boys are freed from the male rules.

Over the course of researching and writing this book I have spoken to scores of boys and men about their experiences of living with these rules, as well as to many women about their experiences as mothers, partners and friends. In defiance of the stereotypes that they are saddled with, the boys and men spoke eloquently and eagerly. Some are struggling to cope with living within those confines; others are breaking free from them. A number are at ease with themselves and with girls and women as peers. I have spoken to schoolboys passionate about dismantling male stereotypes, young men who have left lives of criminality behind, fathers who have embraced their role within the family and men in their later years who are still forging new friendships and contributing to, and learning from, their communities. I have also spoken to campaigners and policy experts who have thought long and hard about the challenges that face modern men, as well as to individual, high-profile men who have encountered some of those challenges themselves and talked to me about what they have learned on the way. They represent a wide range of backgrounds and opinions, proof in itself that the male experience and perspective is as diverse as that for any other group.

While a stereotype of masculinity dominates our culture and is held up as the gold standard, complexity lies beneath. Conflicting ideas about masculinity can be found from one man to the next and even within individual men. In 2014, as I was beginning to think about this book, Tate Britain held an exhibition of British Folk Art:

exuberant and skilfully crafted objects and images created by artisans and others drawn from 'the masses'. Among the shop signs, banners and ship figureheads, the quilts stood out as particularly intricate and careful works. Communal quilt-making helped pass the time for servicemen in the nineteenth and early twentieth centuries. Navy men were expected to know how to repair sails and uniforms, and quilting was promoted as a leisure activity, to distract sailors from the vices of drink and gambling. The exhibition included a 1905 photograph of a group of sailors, their heads bent over sewing machines. The highlight was an exquisite, jewel-coloured quilt made from scraps of old uniform, stitched together by injured soldiers during the Crimean War. Such quilts embody the complex and contrasting nature of masculinity: these men of war passing their convalescence engaged together in the most delicate and domestic of activities.

Male ways of being continue to be multi-faceted and contradictory. This comes through in the modern framing of male culture, a series of blown-up snapshots shifting from one exaggerated construction of manhood to another. In the 1980s portraits of men revolved around the importance of work and cash, from the 'loadsamoney' lads-done-good to *Boys from the Blackstuff*'s Yosser Hughes ('gizza job') who lost his livelihood and his sense of himself as a man along with it. The same decade saw the brief appearance of the quiche-eating New Man, a trend that quickly came and went (not least because women were ambivalent about losing 'real men'). It was replaced by the reassuringly masculine New Lad (lager, *Loaded* and largin' it) of the 1990s and early noughties. He in turn was overtaken by the moisturising Metrosexual. The current decade's Lumbersexual bearded hipster is an affected and resolutely metropolitan take on the log-chopping life of the rural workman. His pumped and primped contemporary is the Spornosexual: a term coined by the writer Mark Simpson (who earlier conceived the Metrosexual) and which neatly captures this new breed of man – half sports star, half porn star and 100 per cent ripped.[10] On the face of it the Lumbersexual and Spornosexual make odd bedfellows. Yet both, in their own way, combine grit and grooming: modern men are pulled in opposite directions.

All these representations – broad sketches though they are – show a restlessness among modern men and, latterly, a desire to move away from the rules they are expected to live by. Men can now gain kudos from being geeks, book nerds or musos, as well as through the well-worn route of physical and sexual prowess or impressive earnings. Gay men in the public eye are broadly accepted and admired, including those working in ultra-masculine fields such as sport. Men are encouraged to be 'hands-on' fathers and are a common sight accompanying their children to parks, leisure centres and libraries, at weekends at least. Nonetheless, the male rules still loom large, as the research and experiences I have gathered together will show. We expect boys to be boisterous rather than bookish, we think boys and men have fewer emotional needs than girls and women and we are more supportive of fathers as main earners than as main carers. Society still cleaves to the masculine stereotype. This is certainly difficult for those men who reject it. It is also difficult for those men who try to live up to it. The rules are so rigid that it is inevitable they will find themselves wanting.

If we want boys and men to be true to themselves without loss of self-esteem, to express emotion and empathy, to be respectful towards girls and women, to contribute positively to the community, to build strong friendships and to take their family obligations as seriously as those of work, then we need to make these things happen. We cannot assume because of the small advances made that progress is inexorable. From predictions of the end of men through to Grayson Perry's insightful exploration of masculine identity by way of ceramics, there is growing recognition that the state of masculinity requires fresh assessment. As much as modern phenomena such as the rise of internet pornography, social media misogyny and the militant men's rights lobby cause concern, they also provide the impetus for change. In tandem with this, the gains made by women in education and the workplace, the desire of modern men to be involved in family life, the growth in liberal attitudes on sexuality and different ways of being, and the dynamism and demands of contemporary feminists provide fertile ground for such change to take place.

In the week I set out to write this introduction I noticed a new ad campaign on buses: the actress and equalities campaigner Ellen DeGeneres surrounded by a diverse and confident group of girls promoting a new range of clothes by Gap. GapKids x ED, states the PR blurb, is 'an apparel collection and social movement ... that encourages girls everywhere to be themselves, do what makes them happy and take pride in who they are'.[11] Although the co-opting of girls' empowerment is a corporate sales strategy, it is at least proof that this agenda is now mainstream. With these arguments firmly established, it is time to widen the focus to include the liberation of boys from the stereotyping that harms them in childhood and beyond. They too deserve to be themselves, to do what makes them happy and to take pride in who they are.

In their different ways, the people I have interviewed for this book point to how we might re-imagine life for boys and men. Those who have been able to shrug off the masculine mantle have experienced profound benefits. They have realised that the male rules do not express who they are. They do not have to live by them, nor do the other people in their lives have to put up with them doing so. These men have championed equality, left gangs, mentored other men, thrown themselves into the lives of their families and communities. They have opened themselves up to nurturing others and they in turn are nurtured as a consequence. They have shown what boys and men can become when they are free to be who they want to be.

1. TOUGH START
Early Boyhood

You can't tell a book by its cover (or a child by its sex)

'I was quite upset when I was told I was having a boy,' says Natalie, who is mother to an eight-year-old son and a five-year-old daughter. During our conversation it is clear that Natalie is alive to the perils of stereotypes. She has had to face up to her own deep-rooted assumptions since becoming a parent. 'I had lots of sexist ideas about what a son would be like. I thought he wouldn't be as loving as a daughter, that he wouldn't be interested in talking and that he would be incapable of sitting still. And now I realise that he does all of these things. I am slightly surprised. And I feel a bit bad about that!'

Natalie is far from alone in thinking that a child's sex predicts its character. During my two pregnancies, the question I was most often asked by acquaintances was whether I was expecting a boy or a girl. I obligingly answered that I didn't know the sex the first time around (my husband and I went on to have a son) and, the second time, that it was a girl. What I really felt like saying was: 'Why does it matter? What difference does it make if we have a son or a daughter? Will we paint his bedroom blue and invest in infant football kits if it's a boy? Or buy frilly tights and some of those pointless hairbands for bald baby heads, if it's a girl?' Yet clothing and colour schemes are just the start of it. Our pre-birth expectations of a child, as shaped by its sex, go much deeper. They extend to its very personhood and the characteristics we imagine it will possess. Girls will be compliant, passive and in touch with their feelings, to the point of being a little over-emotional and intense. Boys will be assertive, domineering, active and emotionally uncomplicated.

Many parents buy in to pre-birth determinism. Mothers who know they are pregnant with a boy are more likely to describe the fetus's movements as 'strong' or 'vigorous' than those expecting a girl or those who do not know the sex.[1] Sonographers carrying out antenatal scans will describe the fetus as 'pretty' or 'handsome', or even 'just like his dad'.[2] For her book *The Gender Trap*, the American sociologist Emily Kane talked to adults about the activities they imagined engaging in with prospective children. Their thoughts were almost comically stereotypical. Men talked of being able to take sons to the match or off camping, whereas women anticipated spending quality time with their daughters in shopping malls.[3] As we will see in the next chapter, Frank, a father of two sons from Somerset, has very thoughtful views about the emotional needs of boys from his perspective as both a parent and a teacher. Yet when we spoke he was also honest about his assumptions regarding his sons' interests: 'A bit of me makes a slight presumption that boys are more likely to play a lot of sport, be into football, go surfing, get into long-distance running, be up for climbing, doing active things particularly. And then the rough-and-tumble stuff, being up for play fighting, as well as building Lego, being interested in Scalextric, all the things I've always loved.'

Emily Kane's work shows that this Boy's Own focus on male physicality often runs alongside a belief that girls will be more family orientated than boys, a view reflected in other research with prospective parents.[4] This is one of the earliest ways in which we position boys as more distant and emotionally disengaged. Adults both pre-empt the characteristics and interests a child will have, and – crucially – *not* have, according to its sex. Carys, who has a daughter in her early twenties and two teenage sons, is one of many mothers who spoke to me about their hopes for a special bond with their daughter, reasoning that daughters stay closer to their mothers in adulthood. 'I was very happy to have a girl first. I am the oldest and I was close to my mum growing up, and I thought it would be the same with my daughter.' But things don't always happen that way. As it turned out,

Carys tells me, 'It is not the case that I am closer to my daughter. She's great and I love her but we are very different.'

When I was expecting my first child a friend commented that it was probably a girl because I felt protective towards it, the logic being that if it were a boy I'd make like the Spartans and leave it to fend for itself. I found the remark baffling, but the assumption that boys will need less care crops up elsewhere too. The comedian Rob Delaney, in a witty, moving piece about having boys, explains that before he had children he had hoped for girls. 'I just thought girls would awaken the fathering instinct in me faster or more thoroughly or something … Does it follow that boys just raise themselves? No attention required?' But when his first son was born, 'I felt every molecule in my body explode, reform and realign as a capital-D Dad, whose sole purpose was to bludgeon this tiny person with love.' As Delaney says, 'It is instructive to examine your feelings very closely when you find out the gender of your child.'[5] Even before we meet our children, we make huge assumptions based on their sex. The way in which we talk about boys, and compare them to girls, gives the impression that children are born with fixed characteristics that clearly differentiate one sex from the other. Yet although children are born with a variety of nascent personality traits and aptitudes, there is little firm evidence that this is dictated by their sex.

'Gender equality' is an oxymoron

Sex is the operative word here. Sex is essential: it is dictated by chromosomes and it is apparent in our genitals and internal reproductive organs. The vast majority of people are born either of the male or of the female sex (the exception being a very small percentage who are born with disorders of sex development[6]). Gender is a social construct. It refers to the identities and roles that people have imposed upon them and which they adopt because of their sex. So, girls may learn to be caring and boys to be assertive because these are the gendered behaviours that society expects of their sex. Crucially, in a male-dominated world, gender is designed to keep men in charge: it is a power structure that maintains the patriarchal world order. The distinction between sex and gender is clear and straightforward yet the two are, often unwittingly, used interchangeably in everyday language (gender balance, a baby's gender, gender equality). But the term 'gender equality' is nonsensical – there can be no equality in a gendered world. Conflating 'sex' and 'gender' is not simply sloppy or euphemistic (why mention the lewd word 'sex' when you can use the much blander 'gender'?). It embeds the erroneous belief that gender is inherent, fixed and binary: that it stems from our sex. But who we are and who we have the capacity to be are not (and should not be) dictated by our sex. Our options are much wider than that.

Hard-wiring and other hocus-pocus

Over the past twenty years, the application of brain organisation theory to humans – that is, the notion that in the majority of cases our brains are organised as 'male' or 'female' according to our sex, and that culturally masculine and feminine qualities emerge from these male and female brains – has lent credence to home-spun beliefs about inherited sex differences. Perhaps the most famous proponent of brain organisation theory as applied to humans is Simon Baron-Cohen, Professor of Developmental Psychopathology at Cambridge University. In his popular science blockbuster *The Essential Difference*, he advanced the idea that the 'female brain' is 'hard-wired' for empathy, while the 'male brain' is 'hard-wired' for understanding and building systems – empathising–systemising (ES) theory, in short.[7] When Baron-Cohen's book first came out it captured the public imagination, lending the gloss of scientific proof to the theme of earlier self-help books in the vein of John Gray's wildly popular *Men Are from Mars, Women Are from Venus*, published in 1992.

The idea is that differences between the sexes can be traced back to fetal exposure to testosterone (the process by which male genitalia are created in the womb). Boys are born with different brains from girls as a result of the higher levels of testosterone to which they have been exposed. These differences are then played out in contrasting behaviour and abilities. Hence boys and men are more aggressive, and more adept at intellectual tasks such as mental rotation (turning objects around in the mind), while girls and women are more empathic and more able readers and writers. Yet the truth is far more complicated: there is a mass of detailed and sometimes conflicting evidence within this field and there is much still to be investigated and learned.

Over recent years brain organisation theory has been very effectively challenged by a number of respected neuroscientists, psychologists and others. Importantly, these critics do not rule out neurological differences between the sexes, caused by testosterone or otherwise: with so much yet to discover this cannot be discounted. However, they do question the evidence that, in humans, fetal testosterone guides complex and sometimes culturally shifting gendered behaviour and characteristics, pointing to significant flaws in experiment design and inconsistency in conclusions.

As the academic psychologist Cordelia Fine argues in her sparky, rigorous book *Delusions of Gender*, 'The sheer complexity of the brain lends itself beautifully to over-interpretation and precipitous conclusions.'[8] Fine painstakingly unpicks the flaws in a range of scientific experiments that claim to prove sex-linked, biological influences in the neurological and behavioural make-up of boys and girls. Both she and Lise Eliot, neuroscientist and author of *Pink Brain, Blue Brain*,[9] alight on

Baron-Cohen's now-infamous study of 102 newborn babies who were shown a human face and a coloured mobile with a ball hanging from it. In the experiment, the boys looked at the mobile for longer while the girls spent more time looking at the human face, apparently supporting ES theory. But the difference in time spent on each was very small. Boys spent an average of 52 per cent of their time looking at the mobile and 46 per cent looking at the face, while girls spent 41 per cent of their time looking at the mobile and 49 per cent at the face. They both also spent time looking at something else entirely. This minor (if statistically significant) difference shows that, on average, boys and girls like looking at both moving objects and faces; hardly startling news.[10]

Eliot and Fine note many methodological flaws in the experiment, the most serious being that few efforts were made to ensure that the researcher carrying out the tests did not already know the sex of the baby, which might skew the findings.[11] Despite this, Baron-Cohen and his team claimed, in writing it up, that the results 'clearly demonstrate that sex differences are in part biological in origin'.[12] Yet years later, neither this research team nor any other has been able to replicate these first findings.[13] Rather, the results fly in the face of a number of previous and subsequent studies that have found no evidence of a difference between the infant sexes' preferences for objects versus faces.[14] For instance, a 2013 experiment presented four- to five-month-old babies with images of human and doll faces and real and toy ovens and cars and found both sexes preferred the faces to the objects.[15] Lise Eliot points out that across the board studies measuring empathy show the differences between boys and girls to be very small, and in fact 40 per cent of boys are actually more sensitive to others' emotions than the average girl.[16] Nonetheless, the findings from this one experiment from Baron-Cohen's team have since been used by commentators in the field to explain 'pretty much every social and cognitive sex difference ever described',[17] including the career choices of men and women years down the line.[18]

The typically higher level of testosterone that boys are exposed to in the womb is frequently cited as the source for boys' supposed physical and competitive natures. 'It's all that boy energy!' parents declare as their toddler sons spend the afternoon running races with each other in the park. In *Brainstorm: The Flaws in the Science of Sex Differences*, Rebecca Jordan-Young, a Professor at the Department of Women's, Gender and Sexuality Studies at Barnard College, reviews hundreds of studies that claim to have found evidence of 'hard-wired' differences between the two sexes, in the main related to prenatal testosterone. She is scrupulously fair in her assessment yet finds these studies collectively wanting. One influential study (the design of which, she is at pains to point out, was excellent) found a small correlation for girls between exposure to high levels of testosterone in the womb and more masculine behaviour (as measured by interest in supposedly boyish toys and games) but no such correlation for boys. Yet in separate experiments carried out by Simon Baron-Cohen and his team the opposite finding was reached: there was a link for boys but none for girls. Jordan-Young is open to the idea that testosterone levels may affect the brain and behaviour, but she points out that we do not have the answer yet to how they impact on children, and that the information gleaned so far from these and many other studies is contradictory.[19]

Cordelia Fine and Rebecca Jordan-Young have, together with their colleagues, set out critical points to bear in mind with sex/gender research. Although they do not dispute that sex-linked biological influences may have some effect on behaviour, they argue that this does not show up in a binary way between boys and girls. Rather there is substantial overlap in the range of abilities and characteristics that boys and girls exhibit. If these were plotted along a continuum some boys might be at one far end and some girls at the very opposite end but the vast majority would cluster in between. This holds true in a great variety of areas, from range of vocabulary, reading comprehension and understanding facial expressions (abilities that girls are often assumed to excel at) to spatial visualisation, competitiveness and domineering behaviour, usually associated with boys and men. The variance within the sexes is just as great, if not greater, than between the sexes. There is even 'non-trivial overlap' between the sexes in supposedly very masculine behaviour such as physical aggression.[20]

When it comes to the make-up of the brain itself, these academics stress that its characteristics cannot be predicted on the basis of whether a person is male or female. Rather, each brain is made up of a collection of features, unique to that individual. There are not just two types of brain.[21] As the psychobiologist Professor Daphna Joel puts it, we all have 'a mosaic of "male" and "female" brain characteristics' as well as an 'array of masculine and feminine traits'.[22] Furthermore, the features of the brain are not fixed. The brain adapts to new events and experiences, so any differences between the brain of an individual male and that of an individual female may have developed over time rather than existing from birth.[23]

Despite this, some scientists and media commentators promote simple and misleading messages about sex differences in the brain rather than the complex truth. In 2013 Ragini Verma of the University of Pennsylvania and colleagues published research comparing the neural connections within the brains of males and females. The results showed that the differences in connectivity between the sexes were modest and the overlap significant.[24] But this got lost in the academic telling – and media retelling – of the story. Despite their modest findings, the researchers boldly claimed that, 'these results reveal fundamental sex differences in the structural architecture of the human brain'.[25] In the university's press release about the research, Verma asserted that the study, 'helps provide a potential neural basis as to why men excel at certain tasks, and women at others'. The press release went on to suggest that this might explain why in general men are (supposedly) better at navigating and women at multitasking.[26] In fact, there was absolutely no evidence of this convenient 'potential neural basis' for the gender roles of men and women in the study's findings. The researchers overstated the differences found between male and female brains, and suggested that these may explain differences in male and female behaviour, without any data to back up these claims. Yet the media ran with it anyway. 'The hard-wired difference between male and female brains could explain why men are "better at map reading",' announced the *Independent*. 'Scientists have drawn on nearly 1,000 brain scans to confirm what many had surely concluded long ago: that stark differences exist in the wiring of male and female brains,' opined the *Guardian*.[27] Although much of the reporting of this study claimed that the research concerned differences between the brains of men and women, it was actually conducted among eight to twenty-two year olds. The study found 'only a few' connectivity differences between the sexes before the age of thirteen, with the differences 'more pronounced' from fourteen onwards.[28] It would therefore appear to support the notion of the plasticity of the brain – that it responds to the different treatment to which girls and boys are subject. It may also simply reflect the fact that girls mature earlier than boys during puberty. It certainly does not offer proof that men are born better map readers, and women better multitaskers. One year later, another study found that wiring differences were driven by brain size not sex.[29] This study failed to generate the same mainstream media excitement as Verma's.

Ultimately, as Verma's study itself shows, beyond sex chromosomes, genitals and gonads, the differences between the sexes are not essential – that is, they are not clearly distinguishable, internally consistent, fixed and universal.[30] So what does this mean for our perception of the day-to-day behaviours of children? In their comprehensive survey of existing research on sex, gender, brain science and socialisation, the psychology professors Judith E. Owen Blakemore, Sheri A. Berenbaum and Lynn S. Liben draw conclusions that directly contradict the deeply embedded stereotypes about young boys and girls. For instance, they find that there is very little difference in the emotions displayed by children in the first two years of life – if anything, boys have more intense emotions, are more expressive, require more soothing and cry more frequently. Girls' early language development tends to be slightly ahead of boys' but boys then catch up. Infant boys' activity levels are generally only slightly higher than those of infant girls, and there is only a small – if any – difference in neuromotor skills (such as gripping a pencil or maintaining balance), with girls having the slight edge, though the evidence is inconsistent. Three clear overarching messages come out of their review, all of which echo the principles emphasised by Cordelia Fine and her colleagues: there is extensive overlap between male and female behaviour and aptitudes; the brain changes over time according to what happens to a person; and there is much that is not known about the brain and its influence on behaviour.[31]

Yet, the myth of 'hard-wired' differences persists. They may be trained to be objective thinkers, but scientists are not immune from stereotypical thinking. Nor are those who report on their work. When background assumptions reflect the wider beliefs of the time they are more likely to go unnoticed. Thus in the nineteenth century the fact that men's brains are larger than those of women was taken as evidence that men were the more intelligent sex, befitting contemporary social views. We now know that the sexes are equally intelligent.[32] The persistence of these myths also has much to do with the eagerness of a media that will not let go of the simplistic Mars and Venus narrative. Even within the academic publishing world, studies that 'prove' a difference between the sexes are more likely to see the light of day than those that do not.[33] When it comes to the mainstream media, lack of scientific knowledge, journalists' willingness to fall in with dominant narratives and the increasing pressure on academics to get wider attention for their work (and thus prove its public impact) can make for stories that badly misinform the public.

Serial parenting gurus are only too happy to jump on the sexist bandwagon, seeing the money-spinning potential in wheeling out another book of tips, largely the same as their original unisex version, but with 'boys' or 'girls' slapped on the cover. In his book *Raising Boys*, Steve Biddulph advocates that boys should have a strong relationship with both parents, as well as structure and order in their lives. This sounds like common sense – but would not the same go for girls?[34] 'Boys are different' the front of the book announces. Yes they are different – from each other, over time, before and after they have had a good night's sleep. But to imply in such a blanket statement that all boys are different from all girls, in every way and for ever, is simply wrong.

'I was amazed at how quickly he became a boy'

For the rest of us, whether we have children or not, buying into the notion of fundamental differences in the aptitudes and behaviours of the sexes is the easy option. It is simpler to go along with the dominant beliefs of our society than to question them. It saves time spent struggling against the tide and it protects us from others' scrutiny. Most of all, it stops us from having to ask hard questions of ourselves about our own choices and assumptions. Even some who consider themselves aware of the pitfalls in pigeon-holing boys and girls sign up to these beliefs. Kate, the mother of a son and daughter from the Midlands, tells me, 'All my family think I am a raving feminist. I will say something and they'll go, "She's off again!" We live in a white, male patriarchal society and it sets gender stereotypes very young.' She then says, 'My boy and girl are very different by nature and I wouldn't have believed it if I had not had my own children. I bought my son a doll but I was fighting nature. He wants to play football and rugby and to fight.' Mandy, who also has a son and a daughter, thinks she too is powerless in the face of her children's natural and sex-defined interests: 'My son is very much a boy and he is very different from my daughter. I was amazed at how quickly he became a boy. He is really into football. That was apparent from day one. And I'm not sure where he gets it from. His masculinity came from within – it was naturally there. It's nothing I've done.'

Based on a child sample size of one, two, three or possibly slightly more if they take extended family or friends into account, many parents readily sign up to a restrictive view of the interests and capabilities of their children. Among parents with both boys and girls there is a tendency to see differences that exist between all children through the prism of their sex. This is not true for every parent, of course. Bridget and her husband have two young children, a boy and a girl. 'The average boy might be more physical than the average girl but there will be lots of girls who are physical too, and also boys who aren't,' she says. 'In any case, it is magnified by nurture.' Boys are not clones of one another, their characters and traits are infinitely varied. 'They couldn't be more different,' says Jane, a mother in Manchester with two boys. 'They are the complete opposite in many ways. My oldest son is not into sport. He's very academic and very self-contained. He has strong friendships but it's within a small group. My other son is bright but he's not intellectual. He's very sporty. The last thing he could do is sit on his own. They are very, very different to each other.'

Let's focus on what we can change

The debate on the sex-linked biological influences that might exist – and their extent and source – will continue among scientists, parents and commentators for decades or more to come. It is a fascinating and fiercely contested field. But it is also one that should be kept in proportion. Whatever one's stance on the issue of biological influences, there is broad consensus that how children are brought up has a profound effect on their behaviour, interests and abilities. After all, this is what lies behind our collective concern about approaches to parenting, children's friendships, the quality of formal care and teaching they receive, and the messages they may pick up through television and the internet.

Parents influence their children all the time, guiding them to what they consider to be appropriate ways of being, whether they are conscious of doing so or not. As Amy, the mother of two young boys who blogs at 2boys1mum, remarks to me, 'People say it doesn't matter what we do, it is his natural urge to be a boy, you can't suppress it. Whereas I think, I want to suppress society's urges to make him into "a boy".' We 'make our sons into boys' through the things we buy for our children, the way we interact with them, our explicit instructions and the models of behaviour that we enact as parents. From their earliest days boys are left in no doubt as to what is expected of them. A baby boy will make a half-hearted grab at a soft ball and those around him will laugh and predict he will become obsessed with football. Or he will push a teddy out of the way and his boisterous, determined nature will be noted. Any behaviours that do not comply with our expectations are overlooked.

This drip, drip, drip of parental influence shapes the daily lives, experiences and attitudes of children. Parents Ros Ball and James Millar, tweeting as @GenderDiary, record the many small, and not so small, ways in which people treat their young daughter and son – and other girls and boys – differently: from the hairdresser who tells their daughter that she is going to make her look 'like a princess' to other parents allowing their sons' domineering behaviour to go unremarked. 'Our kids weren't born different,' they write in *The Gender Police*, their book of collected tweets, 'it was the world around them that was treating them differently.'[35] The academic psychologist Dr

Ben Hine describes this to me as the 'innocent socialisation process' – the supposedly benign and very subtle differential shaping of our male and female children: a passing comment, a particular tone, a smile or a frown. This process eventually leads to a social gulf between boys and girls, and later men and women. As such it amounts to an under-pinning of patriarchy, subordinating women and signalling to men that they are expected to be emotionally shut off and in charge. The very fact that many of us are unaware of this 'innocent' socialisation demonstrates how pervasive it is. It is the background to our lives.

The all-encompassing scope of this process, and its cumulative effect, is breathtaking, as a wealth of research shows. From infancy, boys are regarded by parents as larger, stronger, more athletic, less emotional and more capable – whether there is evidence for this or not.[36] In one experiment mothers with eleven-month-old babies were asked to estimate their infants' ability to crawl down a ramp. Those with baby boys thought that they would crawl steeper slopes than did those with girls. In fact, the boys and girls were equally good at crawling down equivalent ramps.[37] Another study found that mothers with newborn sons commented on their broad hands, large size, athletic look and serious appearance.[38] Parents from the early years are more tolerant of risk-taking behaviour in boys than in girls, even actively encouraging it. They are more likely to encourage their sons to play sport[39] and believe they have greater sporting talent than their daughters.[40]

Boys and their toys

The material environment that parents create for children is also highly gendered. One study of children's toy collections found that boys had more 'toys of the world' like vehicles and machines, whereas girls had more domestic-centred toys, such as dolls and housework role-play paraphernalia.[41] When parents are observed in playrooms with their children they are more likely to choose toys considered masculine for boys and feminine for girls. This is especially true of fathers. They are also more likely to respond positively to children when they choose the 'correct' toy. This could be such a subtle sign of approval – perhaps a smile or a touch – that parents may not even realise they are doing it.[42] Even in their first year, babies are aware of the emotional responses of those caring for them, and pick up on cues such as tone of voice and facial expression as a guide to which toys to play with and which to ignore.[43] A study that compared mothers' and fathers' reactions to their three- and five-year-old children playing with both sex-stereotyped and non-sex-stereotyped toys, found that when boys played with ste-reotypically male toys they received mild approval from their mothers and strong encouragement and reward from their fathers. By contrast when boys played with toys that were stereotypically associated with girls they were actually encouraged by their mothers but strongly discouraged by their fathers, with older boys reprimanded particu-larly vehemently. Fathers were harsher in their treatment of sons than daughters.[44] Yet, when left to choose toys for themselves, there is a size-able overlap between the types of toys young boys and girls play with, even with those totems of male and female play – trucks and dolls.[45]

The debate provoked when former Westminster Equalities Minis-ter Jo Swinson suggested encouraging boys to play with dolls (on the basis it would foster and normalise their nurturing abilities) shows how deeply gendered and conservative parts of society remain on this issue. 'Even the government can't force boys to play with girls' toys', pronounced the *Daily Telegraph*.[46] Boys have 'little natural impulse to do so', its journalist stated, 'interfering parents must be stopped'. Presumably he did not mean the 'interfering parents' who steer their sons towards 'boys' toys', often pulling them away from the dolls they happily played with in the first year or so of life.[47] Josh Lee is a father and the main carer for his young daughter. He set up the organisation

Bristol Dads, running drop-in play sessions for fathers and their children. He would go one further than Swinson in counteracting male stereotypes: 'If I push a buggy and change nappies, then why shouldn't a little boy play at doing the same thing? What I would like to see is positive action, like men playing with dolls with their sons.'

In the early 1970s, around the time I was born, the American actress and activist Marlo Thomas cooked up the brilliant *Free to Be ... You and Me*, a book and album for children, celebrating a world with no gender boundaries. The stories and songs were inspiring and witty and the music thrillingly catchy. A big television star at the time, Thomas was able to call on the talents of friends and colleagues such as Alan Alda, Mel Brooks and Diana Ross for the project, lending it extra sparkle. One of the songs on the album was 'William's Doll', inspired by the 1972 children's book of the same name. The book and the song describe William's longing for a doll, the mocking of his brother and best friend, his father's attempts to interest him in more supposedly appropriate toys and finally the intervention of William's grandmother, who gives him a doll and explains that this will prepare him for caring for his own children in later life.

It is sobering to think that over forty years later, and despite increasing awareness about the role of fathers in children's lives, a boy playing with a doll is still such a touchy subject. Rather than inching towards more progressive attitudes about boyhood interests, we have gone backwards. A revealing, small-scale piece of research casts light on boys' doll play in particular. A group of researchers came across a file of written responses to reading *William's Doll* from a primary-school class in 1975. They then set out to compare them with the thoughts of a class of contemporary children, returning to the same school in 1997. Among the boys who responded, one third reacted negatively to William's wish for a doll in 1975. This increased to two thirds in 1997. Seven boys in the earlier sample agreed that it was a good idea for William to have a doll in order to learn to care for babies. Only one boy put forward this argument in the late 1990s. The most common reason for reacting negatively to William's wish for a doll was that it's a girl's toy and boys shouldn't play with one. This argument was put forward by both boys and girls, with a slightly larger proportion of children doing so in 1997. As one boy from the later class wrote, 'He was only interested in playing with his doll, which I think is kind of weird. I would have chosen a M16 K. A. 60 violator assult [sic] rifle.'[48] Interestingly, a separate piece of research has found that, when reading a story to their child (aged between three and seven years), mothers are more likely to challenge sexist stereotypes with their daughters than with their sons.[49] Yet on the basis of the *William's Doll* research, it seems that boys could do with just such a mind-broadening intervention. The study of story-reading also found that children themselves shifted between endorsing and challenging sexist stereotypes, demonstrating that it is all to play for in terms of shaping children's attitudes, at a young age at least.[50]

It is glib and easy to romanticise the liberal parenting and equality agenda from the days of my own Clothkits-clad youth in the seventies and eighties. Digging deeper into my memory, I recall the delight of my sister and I when our grandparents brought back mini flamenco dresses for our Barbies from a tourist market they visited in Torremolinos. Nonetheless, as the *William's Doll* research suggests, we were living in a relative golden age of toy gender neutrality. Lego's wonderful advert from 1981, featuring an impish girl with plaits and dungarees clutching her assembled Lego structure, has gone viral in recent years and is emblematic of that time. The American sociologist Elizabeth Sweet has analysed the toy selection in Sears catalogues from the early 1900s to the present day. She has found that gender neutrality gradually gave way to increased segregation between 1905 and the 1960s. This then reversed in the seventies and eighties (with boys modelling toy vacuum cleaners and girls playing with She-Ra).[51] Not that it was a unisex nirvana: looking at Argos catalogues from the same era, there are girls poring over toy kitchen sets while boys brandish guns. But what is noticeably different is the lack of the blue/pink colour-coding that is now endemic, the explosion of which Sweet traces back to the mid 1990s.[52] Sweet suggests that colour-coding is chiefly a hard-sell device employed by manufacturers. This coding makes great commercial sense for the toy industry, opening up the possibility of selling two distinctive sets of toys into families with children of both sexes. The stock in the toy section of many supermarkets and department stores exemplifies this, with rows of pink princess gear and domestic role-play kit on one side and action, science, gross-out (slime) and noise-orientated toys on the other. Even toy cash registers and telephones are available in pink and blue. Bridget, mother to a young son and daughter, ponders the intensification of this segregation: 'It is definitely worse now than when I was a child. Adults are perhaps less divided by their sex than in the past but I wonder if they project it more onto their children.' In doing so, while the adult sexes may inch towards equality, they risk inhibiting progress in the next generation by constraining the eventual career choices boys and girls make. By the time they are at primary school, children have clear ideas about which jobs are appropriate for men and for women, informed in part by the role-play games and toys to which they have been exposed.[53] The hostility towards pink that the colour divide provokes among boys is particularly troubling. As Ros from Gender Diary told me, 'Hating pink is a misogyny in itself. It is really sad for boys that being anything like a girl is so shameful.' When boys say they hate pink or anything else deemed girlish, they are likely to be motivated primarily by the wish to fit in with other boys. But, in seeking this acceptance, they cast themselves as a higher class apart from girls.

I meet teenagers Liam, Clare and Annie just after they finish school one afternoon in Cambridge. We spend an hour or so talking in a nearby café before they have to catch the bus home, their bags bulging with books for revision and homework in the run-up to summer exams. Liam has clear memories of his parents' 'interference' in his toy choices. 'Everything was knights and castles and action figures. It was definitely a case of them steering me into it. I loved stuffed toys but if I was seen veering towards a pink cat or something they pushed me towards the brown bear instead.' His friend Clare recalls, 'There was a pink toy section and a blue toy section. When I went shopping we went to the pink section and that was that. My mum wanted to get us all a doll when she was expecting again. But my dad said my brother wasn't allowed one as it would turn him gay. He was only two or three at the time so she bought him one anyway. But it was a controversial doll.'

Groups such as the excellent Let Toys Be Toys, formed in 2012, have mounted effective campaigns to get stores to rethink their classification of stock, with the result that companies such as Tesco, Debenhams and Boots have stopped labelling goods as either for girls or for boys. Their books arm, Let Books Be Books, has persuaded nine publishers to do the same. This battle has gained a great deal of media and online attention. Yet much of the wider debate on colour-coding and toy segregation centres on how they limit girls' horizons rather than boys'. Toy kitchen equipment, nurses' outfits, beading kits and baby dolls are all worthy play items in themselves but when they are marketed solely at girls, with the girls modelling the toys on packaging dripping in pink, they perpetuate a stereotype that is home-focused, caring, quiet, decorative and nurturing. Equally, the toy guns, cars, action figures and work benches targeted at boys fuel a perception of them as combative, noisy and active. Many of these qualities have much to be said for them, others are fine in moderation (even being combative or decorative can have its place), but it is the relentless reinforcement of a limited range of qualities for each sex that's so restrictive, for boys as well as girls. As Amy, who has two boys with her husband Ed, says, 'The focus is on encouraging girls to be what they want and to play with a range of toys. But there is very little about boys out there – making the case that we should be encouraging them to be nurturing and caring, or to aspire to be a nurse.' Perhaps it is a lack of appreciation of the effect that gender has on boys. When I met Ros and James from Gender Diary, Ros explained how she was very alert to stereotypes when she first had her daughter but less so when she had her son. 'It was partly because I just had less time, but also because he was a boy.' 'I worry about it less with a boy because it doesn't hold boys back,' James added. 'Well, it does,' replied Ros, 'but in a different way.'

An emotional education

The debate about toys is a familiar one, though nonetheless serious. What is more startling is the way in which parents teach the sexes about 'appropriate' emotions. Boys and girls are born with a capacity and wish for close and responsive relationships and both sexes are attuned to their own and others' feelings.[54] Yet studies show that mothers and fathers are less tolerant of displays of emotion in boys, particularly crying and expressions of unhappiness or fear, taking a more punitive approach to them than with girls.[55] A review of existing academic studies on shyness published in 2014 found that parents also respond more negatively to shyness in sons than in daughters.[56] At the same time, they are more accepting of anger in boys than in girls. Research from 2005 in which mothers, fathers and children were observed as they played a competitive game revealed that fathers specifically paid more attention to displays of anger from boys and displays of 'submissive emotion' among girls.[57] This echoes earlier research showing that, in daycare and preschool settings, adults respond to assertiveness and aggression in one-year-old boys more readily than they do in girls. At that age, there is no difference in the behaviour of the two sexes. But, one year later, their behaviour does differ as boys learn to be more assertive and aggressive in order to provoke an adult response: in their gendered interaction with one-year-old children, it seems these adults create gendered behaviour in the young.[58]

Researchers in another study found that whereas mothers discussed anger with their sons when recollecting past experiences, they never did so with their daughters.[59] Parents also use fewer emotion-related words with boys. In one longitudinal piece of work, academics recorded and then examined the conversations of mothers and fathers with daughters and sons at home while they talked about past special occasions where they had all been present (such as a big outing or family celebration). The families were studied when the children were three, and again two years later when they were five. Both mothers and fathers used more emotion words when talking to their daughters on these occasions. Aged three, the boys and girls used a similar number of emotion words, but by five girls used them more frequently than boys, particularly with their mothers.[60] These findings are consistent with many other studies.[61]

Physiological measures of emotion (heart rate, blood pressure and so on) show no clear differences between boys and girls. However, girls are more likely to display emotion than boys, except of course anger, which boys are encouraged to display more often than girls.[62] Boys have the same emotions as girls but they learn not to express them. Girls are also more likely to report feeling sympathetic or empathetic – and this increases with age, indicating that girls learn to conform to what is expected of them. A literature review of studies of empathy found that women scored significantly higher than men on the empathy scale when levels were self-reported but the same as men when their empathy was being scored unobtrusively by others.[63] A number of the parents I spoke to said their sons were less complicated than their daughters, who they described as more intense or difficult. This may have something to do with the fact that we encourage suppression of feelings in boys and demonstration of feelings in girls. Through the influence of their parents, boys begin to see emotions as feminine. For many of them, 'feminine' is synonymous with 'inferior' and so to be avoided. This process alienates boys from themselves and from girls. Even highly self-aware parents can slip up. Indigo, the mother of two young sons in Brighton, who in our conversation talked passionately and wryly of the influence of parents, admitted, 'I have said to them before – and then regretted it – when they used to run around screaming, "I didn't have boys so you could run round screaming like girls!"'

It is not just in talking about emotions that parents treat boys and girls differently, but in everyday conversation. Mothers speak to infant sons less than they do to daughters – and there is mounting evidence that this is the case for fathers too[64] – indeed, this behaviour from parents may go some way to explaining boys' slower early language development.[65] Mothers are also more conversational and supportive in their talk with daughters.[66] These stereotypes soon become internalised. The types of role play that parents engage in with their children also affect the conversations they have. Playing with dolls and other 'social pretend play' (such as playing at shops or housework) entails more complex language use. This type of play is more likely to be initiated with daughters than sons. Playing with vehicles often leads to more imaginative sounds as the participants imitate vehicle noises, but it involves less expansive language use. It is this type of play that parents are more likely to participate in with their sons. Again the potential origins of boys' slower language development begin to emerge.[67]

'Busy, filthy, sweaty boys'

The early formation of gendered behaviour is seen in other types of play. Studies show that in infancy physical play is equally common among boys and girls. But rough-and-tumble play, which tends to start just before children turn school-age and continues through to early adolescence, is more frequently found among boys than girls. One of the most significant predictors of children playing rough-and-tumble with their friends is having had a father who played this way with them when they were younger. Fathers are more likely to engage in rough-and-tumble with sons than daughters. Thus, fathers' rambunctious play with their sons contributes to boys' more active play with their peers as they grow up.[68] Nadine, who has one son, says, 'Before my son was at school I would sometimes meet up with other mothers who had girls. He would encourage them to play rambunctiously. The girls enjoyed it but the mums always disapproved. All children have that energy and we accept it in male children but it causes anxiety if girls are like that. Girls are always being shushed and told not to take up too much space. Yet we accept that boys have little control and think it is cruel to squash them. We want to see busy, filthy, sweaty boys, running their energy out, but parents are uncomfortable seeing that in their girls.'

The perceived physicality of boys may be one of the reasons that parents, especially mothers, behave more harshly towards them than girls and are more likely to punish them physically.[69] Beth, a mother in Dover, has two sons and a daughter. She is admirably honest as she mulls over her approach to discipline with her children, correcting herself on reflection as we speak. 'I don't hit the children,' she begins, 'I feel they get the same tone and treatment, although I am conscious of boys needing to know their place. I have probably manhandled the boys more than the girls. And I probably did that because they are boys,

because they are in a physical world. Yes, thinking about it, I have han-
dled the preschool years differently.' One longitudinal study tracked
over 700 children, measuring their temperaments, relationships with
their mothers and fathers and their parents' approach to discipline over
ten years. At the start of the study there was no difference in the temperaments of the boys and girls involved. By mid-childhood the boys
had become more difficult, reacting negatively to harsh discipline. The
researchers found that the boys reacted particularly badly to such discipline when it was meted out by their mothers and suggested that boys
are sensitive to what they view as 'female aggression'.[70] This points to a
'feedback loop' of gendered behaviour and expectations: mothers are
harsher with sons because they think they can cope with it and that
they need reining in more than girls; boys are more hostile to mothers'
strict discipline because it goes against the stereotype of the compassionate, maternal figure and of women as the submissive sex.

But the son/father dynamic is of course a crucial one too. Fathers
police their sons' behaviour more strongly than mothers, and are
more watchful of their behaviour than that of their daughters. The
more stereotypically masculine a father, the more strongly he will
encourage supposedly masculine behaviour in his son and discour-
age anything supposedly feminine. Boys with such fathers are more
likely to exhibit aggressive and very active behaviour.[71] They grow up
with a male chorus of approval when they conform to stereotype:
that's my boy, such a boy, a real boy. In one American survey, 76 per
cent of men admitted using phrases such as 'man up' and 'be a man'
towards boys.[72] Frank, the father of two sons, says, 'Some of the dads
on the edge of the football pitch are awful. You hear dads say to their
own sons, "Don't be soft" or "Don't be a wimp". They shout at the
referee and set a really bad example.' Lisa is the mother of two boys
from Sussex. She tells me, 'I have taught my husband that he can't say
things like "Man up!" and "Don't be such a girl!" to the boys. He used
to say it because he is a sports coach and that's the world he is used to.

I hate it. I don't want the boys to have that mindset. I want my boys to know that if it hurts, it's fine to cry.'

The militant monitoring by some fathers of boys' behaviour sheds light on another deep-rooted trend. Tomboys are tolerated, perhaps even celebrated, by parents in a way that boys who display supposedly feminine interests and behaviours are not. The fact that there is no male equivalent for 'tomboy', a term that is now generally used quite casually and neutrally, is itself evidence of this. 'Sissy' is perhaps the most commonly understood male comparative – most of us would know what somebody was implying if they used it. But it is a loaded, pejorative word. Why is the tomboy accepted and the sissy reviled? As with most things in life, patriarchy is at the heart of it. Being a tomboy shows grit and vim. It is ambitious to want to act like a boy: give the plucky little girl a pat on the head. But being a sissy? It is wet, it is pathetic, it is beneath a boy. Ian McEwan captures the contrast precisely in his novel *The Cement Garden* when Julie says to her brother:

> 'You think it's humiliating to look like a girl, because you think it's humiliating to *be* a girl … Girls can wear jeans and cut their hair short and wear shirts and boots because it's okay to be a boy; for girls it's like promotion. But for a boy to look like a girl is degrading, according to you, because secretly you believe that being a girl is degrading.'[73]

Despite all our concerns about girls, there's a greater range of accepted ways of being a young girl – princess, arty, sporty, swotty, tomboy – than being a young boy. Young boys can be sporty or geeky (Lego, coding, Beast Quest) and thereafter they begin to run out of socially acceptable options.

In her interviews with parents, the sociologist Emily Kane found that the steers parents give to children also stem from fears that, if they allow boys to play in a supposedly feminine way, they might encourage homosexuality. One of the parents she spoke to commented that it might be 'bad' for his son to take an interest in 'things meant for girls' because 'his sexual orientation might get screwed up'.[74] I wonder if fathers also fear that a lack of suitably manly behaviour in their sons will in some way reflect badly on them: both on their parenting and on their own masculinity. Joel is the father of two sons now in their early twenties, the oldest of whom is gay. Thinking back to when his gay son was very young, he tells me, 'Sometimes I would pick him up on stuff. I'd say, "Why are you talking like a girl?" Perhaps I shouldn't have done that. But it was frustrating as a dad. I didn't particularly like it. I felt embarrassed. That's the truth. It's not a nice thing to say. But the truth is you feel conspicuous.' Alice, a mother of three sons based in Edinburgh, remembers a family visit to some friends with daughters when her boys were small. 'The boys all made a beeline for the pink fairy dresses in the dressing-up box. We were about to go into town and the boys wanted to go in their outfits. My husband said, "No son of mine is going into town in a fairy outfit!" Dads are very conscious of that sort of thing, I don't know why.' To the extent that parents see children as a reflection of themselves, for men that can include their masculinity.

Not every father is resistant to his son roaming beyond the conventionally masculine. Ed and Amy have two young sons. Ed tells me of the eyebrows raised when his two-year-old son asked to dress up as a witch at Halloween. This prompted Ed to put on a dress too to ensure that his son felt comfortable. 'I wanted to make it clear to him that whatever interests he has, we will support him. There will be zero prejudice from us. It was a great way of doing something fun. From his point of view it was just a game. And for me, well, if there was any game that I wasn't going to join in, it wasn't going to be that one.'

Ed's story is reminiscent of that of Nils Pickert, the admirable German father of a five-year-old boy with a fondness for wearing dresses who made the headlines by donning a skirt himself to ensure his son felt confident enough to withstand any teasing. In one piece on the Pickert story, I came across this below-the-line comment from a man who wasn't supported in his childhood choices by his father. It is an emotional read:

> Thirty years ago, I WAS that boy. I was wearing dresses and skirts, I had long hair, I wanted to wear make-up … My father was not happy about this. He wanted a 'real' boy, like my brother was … he took me to ball games and other activities to butch me up. I always failed and I hated seeing that look on his face, when his sissy-son had embarrassed him in public once more … Needless to say, none of this butched me up or turned me into the boy my father wanted me to be. It just made me feel unloved, ashamed for what I was and I became a very unhappy kid … Just a little love and support would have given me the backbone to be proud of who I was and maybe one day even stand up to those bullies kicking my teeth in every other day. Because I would have known I didn't deserve that.[75]

Siblings also play their part in reinforcing stereotypes. As we might imagine, if a boy has an older brother he will behave in more stereotypically masculine ways and in less stereotypically feminine ways than a boy with an older sister. Older brothers influence younger sisters in the same way: having an older brother is associated with both more stereotypically masculine behaviour and less stereotypically feminine behaviour for girls as well as boys. This is yet more proof that these elements of our being are largely acquired rather than the result of sex-linked biological influences. Interestingly, older sisters hold less sway over younger brothers than older brothers hold over younger sisters. Boys with older sisters develop more stereotypically feminine behaviour than those without an older sister but the level of their stereotypically masculine behaviour is comparable to singleton boys, although lower than for boys with older brothers. As with the tomboy/sissy comparison, the higher social value of boys and boyishness means that boys are less influenced than girls by older siblings of the opposite sex: older sisters carry less authority than older brothers.[76]

The actor Charlie Condou has a daughter and a son, whom he co-parents with their mother, his friend the actress Catherine Kanter. The children spend half their time with Catherine and half with Charlie and his husband, Cameron Laux. I met Charlie to talk to him about his experience of being a gay father. One anecdote seems to encapsulate perfectly the experience of boys influenced by their older sisters, yet with half an eye to the other boys around them. Charlie told me, 'My son went to a birthday party recently in the park. So he put on a party dress – a pink nylon Disney dress – because that is what his sister wears to parties. And he also took his football. He raised a few smiles as he stomped along the pavement with his football and dress. I don't mind at all. But maybe that's because he's three. What about when he is thirteen? Would I worry then? I probably would worry about the reaction to it, if he were dressing conspicuously. I hope it is that and not just me justifying my own prejudices.'

Screen time

In the sibling study just discussed, the younger siblings were three years old. But even at that age the influences on children extend beyond the family, most notably through the media. The average three to four year old in the UK watches fifteen hours of television a week, spends seven hours a week on the internet and six hours gaming.[77] Research into the content of children's television across a number of countries, including the UK, has found that male characters tend to be central, combative figures in stories and series, and that there are twice as many male as female characters.[78] The television industry has been accused of sexism that encourages girls to be passive and to play second fiddle to more active boys. As a result, some new female characters have been introduced into popular television (think Disney Junior's *Doc McStuffins,* or the female *Swashbuckle* pirates and *Nina and the Neurons* on CBeebies). Yet although the male characters dominate, they are one-dimensional creatures, rarely shown in caring or nurturing roles, for example.[79] They are too busy vanquishing the enemy or setting off on adventures to look out for their nearest and dearest. Characters such as CBeebies' Charlie, who playfully and affectionately looks after his little sister Lola, or the equally matched (give or take a royal title) Ben and Holly on Channel 5, stand out because they are exceptions. The likes of CBeebies' Tree Fu Tom, the boys-y dogs in Nick Jr's *Paw Patrol* and gung-ho Jake leading his *Neverland* pirates on Disney Junior predominate. A study of violence on children's television in Britain across eight channels found that 39 per cent of the programmes contained violence. Of course, the violence on children's programmes is generally cartooned and sanitised. But the perpetrators of the violence were mostly male.[80]

The adverts between the programmes on commercial stations reinforce this sexist world view. Girls skip through studio-simulated butterfly meadows comparing glittering pink shoes while tinkly music plays in the background. Or they lie across a bed decked in pastel bed linen, combing the hair of a princess or a pony or a troll. Boys, meanwhile, aim guns or water pistols at each other, or set competing remote-controlled trucks on a collision course. It ends in destruction and that is the point. The volume is up ten notches, compared to the world of glittering pink shoes. Noise, action and aggression are for the boys.

The recent phenomenon of 'unboxing' videos, in which disembodied hosts film themselves unpacking toys and posting their running commentary on YouTube continues this gendered trend. Female hosts (mainly adults, with only elaborately manicured nails on show) unwrap the latest Sofia the First or My Little Pony merchandise, exclaiming at how much cuter the new models are. Their male equivalents begin with a blokeish 'What's up, guys?' to the watching bros (four-year-old boys eating their pre-nursery Cheerios) before launching into a specifications analysis of the new Hot Wheels model. The most-watched hosts are reportedly worth up to $5 million. This is calculated on a fee of $4 per 1,000 views: an awful lot of hits from the young fanbase.[81] The media and its merchandise spin-offs are so pervasive, even in very young lives, that the attitudes and assumptions that lie within its content are bound to have an effect on the children watching. Ros from Gender Diary tells me of a party that her daughter and son were recently invited to: a Superheroes and Princesses party in which there were separate Spiderman and princess cakes and two sex-segregated bouncy castles.

Given how much the early differences between the sexes are dictated by environment, with parents the most consistent presence in young children's lives, why are we so resistant to accepting the extent of our influence and to scrutinising the ways in which we perpetuate stereotypes? Perhaps it is because it would be such a huge undertaking to question – and up-end – the way in which our society is structured. It would entail a root and branch overhaul of patriarchy, and honesty about our complicity in it. That is a daunting and possibly frightening prospect. It is much easier to go with the flow, to join the chorus of 'boys will be boys', perhaps with the occasional carp on the sidelines to ease our consciences. Instead of taking responsibility, we opt for the quiet life. But by doing this we are preparing many boys for a life of more limited choices and emotions, risking unhappiness as they attempt to live up to a rigid image of manhood and to cleave to a stunted world view. If we could re-imagine what it is to be a boy from birth we would save them and everyone else a lot of heartache. As Amy says, 'My boys will be adults one day; they may have children of their own. And I want them to feel free to live their lives as they would wish and to have the same respect for women as they do for men. I believe that the values we are instilling in them will make a difference.'

Seizing the initiative

As a society we recognise implicitly the long-term effects of how we raise our children in the early years. Think of all the column inches and parental conversations about encouraging children to share possessions with others or the merits or otherwise of early formal childcare. Yet we still believe that there is something instinctive about boys reaching for trucks and girls reaching for dolls, or boys' liking for dinosaur T-shirts and girls' desire to wear pink. But these are just the norms and constructs of our time: it has not always been this way and it will change. Today we look back at racial segregation or the days before women had the vote and wonder how it could have been that way. Yet those laws and practices reflected commonly held views of the era. In a generation or two, we may shake our heads at the current social and cultural segregation of boys and girls and wonder what we were thinking. By encouraging boys to be active and dominant, to suppress their emotions and to reject interests associated with girls, we risk pushing them towards a future in which their self-esteem relies on climbing hierarchies, their interactions with other men are characterised by jockeying and unease, they are unable to recognise or express their true emotions and they regard girls and women as alien and inferior.

In our roles as parents, extended family, members of the community and others who come into contact with young children, we must think harder about our influence over the way boys behave. So much debate is focused on the extent of biologically influenced differences between the sexes. As this chapter has shown, the commonalities between them are far greater than any differences. While the research and debate on brains and behaviour continues, we ourselves can make an immediate and lasting impact on the lives of children. We can show boys that they have so many more options than the dominant male stereotype suggests. We can do this through challenging those stereotypes that we encounter, rejecting them in our own actions and accepting individual boys for who they are. Parents such as Amy and Ed and Ros and James are already doing this in their daily lives: from the range of toys and activities they expose their children to, to encouraging them to question the gender constraints they encounter – like the instruction for boys to dress as superheroes for a party. As Josh Lee , the founder of Bristol Dads, suggests, men playing with dolls with their young sons would make a very powerful impression yet it is a simple plan that almost every father could put into action. Beyond the family – from shop workers selecting and displaying children's toys to community volunteers running drop-in play sessions – everyone has a role in dismantling the rigid expectations placed on boys. Boys can be active and they can be quiet, they can play with trucks and they can play with dolls, they can laugh out loud and they can burst into tears. They can do any of these things, and that is fine. Releasing boys from the male rules will make a fundamental difference to their lives now and their expectations for the future.

2. FROM INDULGENT SMILE TO CURLED LIP

Schooldays

Playground politics

'My youngest son used to dress up in fairy outfits when he was two or three,' remembers Indigo, a mother of two boys. 'Now he has a weapons box and runs around in army gear.' Going to school brings a step change in how children's identities develop. Early childhood experiences in nursery or other forms of childcare have hugely important developmental influences, but it is at school that children start to look beyond their parents to inform their sense of who they are. There they encounter a set of influences that rival those of their parents: classmates and teachers who establish new norms and ways of behaving.

One of the clearest changes is that children begin to socialise almost exclusively in single-sex friendship groups. The first signs of this occur in the preschool years and it is girls who tend to gravitate towards other girls first, with boys following suit later. The rough-and-tumble play fostered among boys becomes off-putting to some girls who are discouraged by adults from joining in. Girls vote with their feet and keep their distance. By the time they reach school the vast majority of children spend the bulk of their time playing with others of the same sex.[1] This does not change until adolescence.[2] As Indigo says, 'My youngest son's best friend at nursery was a girl. But when he arrived at school he migrated towards the boys. He is very sporty, much more so than my other son. And he is more easily influenced by his peers. He is in a very boys-y class. They play armies and Power Rangers. He has left the world of fairy outfits behind. He is mortified when we mention it. He wanted to fit in and be one of the boys.' Charlie Condou, whose son will soon start school, agrees, 'My son has always emulated his older sister – dressing up as Cinderella and playing with Barbies. But about a month ago he discovered Spiderman, the Hulk, Batman and rolling around on the floor – all that suddenly hit. When he started nursery his best friend was a girl but he's stopped talking about her. It's only boys now. Has he seen that boys don't play with girls or is he growing up and feeling more affinity with boys? It is difficult to tell.'

It is to be expected that children will begin to self-segregate in this way. Not only have they been brought up to play differently but they will learn from older children and adults that, on the whole, girls and women have female friends and boys and men have male friends. Within many primary schools, repeated distinctions are made between the two sexes, often in quite subtle ways, such as splitting children into boys and girls when lining up in the playground or for specific learning tasks. Research shows that simply sorting children into groups of boys and girls in class – even if both sexes are treated equally in every respect – is associated with children developing stronger gender stereotypes than when they aren't organised in this way.[3] Taking their cue from the adults around them, children increasingly understand that their sex is a significant point of similarity or difference. Much same-sex bonding over shared interests is hugely enjoyable and comforting for children. They find joy in mutual passions and friendships. Particular pastimes, toys and games are useful short-cuts to seeking out like-minded playmates. But because of the social construction of gender, these often run down restrictive, sex-divided tracks, with football, Lego and superheroes for boys, and dolls, My Little Pony and fairy tales for girls. Emily Kane found that, by the age of four, children start to regulate their own behaviour, fitting in with the dominant culture. So boys start to play only with those of their own sex and define their favourite pastimes in opposition to girls.[4]

Research suggests that it is the most 'socially sensitive' girls who first avoid the most boisterous boys, who in turn seek out other boys of the same ilk. Those around them then fall in with this pattern.[5] As their friendships develop, girls are prone to 'co-rumination' – that is, talking over and dwelling on their problems. This provides emotional interaction and support although it may also lead to introspection. At the same time, boys encourage each other in loud and active play. They often greatly enjoy this but it can crowd girls out of the playground.[6] 'My son tells me that the boys run around with a football at break time and the girls stand at the edge and talk,' says Natalie of her nine-year-old son. This pattern of play also denies boys quieter and more reflective time. Likewise, girls might benefit from letting their hair down and running around once in a while. As it is, playground activity becomes gendered.

A number of parents I spoke to said that their sons had female friends outside of school – often old playmates from the preschool years – but that they tended to keep these friendships hidden from their male social group. Natalie tells me, 'My son says it's not done to speak to girls. It would be socially shocking to speak to a girl. He does get on with girls and he feels it is a bit limiting to be able only to play with boys. The girls won't play with boys either. He has a friend at school who is a girl but they would never play together in the playground, only after school.'

Natalie notes that girls observe this segregation as much as boys, and both groups develop an 'us and them' mentality. Indeed, as we have seen, it is girls that begin to peel off in the first place. But boys still hold the upper hand: although girls initiate the segregation, boys begin to police it more vehemently, and are much less likely to let girls into their group than vice versa.[7] They believe they have more to lose in status by fraternising with girls. This would explain why the friendships that boys have with girls must be kept secret.

For those boys who do hold on to friendships with girls at this age, they are often very rewarding and steadfast bonds. Josh, a university student in the north-east of England, went to a school in Scotland, where there were just nine pupils in his class: five boys and four girls. 'It was a very stable group,' he tells me. 'We all went on to the same high school and we are all still in touch. Some of them have kids now and the children call me Uncle Josh.' As in Josh's case, sometimes mixed-sex friendships come about because of circumstances. At other times it is because of the particular culture of the school or perhaps the outlook of local parents. Tom, who lives in Devon with his wife and three children, tells me, 'We live in a very liberal area. Lots of boys have shoulder-length hair and there's no real need to be doing boy things. My son doesn't behave in an aggressive way and nor do the boys he mixes with. They are very gentle and happy in their skin. He still has good friendships with girls at school.' It may also be down to the choices of individual children. Kim, the London mother of a boy and a girl, says of her son, 'He is the very youngest in his age group. When he got to school the boys just seemed too much for him. They were very boisterous and wild. He gravitated towards girls.' There is, though, a distinction between the mixed-sex groups Tom describes and boys who do not socialise with other boys. Kim is aware that this marks her son out: 'He is not bullied for who he is but he consciously does not make an effort to be friends with the boys. He actively shuns them. I don't know if it is because he feels nervous about whether they will accept him or because he just doesn't like being with them.'

There is evidence that boys socialise in larger groups than girls, who tend to pair off, or get together in threes.[8] This goes some way to explaining the jostling that occurs among male friends, as boys scramble to secure a position in the pecking order. Eleanor, a counsellor who works with boys and girls in secondary school, says that much of her work concerns supporting boys as, 'They try to find out their place with their peers. Sometimes there is jockeying within friendship groups and sometimes they are good friendships: a friend might even suggest to a boy that he comes to see me. But often I see boys who are having to accept they are not one of the pack and asking themselves, "What do I do with that?"'

Prompted by expectations of competitive and assertive behaviour, boys issue instructions to each other and openly rank their own and others' abilities in a variety of activities as they size up who goes where in the hierarchy.[9] Mandy says of her son, 'He's in that pack at school. It ebbs and flows and there are struggles and fights to see who is the leader. One boy has commanded the whole class: he can turn his favour on or off. My son would love to be the one in charge. He is consumed with concern about it.'

One of the ways that high-ranking boys maintain their position is by forcing those in the lower ranks to do their bidding and by tormenting boys outside the group. High-ranking girls do this too (the film *Mean Girls* was, after all, based on a non-fiction book – Rosalind Wiseman's brilliant *Queen Bees and Wannabes*). But for young boys physical aggression is more likely to be one of the ways that they exercise this control, while girls favour the 'social' or 'relational' aggression method. (Both sexes are, of course, capable of either approach and in fact boys tend to ditch physical aggression and switch to bitching and eye-rolling as they grow older.)[10] Children at the top of the tree – again, especially boys – are particularly watchful about maintaining boundaries with the opposite sex. This is seen as a sign of social competency by peers.[11]

All friendships involve jockeying for position to some degree. But it is the criteria for allotting a place in the hierarchy that differs between the sexes. Boys tend to be judged according to very stereotypical, masculine parameters: who is strongest, fastest, biggest, loudest and best at sport? As we know, from a young age, boys are more likely to receive affirmation if they engage in active and rough-and-tumble play and other activities popularly associated with boys. In contrast, boys who engage in activities associated with girls are much more likely to end up being rejected by other boys and playing alone.[12] Ben, a civil servant in his twenties who lives in London, remembers this dynamic from his own schooldays. It was, as he describes it, a culture of, 'conform or die. It was a difficult space to grow up in, although I did push back as often as I could. From an early age boys are given very clear messages about how they are expected to behave and you are confined within that shell. It's really limiting and constantly re-enforced.' In this world of mirroring and reward and punishment, single-sex friendships reinforce stereotypes. The more time boys spend playing with other boys the more stereotypically boy-like their play becomes.[13] In fact, their group play is more sex-stereotypical than that of girls.[14]

So what do boys learn from the jostling and judgement of their peers when they start school? Dr Judy Chu is a lecturer in the Human Biology faculty at Stanford University. She carried out an intriguing study of boys, closely observing and interviewing them over two years, from their entry into school at the age of four. Chu followed the group as they negotiated the social challenges involved in the transition. She found that notions of what it is to be a boy are defined and fixed early on. As boys scramble for their place in a group they attempt to enhance their standing with others by demonstrating their adherence to stereotypical masculinity. They do this in part by open shows of competitive, highly physical and stoic behaviour. In her book *When Boys Become Boys*, Chu recounts the following exchange, in which she quizzes members of the group on the jobs they would like when they grow up:

ROB (*softly*): I'm going to be in the army.
JUDY (*interested*): You are?
MIKE (*cautioning*): Then you'll get killed.
ROB (*unconvincingly*): I don't care.
JAKE (*emphatically*): Yeah, I don't care. That's what I want.
JUDY (*to Jake*): You want to be in the army?
JAKE: Yeah, and I want to get killed.[15]

It is through such overtly macho declarations that the boys become 'boys'. Ironically, as Chu points out, by suppressing their emotions in order to prove their masculinity and forge bonds with other boys, they reduce their ability to make intimate connections with those they are trying to befriend. The influential masculinities researcher Michael Kimmel, Professor of Sociology at Stony Brook University in America, argues that boys censor their own behaviour and monitor that of others because their masculinity is always under scrutiny and liable to be called into question by others.[16] As well as limiting choices, this process of restricting and policing masculine behaviour defines boys in opposition to girls. 'I don't have friends who are girls, because I play with the boys,' says one of Judy Chu's group simply. Another boy says to Chu, 'Boys really like weapons and stuff and the girls really like dolls and stuff like that.' Chu asks if the girls ever play with weapons: 'No.' Do the boys ever play with dolls? 'No' (emphatically, with a 'wah' sound at the end for effect).[17]

Chu rightly cautions against viewing the boys as passive recipients of masculine socialisation: they are more canny and self-aware than that. They realise what they are doing (consciously demonstrating stereotypical boy behaviour) and why (in order to gain acceptance within the group). They also understand the immediate, personal cost involved, restricting the way they express themselves and the activities they take part in. Some even try to put up resistance but ultimately the choice is to act like a 'boy' and be part of the group, or to be less constrained but also less accepted. As Chu notes of one of the boys she studied, 'as Rob tried to figure out how he could preserve his relationships and also preserve his sense of integrity, he learned and gradually came to accept that it might not be possible to have it both ways ... Forced to choose between being a part of the group and being autonomous, Rob ultimately chose the latter.'[18]

Sports scores

I first met Ben as part of a group of male, twenty-something volunteers for an organisation called Great Men that runs workshops with schoolboys, challenging gender stereotypes and promoting equality between the sexes. Sarah Perry, who set up the project, arranged to introduce me to them in a pub in east London. An evening spent discussing gender politics may sound quite dry but I had soon filled half a notebook as the group animatedly told me about their reasons for signing up and their observations from the sessions they have run. 'People are worried about fitting in and the price they will pay if they break out of that shell,' Ben said. 'They want to keep their friends so they keep on conforming. But really everyone in that group is behaving the way they are because they feel that is what is expected of them. It doesn't matter if they are the most dominant person or the weakest. They are all pretending to some degree. Nobody feels able to be who they really are.'

Sport is a central means of gaining status and proving yourself as a 'boy'. It is a dominant feature of school life, for good or ill. In one study of pre-adolescent peer relationships, researchers found that athletic ability was the primary factor in determining boys' social standing. At many of the schools they visited the best sportsman was also the most popular boy in that year.[19] For many, sport is a source of huge enjoyment and camaraderie. Andy, an apprentice in Newcastle in his late teens, says, 'I had a fantastic childhood. A lot of that was down to sport. I'd really encourage boys to play sport. It gets you out, you make friends and it keeps you fit.' Neil, a father of two from Lancaster, says of his son, 'He loves playing football because of the friendships it's given him. Sport is very important in his life. It gives him great enjoyment. He loves being in a team and he's gained skills from being a team player and a leader. It's great for his confidence and he's developed communication skills through it too.'

Others have a different experience; the flipside of sport bringing people together is that you can feel left out if you are not involved. As Matt, who lives in Kent with his wife and two children, explains, 'I do think my son and I have a social stigma in that we are not into football, rugby or any team sports really. I did play as a child but I didn't enjoy it and my son is very resistant too. Is that because I don't like it, or is it because he genuinely doesn't like it himself? I don't know. Even now I can feel at a disadvantage when friends are talking about sport. So I would rather he could play and talk about football. I felt when I was younger that it held me back slightly.'

Matt doesn't appear to have suffered much from his lack of sporting prowess, yet it is interesting to see how it still hangs over him. The same is true of Abel, who is in his late twenties and works in the City. 'As I grew up I always had lots of friends but I didn't fit in with one particular group. At school, the boys stick with the boys and the girls stick with the girls and you are forced in to doing things that you are not particularly interested in or good at. Sport was definitely an obstacle for me. I wasn't good at it. There's a caste system in school. When my friends were all playing football I was a bit stuck. I was lucky because I stepped up in other areas – I was confident and a comic. But for some, if they are not good at sport then they are not one of the boys.'

Like Matt and his son, Abel and his dad shared a lack of interest in football. Abel is firmly of the view that the way he was raised was fundamental in shaping his attitude towards sport. 'My dad was not into sport either,' he says. 'You can be a natural at something but if it is not honed from a young age then it won't develop. My dad loves motor racing. I used to watch Formula One with him and I still love it because he instilled it in me. What is stamped on you at home makes a difference. My younger brother is more physical than me. My dad was at home more by then and took him to matches and played football with him. It is about the way you are brought up and what is considered important at the time.' As Abel found at school, sport is not necessarily the be-all-and-end-all. Social confidence and a 'cool' appearance or attitude go a long way too. But if you cannot call on these other assets either, it can be very hard. Ian, a father of two, thinks back to his time at primary school. 'My perception was that other boys were more aggressive and I felt inadequate. It began to coalesce into a belief that I wasn't much good at being male. Boys were meant to show physical prowess and social prowess, being able to be a bit insensitive, to not care. In some ways that isn't a bad thing. I felt I was oversensitive. I excelled academically. But it was the opposite with sport and I was teased and bullied.'

What should parents do?

Many parents wrestle with how best to support their sons, given these profound pressures to fit in with a rigid version of boyhood. When Liam, who we met in the last chapter, was perusing the stuffed toy selection and being guided by his parents towards brown bears and away from pink cats, he felt they were doing this out of a misplaced sense of his best interests. 'I think they were afraid of what my friends would say. They should have said, "So what?"' But most parents want to save their children from enduring stigma or peer-group exclusion. Amy, the mother of two boys who are not yet in school, tells me, 'I am aware of others' reactions. One of my sons had dress-up day recently at nursery and I had a sinking feeling that he would want to wear his pirate dress and would end up being mocked by the older children. I was so relieved when he said he wanted to go as a dinosaur. That is awful. I shouldn't have to think that. But you do want to protect them. I worry about him starting school. He doesn't have particularly feminine traits or interests but if he did I would so whole-heartedly want to encourage him, but I would also worry about the reaction of others.' Tom from Devon says of his son, 'He is very sensitive. He can be incredibly smiley and happy, but it can be thunder and lightning too. He is a soft and gentle boy and he will burst into tears very, very easily. I was exactly the same when I was a child. I was told by my sisters, "Don't cry, it's embarrassing." I do occasionally say to him, when things are tough with his friends, that it is sometimes better if you don't show you are upset as it may encourage others to tease you more.'

The penalty paid by children who don't fit in is not just a social one, but potentially a physical one too; as we've seen, boys use physical aggression to maintain hierarchies. Dr Andrew Irwin-Smiler, a psychologist and therapist specialising in masculine behaviour, comments, 'One of the very real ways that gender gets policed, at least among guys, is this perpetual threat or joke of "somebody's going to kick our ass". It's kind of always there, and guys know it.'[20] Parents face a hard choice. Do they risk their child becoming a victim by encouraging him to resist the mainstream macho culture? Or do they stand back, allowing their son to get drawn in?

All children, girls or boys, become aware of the social expectations placed on them because of their sex. Parents cannot deny these expectations exist. Indeed it would be unhelpful to do so, since we cannot wish them away. But we can actively support our children by acknowledging these expectations as they arise and then analysing and challenging them, in the hope of showing that it is possible to find your place in the world and stay true to yourself. Judy Chu speaks good, pragmatic sense on this topic: 'One thing we can do is to help kids distinguish between their behaviours and their beliefs. Ideally their behaviours would always reflect their beliefs. But this is not always practical. At times when they feel reluctant to speak up, they can still preserve their integrity by remaining aware of what they really think, feel or want. That is, they can compromise their behaviours without compromising their beliefs. If forced to choose, it's more important for them to know than to say what is in their hearts and minds. That said, we can also help kids to identify and focus their efforts on relationships in which they wouldn't have to choose between being themselves and being with others.'[21]

We all strive to teach our children to behave appropriately, make smart choices, form strong allegiances and build a base of support in their lives whilst maintaining a strong sense of themselves. That is a parent's crucial role – to help our sons (and daughters) find a balance between these social forces and personal needs, setting them up as best we can for their lives to come.

'A man should look like a boss'

It is important to help children find this balance when they are young because parents begin to lose some of their influence when children move from primary to secondary school. The rigidity of the cultural rules for boys and the rigour with which they are enforced also intensify. Aaron, who has just graduated from university and lives in Hull, remembers this transition well. 'At primary school if there was a play everyone wanted a part. As soon as we got to secondary school, I turned up to the auditions and there was only one other boy there. I guess people think it's the age when you are supposed to become a man, so drama's not for me. It changed really quickly.' Frank, who has two boys and is a secondary school teacher, is very aware of the need to counter the negative forces pulling at boys. 'I think the influences that boys are subjected to – the stereotypes and the way that society tries to shape them into highly competitive, physically assertive beings – if you don't temper that with a kinder influence, by teaching them to be aware of others and thoughtful and empathic – then they won't learn it. Boys are terribly affectionate, and instinctively so. They are emotionally aware and sensitive. But you need to enable them to bring that out.'

Adherence to the male rules was evident when I visited a large, mixed-sex state secondary school in east London to watch the work of the Great Men project. When I walked in on the group of fourteen-year-old boys I was to follow, they were working in pairs under the direction of two volunteers on a 'body sculpture' exercise, each boy manipulating his partner into a suitably manly stance and then describing what he had done to the rest of the group:

> BOY: I made this sculpture because I think a man should look like a boss, a proper guy who should be in charge.
> VOLUNTEER: So a guy who is not in charge is not proper?
> BOY: You've just confused me now, sir.

Later that morning, the boys turned their attention to the 'man box', the personality traits that are commonly accepted to make a man, first watching anti-violence-against-women activist Tony Porter's brief and powerful TED talk on the subject.[22] The boys were then invited to make their own, new 'man box', with all the traits that they would like included within it. The boys listed:

Be free
Allow people to be different
Allow us to have choices
If you want to be emotional, you can be
Empathy
Responsibility
Respecting women
If you want to be gay, be gay.

That's so gay

This allusion to the need for greater acceptance of homosexuality among schoolboys reflects the findings of research published by the equality campaign group Stonewall. In many ways, Britain has become a more socially liberal country in recent decades and there has been a marked change in attitudes amongst the young towards gay people and homosexual relationships. Young people are less homophobic than older generations and more sexually experimental. When asked about their sexuality, half of British eighteen to twenty-four year olds now say they are neither gay nor straight but somewhere in between.[23] This is a remarkable transformation in social mores. Yet at the same time, Stonewall's research shows that homophobic bullying is still rife. Gay boys, in particular, are still subject to significant abuse from their peers, usually other boys. Boys in Britain are far more likely to be the perpetrators of homophobic bullying than girls, and gay boys are more likely to be the victims than bisexual boys and girls or lesbians.[24]

Part of the explanation for these apparently contradictory facts may lie in the contemporary use of the word 'gay' as a general put-down, to mean weak and unimpressive. While some have argued that this broadening out of the common definition of the word reduces its potential to offend,[25] groups such as Stonewall are adamant that equating 'gay' with 'rubbish' is part of the problem and that its use remains homophobic and harmful towards homosexual young people.[26] But the most intriguing thing about the common contemporary use of 'gay' is that it is also relentlessly employed to ensure boys are behaving in what is deemed an appropriately masculine way. It is not just directed at homosexual boys and rubbish things, but also at straight boys who do not conform to prescribed masculine behaviour. According to Ben, 'The word "gay" is definitely used to police behaviour. It is used as a warning sign that you are straying from the consensus on how the group should behave.'

In her research into boys' friendships, Niobe Way, Professor of Applied Psychology at New York University, found that while most of the teenage boys she spoke to wanted close friendships with other boys, they worried that being open about it would lead to accusations of being 'gay'. This led to a loss of intimacy as the boys progressed through adolescence.[27] Aaron, a new graduate, tells me, 'From the age of about fourteen or fifteen if there was ever any talk about feelings, someone would punch you in the arm and tell you to shut up.' C. J. Pascoe, associate professor of sociology at America's University of Oregon and author of *Dude, You're a Fag*, dubs this way of policing masculinity 'fag discourse'.[28] In the early 2000s she based herself for eighteen months in a high school in a working-class area of California. There the most commonly mentioned infringements against manly behaviour included dancing, showing emotion and being incompetent at something. Peer groups of boys would call out such behaviour in an aggressive, humorous and collective manner, partly to shore up their own position. Other researchers have even detected a 'compensatory masculinity' among those who fear being labelled as 'non-manly'.[29]

However, beyond the broad 'fag discourse' – which is still at work in schools today – Pascoe is careful to make the point that gay pupils are bullied for being gay. It could be that the bullying of gay boys by other boys is in part a means for the bullies to establish their own position in the social hierarchy – because gay boys are thought not to conform to the rigid view of masculinity so important to adolescent males, they are likely targets. This may go some way to explaining why homophobic bullying is more prevalent among boys than girls.

Pascoe notes that, of the three openly gay boys in the school she studied, it was the one who was the most overtly gay (in dress, interests and manner) that suffered the most bullying, to the extent that ultimately he dropped out of school. When I speak to Charlie

Condou he tells me about his experience of being gay and at school in the 1980s. 'When I was young I was quite effeminate and then at the age of about eleven I realised that the way I was wasn't going to be okay for me. I am not sure if that was because of how people reacted to me or just because at that age I had an internalised homophobia. That's why I think being camp is a brave thing to be. I conditioned myself in a way.' Since Charlie was at school, rights for gay people and wider social attitudes on homosexuality have improved, although the teachers and young men I spoke to painted a mixed picture of the progress that has been made. Frank believes that there is cause for optimism and things have got better: 'I went to a boys' boarding school. It was a hyper masculine environment. The bullying and teasing that happened there were terrible, looking back on it. Boys who were gay or effeminate were savagely, mercilessly treated, perhaps suffering homophobic bullying for years. I have worked in the state sector in so-called challenging schools and I have seen nothing like the way some boys were treated there. Mind you, that was a while ago and times have changed.'

Andrew McBroom is Head of Sixth Form at City of London School, a boys' public day school. I arranged to visit the school to talk to him and some of his pupils who have recently formed a Feminist Society. 'We pride ourselves on turning out boys who are good men,' Andrew remarks. 'The boys tend to be quite enlightened. There are always openly gay boys in the school. They will come to the end-of-sixth-form prom with their partners and no one bats an eyelid.' Indeed, when I meet the Feminist Society that lunchtime, boys are ticked off by others for their 'heteronormative' assumptions on more than one occasion. An alternative form of policing is in place. But this is in contrast to the memories of Barney, a student in Manchester. He also went to a single-sex London public school, which he left just three years ago: 'Two boys have come out since school. There must have been an element of those boys feeling it wasn't acceptable to be gay when they were there.' I tell him about the City of London School prom. 'At our prom, there was not one person who wasn't in a hetero-sexual couple. We are not as progressive as we think.' Lewis, another volunteer with Great Men, says to me, 'On the surface young people are a lot more tolerant. There are more kids who feel they can come out now. But you have to come out in certain ways: in a way that is not seen as threatening. So you might be very performative and camp, so people can put you in a box. But it would be hard to come out and be masculine or in the rugby team.'

This diverse range of experiences is perhaps to be expected given the rapidity of social change: in under thirty years Britain has gone from introducing Section 28 to legalising same-sex marriage. On the whole, young people appear more relaxed than older generations about same-sex relationships. Yet the old stigma still holds some sway among boys at an age when their own sexuality is developing and they are trying to fit in to a social world governed by male rules, with heterosexual assumptions at its heart.

The group of young people that arguably suffers the most from the binary way in which society constructs gender is transgender children. Transgender people are estimated to make up 1 per cent of the UK population, although it is of course difficult to be precise on this point.[30] Over twice the number of male to female transgender people as female to male have considered or taken action towards sex reassignment,[31] although more females to males are now coming for-ward.[32] The Tavistock and Portman NHS Trust is the only UK centre specialising in gender identity issues in children. It has seen a four-fold increase in those aged ten or under being referred to the unit in recent years.[33]

Susie Green is the chair of Mermaids, a group that supports trans young people. She tells me that boys and their parents tend to pick up on gender identity issues earlier than girls precisely because of the more rigid rules applied to boys. On the one hand it is heartening that children are able to discuss the severe emotional turbulence they experience and that parents seek out help. Yet it is also deeply troubling that children feel so constrained by established male or female ways of being that deviation is seen as such a problem: the medical term 'gender identity disorder' is itself an example of this.[34] As Dr Jay Stewart, the Director of Gendered Intelligence, a charity that works with trans youth, told a parliamentary committee at Westminster, 'We live in a world that is very much about being a girl or a boy and never the twain will meet, and trans people complicate the picture of the gender binary.'[35] The suffering is huge for this vulnerable minority: a third of trans adults have attempted suicide at some point in their lives and half of trans young people self-harm.[36] Our rigid gender rules for boys and girls must contribute to these dreadful statistics. Susie says, 'If there wasn't an issue about what toys, clothes or other children kids played with there wouldn't be any major distress. There is a massive amount of prejudice out there, with children being told they are strange and wrong. Everyone is an individual and society should stop pigeon-holing people into a particular mould.'

Susie speaks as someone who has seen this distress up close – one of her children, a daughter, was born a boy. Susie recalls that, growing up, 'My daughter's distress was caused because she was bullied so badly, called a gay boy and a freak. Not having to deal with that wouldn't have stopped her wanting to be female but she wouldn't have taken seven overdoses.' Susie says her daughter has now recovered emotionally and, when we spoke, was working abroad.

On an individual level, for some people such as Susie's daughter, surgery or hormone treatment appears to have transformed their lives for the better. But on a societal level, it should give us pause for thought that the gender binary means the desire to explore an identity more commonly associated with 'the opposite gender', as the NHS unhelpfully calls it,[37] is pathologised. While many support surgery and hormone therapy and others argue the solution lies in

psychiatric treatment, the fundamental problem with society's bifur-
cated view of gender often gets overlooked. This needs to change. As
Dr Stewart says, 'We are going to see more and more stories coming
through where people are really challenging the gender binary, and
that is a challenge to shift cultural attitudes, because we are very regulated in terms of our behaviour and social expectations of what it
means to be a girl or a boy.'[38]

'Looking good is pretty key'

Back at the Great Men session in east London, one of the final exer-
cises the schoolboys perform is 'the mood board' – in which they pull
out images of men and women from newspapers and magazines to
compare the way the sexes are portrayed. It is quite incongruous to see
these teenage boys chatting away in groups around tables as they cut
out the pictures and glue them on large pieces of card, as if they were
doing a nursery collage rather than taking a break from GCSEs. Sure
enough, many of the images of women that the boys come across are
sexualised. 'Whoa!' says one boy as he tears out a picture of a woman
from a men's magazine. Another cuts round a picture of a naked
woman and sticks his tongue between the legs. But some of the photos
of men are overtly sexual too. In between bland agency photos of
men in suits carrying briefcases or snappers' shots of politicians, are
images of male actors, models and sports stars with few clothes on.
'Everyone spends 60 per cent of their day thinking about if they look
all right. I feel self-conscious all the time,' says one boy as he assembles
his images. 'In the morning I think I need to make sure I look my best
even if I'm only going to Tesco or Westfield,' says another.

The contemporary emphasis on male physical prowess has led
to a preoccupation with body image, and the diet and exercise

regimes that produce sculpted, six-pack physiques. Eating disorders are on the rise among boys and young men. Although the number of female sufferers far outweighs that of boys and men (63 per 100,000 of the population and 7 per 100,000 respectively), male incidences of eating disorders have increased sharply since the turn of the century.[39] These disorders take different forms. Boys are more likely to attempt to control their weight by excessive exercise and frequent bingeing and purging, whereas girls tend to restrict their food intake or avoid certain foods.[40] Encouragingly, boys are increasingly willing to ask for help, though many young men with entrenched eating disorders only realise at a late stage that they have a problem, and medics are less likely to spot the condition in male patients.[41] This is frequently because eating disorders remain associated with young women, rather than boys, and perhaps too because young men aspire to a very different physical ideal to girls: rather than being waif-like, boys want to be lean, certainly, but often also muscle-bound.[42]

It is no coincidence that alongside the rise in male eating disorders the popular-culture obsession with the male body has also grown. The ripped look that was once the preserve of weightlifters and *Men's Health* magazine now pervades male celebrity culture. Stars from Hugh Jackman to Justin Bieber display their glistening, buff bodies in photo shoots. David Beckham – the celebrity footballer of our age – seems to flaunt more muscle and fewer clothes with each year that passes. Whether they are taking off their shirts on a pitch or on screen there is an increasing expectation that sportsmen and actors should look not just fit, but pumped. This spectacle is presumably why films like *Magic Mike XXL* get made: its story of a male stripper is light years away from *The Full Monty* or even the cheeky antics of the Chippendales. The transformation of actors like Chris Pratt, once the go-to guy for chubby boy-next-door roles and now a muscle-bound action hero, helps ratchet up the pressure for every man – and boy.

On TV, male reality stars discuss their Friday-night plans while working out together in the gym or casually playing a spot of shirts-off handball in Kensington Gardens. An episode of *Made in Chelsea* or *TOWIE* is not complete without a sequence featuring the male stars' waxed chests and six-packs. It is the men who are objectified in these programmes as much as the women; after all, they are targeting a young female audience.[43] In one scene from *Made in Chelsea*, standing on the sidelines while her latest fling, JP, plays a game of rugby, the marvellously monikered Binky Felstead remarks that it is good to see the boys looking like 'actual men'. For boys growing up now, it would be almost impossible not to be affected to some degree by these ubiquitous images.

Alex Lunn, a teacher at Gosforth Academy, a large state secondary school in Newcastle upon Tyne, told me, 'Programmes like *Geordie Shore*, where the men all have six-packs and tans, are a big influence. We have a gym at the school that is open to sixth-formers and obviously it is a good thing to exercise and be healthy. But going there has become the equivalent of hanging out behind the bike sheds for some boys. They take protein shakes and strive towards goals that they are never going to reach.' Zane, a young man whom I meet at a boxing club in London, tells me that he is influenced by 'fashion and the media. The images are everywhere. Be healthy. Have an Action Man body. Live the dream in Vegas or Ibiza.' 'Looking good is pretty key,' agrees Andy, an apprentice in his late teens from the north-east of England. 'It is one of the most important factors in my friendship group. We take a lot of pride in our appearance. We are not an ugly bunch. I like buying clothes and getting my hair cut. I make sure I stay fit by going to the gym. We do judge people on their looks in my generation. Appearance is high on my list of priorities, after morals and ethics.' Even those who feel they cannot spend hours pumping iron are not left unscathed. 'We don't have the time to go down the gym,' a boy from City of London School informs me, 'but you can't ignore that we have these pressures now in a way that women have had for much longer. It is not just being muscly it's about being thin too. It's a lot easier and less time consuming to lose weight than to build up muscle.' 'We are surrounded by underwear ads and music videos – that's the reality and that can have a bad effect,' agrees one of his schoolmates. 'A lot of my friends – they are fine with not being muscly but they do want to be skinny. Especially as at our age there are people who can eat whatever they want and not put on weight. And for some people who may not naturally have that, they really push themselves to get skinny.' I do not think that any of the teenage boys I knew as I grew up would have come out with such an observation. Even in the age of the male waif shoe-gazer, boys did not seem to care about their weight. A squirt of Sun-In and the odd session on a sunbed was as groomed as it got for adolescent males in eighties Newcastle.

Paul Rudd, the lead actor in *Ant-Man*, has spoken about the intense year-long no-carbs, no-alcohol, all-exercise regime he undertook for the film, that was 'almost kind of impossible to sustain'.[44] Increasingly this is standard for film actors wanting to make it big at the box office. Chris Pratt has said, 'I think it's appalling that for a long time only women were objectified, but I think if we really want to advocate for equality, it's important to even things out. Not objectify women less, but objectify men just as often as we objectify women. There are a lot of women who got careers out of it, and I'm using it to my advantage. And at the end of the day, our bodies are objects.'[45] While male advocates for equality are usually to be welcomed, a climate where both men and women obsess about their bodies is hardly something to be celebrated. Levelling down is not the way to go. As Dr Raymond Lemberg, a clinical psychologist specialising in male eating disorders puts it, 'The media has become more of an equal opportunity discriminator. Men's bodies are not good enough any more either.'[46]

Is there a 'boy crisis' in the classroom?

Concern about school-age boys tends to focus less on the cultural pressures they are under than on their academic achievement, or lack of it. In recent years in the UK, the exam results season has brought a rush of media stories about the unstoppable rise of girls.[47] In 2015, at GCSE, girls in England did better than boys across most subjects, even narrowly outstripping boys in traditionally male subjects such as chemistry and maths.[48] But we should not lose sight of some vital details. Firstly, educational attainment is rising for boys and girls: both are doing better than they have done in the past.[49] Secondly, in 2015 the difference between boys' and girls' achievement at GCSE narrowed very slightly compared to the previous year, with 61.8 per cent of girls awarded at least a C grade in five or more subjects including English and maths compared to 52.5 per cent of boys. The gap is still marked and has closed by just 0.8 per cent, but it was seen as a step in the right direction.[50] Finally, and crucially, a closer look at the data reveals that not all boys are falling behind – it is specifically working-class boys. There are ethnic differences too, and the interaction between social background, sex and ethnicity is a complex one. Ofsted has analysed the GCSE performance of pupils eligible for free school meals, broken down into groups by sex and ethnicity. It shows that in English schools White British and Black Caribbean boys from low-income families perform worse than all other economically disadvantaged groups. The next worst performing group is White British girls from disadvantaged backgrounds. These girls achieve poorer results than low-income boys from all other ethnic groups, except Black Caribbean boys and White British boys. This prompts Ofsted to state that, 'The poor performance of low-income White British pupils is not, therefore, a gender issue.'[51] But the fact is that within each ethnic group, including White British, boys from low-income families do worse than girls. In its 2015 report *Is Britain Fairer?*, the Equality and Human Rights Commission drew attention to the lower educational attainment of disadvantaged white boys in particular.[52] Underachievement is primarily to do with class and ethnicity. But sex is a secondary factor. It should not be overstated but nor should it be overlooked.

Are boys born with a dislike of books?

If we are concerned with boys' educational achievement – rather than, say, the qualifications achieved by disadvantaged children as a whole – then we should focus on two key areas where it is possible to identify a distinct 'problem with boys'. The first is literacy. It is in literacy (that is, reading, writing and spelling) where girls most markedly outstrip boys and this has been the case for a number of years.[53] Some boys love reading and writing and do very well at it. But, overall, when comparing the performance of girls and boys in English at GCSE there is a 15 per cent gap in girls' favour in the proportion gaining A* to C grades. Compare this to the 1 per cent gap in girls' favour in maths.[54]

In a 2012 report, the UK's All Party Parliamentary Literacy Group Commission was clear that 'Boys' underachievement in literacy is not inevitable. It is not simply a result of biological differences'.[55] Rather, it must be linked to the way in which parents bring up boys, as compared to girls. Spending less time in the home talking to boys or encouraging them to sit with a book or even to write their own story will have an effect in the classroom. I frequently hear the opinion being expressed that boys are not as good at – or not as interested in – reading as girls. This belief explains why parents are less likely to read to boys, or to take them to the library.[56] If I find this message oppressive and depressing, what must it be like for a young boy to be exposed to this dreary refrain? The subsequent effect of this parental influence on academic attainment is not limited to English results. As research from the Organisation for Economic Co-operation and Development (OECD) points out, reading is the foundation for other learning.[57] If you cannot read well you will have difficulty with everything from history websites to Spanish textbooks. Perhaps we could stop the rot if we also stopped peddling myths about boys' inbuilt reading aversion.

Subject segregation between boys and girls has been much discussed in recent years in the UK, with a particular focus on encouraging girls to take science and maths to A level and beyond. Unquestionably, more female scientists would be good for the field of science itself, as well as for the individual job prospects of girls and the health of the wider economy. However, there should also be a focus on encouraging more boys to take up subjects such as English Literature. At present, less than a third of Year 13 English Literature A-level students in England are male, making up about 3 per cent of the total year group.[58] Arguably, it is a sign of how devalued literature is in our society that this fact occupies so little space in the debate. The arts may not be the most secure route to a glittering career and healthy bank balance but they pay dividends in other ways.

I learned more about effective, inclusive approaches to teaching English when I visited Gosforth Academy in Newcastle upon Tyne. The hangar-like white structure stands on a main road opposite an Asda supermarket from which, when I arrived, pupils were hurrying out with snacks before their first lesson. The building was extended under the Labour government's New Deal for Schools initiative and the new facilities were opened in 2002 by the then Prime Minister (and north-east MP) Tony Blair. There's a plaque in the gleaming reception area marking the event. During his visit, the

PM attended a language class, speaking in French to the students. He was then driven off in a motorcade, past a jeering crowd of striking firefighters.

Chris Duckett, the Director of Communication, Teaching and Learning, describes the school as, 'thoroughly comprehensive, with ability groups evenly split. It is in a middle-class area but there are pockets of deprivation. It is the most ethnically mixed school in the city and there is an acceptance of difference.' When I talk to two of the English Literature teachers at the school, Alex Lunn and Mark Fryer, they set out in eloquent detail the benefits of studying their subject. 'You learn to express the complexity of ideas,' says Mark. 'You are forced to confront the notion of truth in the world: think of Gatsby, a man trying to be something he is not. It enables a level of self-analysis.' Alex adds, 'It gives you emotional intelligence, understanding of how people work, empathy, the ability to put yourself in other people's shoes, a greater understanding of life and how to communicate.' As Alex spoke it occurred to me that he was listing the qualities that so many people say boys lack. Encouraging boys to acquire and develop their interest in reading and English would pay dividends in purely academic terms, as well as broadening their minds and strengthening their ability to engage with others.

Chris Duckett informs me that there is a smaller than average gap in the achievement of boys and girls at the school.[59] What struck me when talking to the staff there was how they treat all pupils, no matter their sex, as individuals rather than as part of a monolithic group. Alex Lunn told me, 'We have done training on working with underachieving boys but you can end up forming and perpetuating stereotypes. Different individual kids need different things. It is about offering varied activities to engage everyone, so they find it really interesting. And that could be looking at a range of texts rather than getting them to run around.' Katherine Saunt, a colleague of Andrew McBroom at City of London School, also expresses scepticism about a homogeneous approach to teaching boys: 'We are wary of being prescriptive. You do hear the argument that boys should be allowed to get up and run around more, but that's based on a stereotype. Every boy is different.'

Research backs up the approach at these two schools. Focusing on the imagined differences between boys and girls and basing lessons around them actually embeds stereotypes. Children are more likely to conform to stereotype in this environment. Instead, training teachers to be less stereotyping in their teaching produces good results, promoting interaction and positive attitudes in the classroom between the sexes.[60] In mixed-sex schools at least, the barriers between 'us and them' start to come down.

Are boys born badly behaved?

The second area where there is a 'boy problem' is in exclusion from school. In England, boys are three times more likely than girls to receive a fixed-term exclusion and four times more likely to be permanently excluded.[61] Over 70 per cent of those permanently and temporarily excluded from school are boys.[62] Although exclusion affects a small proportion of boys, and the rates have gone down in recent years, its impact is deep and long lasting.[63] Exclusion dramatically cuts educational achievement, which then feeds through into poorer outcomes in later life.[64] Excluded boys have a much higher chance of ending up unemployed, in low-paid jobs or in prison.[65] Over half of prisoners had been temporarily excluded from school. Just under half had been permanently excluded.[66] Educational exclusion has dire consequences.

The great majority of exclusions happen during secondary school but the foundations are laid much earlier. Work by academics at the

University of Kent has shown that by the time girls are four years old and boys are seven, children think girls are better behaved and more academically successful. They also believe that adults feel the same.[67] Yet it may be that those teaching and caring for young children encourage the unruly behaviour associated with boys. This applies at home but it also happens in formal settings. In Chapter 1 I mentioned a classic study that tracked children's behaviour in daycare and preschool and found changes between the sexes over time according to their treatment by adults. At the start of the study one-year-old boys and girls displayed similar levels of aggression and assertion and similar styles of communication. Over the course of the following eleven months teachers and care staff responded to boys' aggressive, assertive behaviour and their loud and intense communication. The response might have involved talking to the boy, attempting to distract him by giving him a new toy to play with or moving him to a different part of the room. All of this demonstrates to boys that behaving aggressively elicits attention and a change in the situation. The adults ignored such aggressive, assertive behaviour in girls. The boys' behaviour worsened while the girls' behaviour improved. It is not possible to be conclusive about the precise reason for the changes in the children's behaviour, but it is reasonable to assume that the teachers' responses contributed to it. The researchers note that it can be difficult for adults to interpret infants' behaviour – for example, what a child intends by a seemingly aggressive act. Therefore, they believe, adults 'use any clues available to interpret the child's behaviour. The sex of the child is one such clue, calling into play whatever stereotypical expectations about boys' and girls' behaviour the adult possesses … Using a stereotype to guide behaviour is efficient in terms of processing information economically, but in doing so the stereotype is perpetuated.'[68] Other studies among primary-aged children have shown a similar pattern of disruptive boys receiving the lion's share of a teacher's time and their disruptive behaviour being permitted in a way that similar behaviour from girls is not.[69] Compliant girls become drowned out by loud boys, while boys learn that being badly behaved is the way to get attention.

In its 2011 study of male mental health, the charity Mind pointed out that boys are often regarded as 'a problem' in an educational, and wider, context.[70] Boys are caught in a double bind here. They have been encouraged to behave in a physical, loud and assertive way from birth, and then they are labelled as problematic for doing so. As Indigo, the mother of two sons from Brighton, says, 'I've lost count of the number of times I have heard people put poor behaviour in boys down to testosterone. My personal view is that boys should not be any better or worse behaved than girls and that that is an excuse developed over time.' There may well be too much sedentary time in classrooms and no doubt both boys and girls – especially at primary age – could do with more exercise in their day to improve concentration and behaviour. But it should also be possible to teach most boys and girls to sit still and focus when required. This is a useful skill for life, not just in the classroom. As the 2012 all-party parliamentary report on reading attainment notes of the boys interviewed, 'Their need to run around and be active certainly didn't seem to dampen their enthusiasm for spending lengthy periods playing computer games.'[71]

The disapproval of boys continues in secondary school. A 2015 OECD study of education systems in sixty countries, including the UK, found that teachers tend to give girls higher marks than boys, even when they are turning in work of the same standard. Teachers 'mark up' girls' work in part because they are predisposed to favour girls whom they expect to be more engaged in learning and less disruptive.[72] This is clearly detrimental to boys. It may be harmful for girls too: a teacher who is wedded to the good, able girl stereotype will be less alert to signs that they are struggling. Girls themselves learn to mask any difficulties they may experience, in order to conform to type. It has also been suggested that conditions such as autism are more likely to go undiagnosed in girls because they take great pains to cover up any autistic traits.[73]

The OECD found that, once again, boys in the classroom soon adapt their behaviour to fit the stereotype of being more troublesome and less accomplished. The report notes that: 'From a young age, boys are less likely to raise their hand in class to ask to speak, they are worse at waiting their turn to speak or engage in an activity, they are less likely to listen and pay attention before starting a project.'[74] As they grow older, boys should be able to see for themselves that this behaviour is inappropriate. But is it any surprise that they act in such a way, given expectations of them are low and their poor conduct commands attention?

This can be a confusing and corrosive environment for boys. Outside the classroom they regard themselves as superior to girls (and thus keen to avoid anything deemed feminine) and their concerns about hierarchy focus on where they stand in relation to other boys. Inside the classroom they are treated as the inferior sex, so they try to take control by acting up. This oppositional relationship between the sexes does neither any good. As the sociologist Raewyn Connell has noted, school discipline becomes a challenge for some boys, and they 'take up the offer' of confronting it. Rule breaking becomes a mark of identity and a means of gaining status and pleasure.[75]

Of course, it is not only boys who misbehave. Helen, a teacher at a secondary school in Sheffield, points out that: 'There are some girls with very challenging behaviour too. But the range of boys who can be challenging is wider. Bright boys can be challenging as well as low-ability boys, whereas with girls, if they are bright they are very rarely poorly behaved. There is a culture of smart Alec, middle-class boys who try to challenge teachers intellectually.'

Boys can not only act up but switch off, buying into the idea that trying hard and caring about school is in some way uncool or even feminine. The perceived lack of respect from teachers may also play its part in disengagement.[76] I first met Ruben at an event on the changing role of fathers. Ruben has a son himself and was speaking as a representative of the Young Dads Collective, a peer-support service for fathers under twenty-five. I arranged to catch up with him again a few weeks later to hear more about his work and background. Ruben was brought up in a number of foster homes in different cities across the UK. As a result, he moved from school to school. He tells me, 'When I was at school being smart was seen as a negative thing. Smart meant weak. Looking back it is such an absurd way to think, to say you are not an alpha male because you are intelligent.' Neil, a father of two from Lancaster, says of his own teenage son: 'He is a clever boy, but he will not apply himself. He has always found it very difficult to navigate being cool and being academic. That is what my wife and I talk about all the time. That's where he's conflicted.' But not all boys switch off: some affirm their identity through excelling academically, or view being clever as a status symbol. Ruben recalls a friend who stood out from the crowd because he flaunted his learning rather than hiding it: 'When I was sixteen, seventeen, me and my friend, we would encourage people to use big words and be competitive about it.' Others like Neil's son will try to keep a foot in the academic and cool camps.[77]

The labelling of boys also affects their well-being. Astonishingly, being a boy is in itself a risk factor for mental health issues in childhood. Eight per cent of children between five and ten years old have a mental disorder, with boys twice as likely as girls to experience these problems.[78] Boys in England are four times as likely as girls to be identified as having behavioural, emotional or social difficulty in school.[79] Mental Health America also reports that almost twice the number of boys as girls are diagnosed with conduct disorder in the US.[80]

For some boys their behaviour will worsen to the point where they risk exclusion. This may well have much to do with factors outside of school, such as an unstable family life. But schools do need to bear responsibility for how they deal with these boys. Teachers' unions are invariably bullish about excluding pupils. 'At the end of the day,' intones Brian Lightman, general secretary of the Association of School and College Leaders, '[Heads] have a responsibility to all pupils in their care and they cannot allow the education or safety of the majority to be jeopardised by one or two pupils.'[81] On the face of it, this may sound fair. But the zero-tolerance argument is undermined by the significant disparities in exclusion rates from school to school, area to area. Some schools are better able to manage challenging behaviour – or are more disposed to doing so – than others. Department for Education figures for 2013 show that, for example, exclusion rates for pupils with special educational needs (SEN) in England range from 3 per cent to 13 per cent from one local authority to another.[82] Having special educational needs is the most dominant characteristic of those who are excluded. SEN children are nine times more likely to be permanently excluded than non-SEN peers and it has been suggested that schools may be illegally excluding children with SEN due to issues such as lack of staff available to support them.[83] There are other alarming disparities within the exclusion data too. Alongside being male, children are far more likely to be excluded if they are poor and from an ethnic minority. In 2013 the then Children's Commissioner for England, Dr Maggie Atkinson, published a study of exclusions. It found that, 'a boy of Black Caribbean heritage with Special Educational Needs (SEN), eligible for free school meals, is 168 times more likely to be excluded from school than a White British girl without SEN, from a more affluent family'.[84]

There is evidence of lower expectations and differential treatment of black boys within school. This is something that these boys themselves are acutely aware of,[85] as are their parents. Tanya lives in London and has one son. He won a sport scholarship to a boarding school in the country when he was eleven. Although he found it a difficult transition she feels it was the best choice for him: 'I knew from my brother all the problems that he had with labelling and I didn't want that for my own son. A young black boy in London: what would that be like for him? His white friends were looking at local schools but I knew it would be different for him. I worried about the prejudice of teachers, as well as the police.' It is debatable whether a young black boy risks encountering more hostility in London than in a boarding school in the country, but nevertheless it is telling that this fear prompted Tanya to take her son out of school in the capital. Prejudice is not always to be found; as a young black student Ruben remembers his teachers as an important source of support during a childhood spent in foster homes: 'I had one or two teachers who were really, really helpful. Two of them even travelled with me from the Midlands to London one time so that I could collect an award.' However, analysis shows that black pupils who are excluded are less likely than excluded white pupils to have a long record of disruptive behaviour, indicating a lower bar for their exclusion. [86]

'Unconditional positive regard'

The Children's Commissioner's report was called 'They Go the Extra Mile' in acknowledgement of the efforts made by some schools to avoid exclusions. Perhaps the most prominent current advocate of inclusion is the remarkable Stephen Drew. Drew was the stand-out star of Channel 4's insightful and heart-warming *Educating Essex*, a fly-on-the-wall documentary about a large comprehensive second-ary school in Harlow. Deputy Head Mr Drew, as he was known to the pupils, stole the show with his dedication, dry wit and endless patience. These characteristics were tested even further in the spin-off series *Mr Drew's School for Boys*, in which he attempted to re-engage a group of boys in the world of school with mixed success. It was only a matter of time before he was running his own school and in 2012 he was appointed head teacher of Brentwood County High School in Essex, where he leads over 1,300 children and 200 staff. Stephen Drew is running slightly late the day I meet him. He explains that he was detained by a minor incident in the school's reintegration unit, where a few of the pupils had decided to nip out for a cigarette. He greets me in the hall and takes me through to his office. Just outside his door we pass a girl sitting at a lone desk. He later explains that she had walked out of his assembly earlier in the day so was currently being treated to a spell of one-on-one monitoring. Stephen Drew takes the behaviour and engagement of his pupils seriously, following their progress closely and often getting involved personally. As he tells me in his upbeat manner, 'Behaviour is my bread and butter, managing behaviour is what I do all the time.'

Stephen Drew's attitude towards his pupils is striking: 'Unconditional Positive Regard for all young people is the starting point for success,' declares his Twitter account. It does not always go to plan. Mr Drew looks pained as he tells me that the school issued a fixed-term exclusion to a pupil the previous term. 'It really upset me. The worry is once you've done it, it becomes easy – you know, I've screwed it up this year so [I may as well keep on excluding].' He explains, 'I'm loath to permanently exclude children. Don't get me wrong, if I have a situation where a kid is impossible to deal with and the parents won't engage at all then sometimes you are left with no choice. But other than that, I have managed to get through seven terms without permanently excluding anyone, and the whole of the last school year without using any fixed-term exclusions, which only 140 schools in the whole country managed, and only about a dozen of those were "ordinary" comprehensive schools.'

So what is the secret of his success? 'Successful behaviour management is so much about relationships and balancing acts and juggling all the plates. I don't think I'm particularly amazing at it. I just work hard at it. To use a very clear example – kids swearing at teachers. I am very, very clear: adults don't come to school to be sworn at by kids. And I say to kids, "I don't care if your parents swear at you, I don't care if you watch it in films: it's wrong and you are not doing it to my staff." But why do kids do it? The vast majority of the time it's their frustration, their anger. But people's reaction to kids swearing can be they actually want a pound of flesh, they want to feel that some dramatic public thing has been done that leads to a kid being excluded. Whereas if you take an immediate dramatic action you actually stop yourself being able to deal with the situation. Because you've got the kid's back up to such an extent that you've damaged the relationship. Now some people will argue – quite fairly – that the kid has behaved in a way that is so appalling, why do they deserve to have you worry about the relationship? But actually, fundamentally, I worry about the kids. There's a bit of me that thinks if you've chosen to work with kids, suck it up. If you've chosen to work with them but you are going to be so damaged if a kid swears at you – actually, you need to go and get another job. We are the adults, we are the role models and we should act like it. And I don't think that a kid should somehow feel that they are being given up on.'

Alongside focusing on teachers' interactions with students, the need for a thick skin and a great deal of patience, Stephen Drew also uses structural resources to prevent exclusions. Brentwood's on-site reintegration centre means that disruptive pupils are separated from their classmates but still remain a part of the school community. 'Although we very, very rarely issue fixed-term exclusions, we do issue what we call "school isolation". They will serve all day in the reintegration centre on the site, and there they are supported and supervised by pastoral staff and inclusion staff. So they still have to come to school, they still have to do their work but they are away from everyone else and they are not impacting on other students. The principle is always reintegration. Our isolation room – where kids sit if they are taken out of lessons – is known as the Reflection and Intervention Zone. I said to my assistant head, "You know everyone will just laugh." But it is meant to be about reflection and intervention. There is always a teacher there and the kids have to come and sit and reflect and talk to them about it. It's not an argument, it's not a fuss, and a phone call is made to the parents to say, "This happened, this is where they are, the detention will be on this day."'

Stephen Drew is aware that his inclusive approach may attract challenging pupils: 'We do have very difficult kids who gravitate towards us. I'm not saying that other schools don't have them as well. But when kids seem to be failing in other schools, we do seem to end up with them and pick them up. I know that kids aren't leaving our school in the same position and going to others because we do hold on to these kids.' For him this openness to all pupils is central to the school's mission: 'There are some schools that make a profound difference to their communities. And that's what I aspire to here: a true comprehensive school that deals with everybody, that welcomes everybody, that doesn't say we'll have the most intelligent kids, we'll have the most this or that, that actually says we'll serve our community, whatever our community is and whatever our community brings us and we will try to provide that true comprehensive education for everybody.'

Exclusions are proportionately few in number, and the levels of disengagement, poor behaviour or particular needs among those who are excluded are not representative of the wider school population. Nonetheless, exclusions shine a light on the damage produced by warped masculinity. The stereotyping of boys may not always produce something as dramatic as exclusion from school, but it takes its toll on their sense of self and how they behave.

Stephen Drew's impressive record – and that of his staff and pupils – is proof that schools can deal with the behaviour of even the most difficult boys. Detractors may point to the below average number of students eligible for extra pupil premium funding at the school or those with SEN, as recorded by Ofsted in its 2013 inspection.[87] Yet Ofsted also noted that the attainment of both these groups of children had improved significantly under his leadership, that behaviour was good and that there was a calm atmosphere at the school. The success of the reintegration centre was also acknowledged. Such improvement in a large school over a short period of time demonstrates the importance of the behaviour systems that school managers put in place. It is possible with concerted effort to enable pupils at risk of becoming alienated to remain engaged in the life of the school and in their own education.

Stephen Drew's approach is a heartening example of the ways in which schools can ensure that the children in their charge feel they belong to, and are respected within, the school community. Even the most challenging boys can stay on track and succeed with the right leadership and support. They are not on a highway to nowhere.

3. OPPOSITES ATTACK
Boys vs. Girls

A show of strength

'The way that boys are brought up and the manner in which they treat women are connected. There's a thread that runs through all of it. How boys learn to behave at school, the bullying and the dominance, the sidelining of boys who don't fit that mould, is linked to later abuse of girls and women. It is all about power.' Sam is another of the volunteers I meet from the Great Men organisation. He holds workshops on sexism and stereotypes in secondary schools, and so has had ample opportunity to observe the attitudes of boys towards girls.

As we have seen in previous chapters, as a society we tend to see gender in binary terms. This means that boys are routinely viewed in opposition to girls: the troublesome vs. the compliant, the loud vs. the quiet, the active vs. the passive. Boys and girls share spaces and go through the same experiences (starting school, moving on to secondary education, interactions with friends, parents and teachers), yet these experiences are shaped in distinct ways according to their sex. Given that many girls and boys are seen, and see themselves, as different from each other, it is inevitable that an element of rivalry and even hostility will grow. Boys also develop a keen sense of hierarchy among themselves and in how they relate to girls. They learn that theirs is the superior sex and that proving their status is important. For some this will entail demonstrating their dominance over girls and women. As Sam says, it is all about power.

When boys are young, this power is demonstrated by excluding girls from play, rejecting anything considered feminine, being self-consciously assertive, aggressive and stoic, and attempting to subvert formal hierarchies (such as that of pupil and teacher). Later, sex and relationships come into it. Boys and young men shore up their status among peers by demonstrable and exaggerated interest in (heterosexual) sex. 'I'm very comfortable talking with my male friends about what we get up to,' says Mark, an A-level student. 'Although sometimes someone will let something slip and get teased about it for, like, the next two years.'

Violence and control

Some boys and young men also choose to display their power through aggression towards, and control of, the opposite sex. For a minority, their sense of themselves as men comes to depend on them physically and emotionally dominating women. This is patriarchy at its most raw. Gender roles and the inequality between the sexes are the foundation stones for such violence. Hyper-masculinity, misogyny and abuse are inextricably linked.

This wish to gain brute domination of women is not solely about demonstrating power over perceived inferiors. It is also about gaining power over perceived superiors – so-called 'contrapower'. For example, a number of pieces of research point to male sexual harassment of successful females, fuelled by a need to regain patriarchal control.[1] In a world where girls are popularly framed as better behaved and academically more successful, some boys – driven by poisonous notions of masculinity – will lash out. Rather than celebrating girls' success, their envy and sense of inadequacy turns into anger.

The statistics for attacks on girls and young women by boys and young men of the same age are horrifying. In a 2015 study of fourteen to seventeen year olds involving five European countries, 41 per cent of teenage girls in England reported having suffered sexual violence and abuse from boyfriends (in the main being pressured into sexual activity rather than being physically forced to do so). This was the highest rate in the five countries covered. Twenty-two per cent reported suffering physical violence, including slapping, punching and being beaten.[2] According to the Office for National Statistics, domestic violence and abuse rates among young people in relationships are higher than those among any other age group. Eleven per cent of young women aged sixteen to nineteen and 13 per cent of women aged twenty to twenty-four suffer domestic violence and abuse. The rates are 8 per cent and 7 per cent for young men respectively (I will look at the deeply controversial issue of domestic violence and abuse against men in the next chapter).[3] In fact, in 2012 the Westminster government changed its definition of domestic violence and abuse to include teenagers, in recognition that it is a significant problem among young people and in order to better identify cases and help ensure victims receive support.[4]

The first survey in the UK of violence and abuse in teenage relationships was conducted in 2009 among thirteen to twenty-one year olds by Bristol University for the NSPCC. The report made reference to a range of research showing that 'boys come under pressure, by peers and wider society, to portray a certain form of masculinity, characterised as controlling, sexually assertive and unemotional'. This peer dynamic means that when boys talk of using physical force against girls it may be met with approval by friends. In-depth interviews with young people for the project found evidence of boys using coercion (most often lying) to get girls to have sex with them. Again, this drew admiration from other boys, reflecting the pressure to come across as sexually knowing and aggressive. At the same time, interviews with teenage girls who suffered physical attacks found that 'violence was something that was routinely used within relationships as a general method of domination'. The study also noted that the young women surveyed often blamed themselves for being attacked, as if in some way they had provoked and so deserved the violence. As the researchers point out, this misplaced sense of responsibility is a common theme among victims of domestic violence and abuse.[5]

While researching this issue I came across a disturbing post on The Student Room (a website for young people at university and college in the UK) in which a female student described an incident with her boyfriend.

> I woke him up from a nap by tickling him and giggling, and he got angry. I didn't realise how angry he was and continued being annoying and mucking around. He got really angry and lashed out, and to try and lighten the mood and make it less awkward I went to tickle him again and he went crazy. He put his hands round my throat, he punched me in the arms and side and he put a pillow on my face for a few seconds. He also twisted my arm until I thought it would break … it really is my own fault for winding him up. What can I do to make sure he doesn't feel terrible/guilty in the morning?

As the moderator responding to the post emphatically pointed out, 'This is NOT your fault.'[6] That the female student in this situation believed she might have provoked her boyfriend in some way – and wanted to ensure 'he doesn't feel terrible' – demonstrates how deeply destructive the notion of submissive, placating femininity is, as well as that of an all-powerful masculinity.

The girls and young women in the Bristol University/NSPCC research who had suffered violence and abuse talked in admiring terms about the 'hard' masculine behaviour of their boyfriends as compared to other young men. They seemed to regard the violence inflicted upon them as a price worth paying for having a boyfriend, particularly one regarded as being able to take care of himself, thus giving him higher status.[7] Further, whereas the great majority of young people say male violence towards women is generally wrong, many also believe it is defensible in specific scenarios, such as when women or girls are perceived to have gone against relationship conventions (for example, lying or being unfaithful).[8] In the international

2015 study mentioned at the beginning of this chapter, 18 per cent of English boys aged fourteen to seventeen strongly agreed with the statement that, 'it is sometimes acceptable for a man to hit a woman if she has been unfaithful'.[9] Clearly, young people's views on the justification of violence are closely linked to gender roles. It is acceptable for young men to be violent as that is deemed within the masculine norm. Likewise if young women deviate from the expected feminine behaviours of submission and fidelity then they should expect to be punished.[10] Research has shown that the more rigidly gendered the beliefs of male adolescents, the more likely they are to practise sexual coercion,[11] underlining the way in which gender drives such male violence towards women, even at this relatively young age.[12]

The great majority of boys and young men will have relationships untainted by violence and abuse. Of those that are violent or abusive, one well-known key contributory factor is having witnessed or been the victim of family violence oneself.[13] This is how such boys and young men have experienced control and power being exercised in the past: they are repeating what they know. However, it is important not to be deterministic about the fate of boys who have grown up with violence. Isla, a mother of one son in his early twenties, suffered domestic violence and abuse at the hands of her former husband. She remarks, 'My ex was violent and bullying. The violence was directed at me, although some of his actions towards my son in the teenage years were very bullying. There's lots of research about replicating that behaviour and I really worried about that, or about my son being so afraid of doing so that it would be impossible for him to have a good, healthy relationship. But that doesn't seem to be the case at all. He is very different from his father and very confident in his own personality.' Many people, like Isla, are aware that violent patterns of behaviour may be passed down within families. Yet in their research, the academics involved in the Bristol University/NSPCC study found that, for boys, suffering and inflicting violence within a relationship was even more strongly linked to peer violence than to family violence. Once again, this demonstrates the pervasive and corrosive effect of male hierarchies and friendship groups built around dominance and physical aggression.[14]

Boys who are violent towards those who are close to them may victimise family members, as well as girlfriends. Both boys and girls in childhood and adolescence report being closer to their mothers than their fathers, very probably because children tend to spend more time with their mothers (an issue that I will come to in Chapter 5).[15] They both also tend to have more rows with their mothers and to be less respectful towards them, which may be a matter of familiarity breeding contempt. But it could also be because they pick up on the lower status of women within society.[16] The tensions between mothers and sons can shift into violence. Child violence towards a parent is not widely discussed but it does happen, and it is mainly perpetrated by boys who behave violently towards their mothers (although girls can be perpetrators and fathers victims too).[17] Accurate statistics on its prevalence are, inevitably, hard to come by and also very variable. Some say it occurs within 10 per cent of families, whereas others say 3 per cent is a more accurate figure.[18] Ben Jamal is the Chief Executive of the Domestic Violence Intervention Project, which works with perpetrators and supports victims of domestic violence and abuse. One of its projects targets eleven to twenty-five year olds who are violent and controlling towards their girlfriends and boyfriends or parents and carers. When I meet Ben, he explains that 'the issue of children perpetrating violence against a parent has come to the fore in recent years. It is becoming a real, recognised phenomenon.' Fascinating qualitative research by a family therapist and psychologist in Australia reveals two particularly common patterns of emotional and physical violence: that inflicted by children on single mothers, having seen their mother suffer violence and abuse at the hands of a partner, and that inflicted by privileged 'over-entitled' children on their parents.[19] His review of the literature leads him to conclude that around 70 per cent of the perpetrators are sons.[20] Ben Jamal stresses the importance of identifying and addressing the needs of children at risk of perpetrating violence. 'You have got to get in early with a treatment response,' he tells me.

The porn panic

It is often argued that the media fosters a climate in which misogyny is seen as permissible, and violence and abuse justified. From music videos to computer games, our popular culture is regularly blamed for leading boys and men astray. Recent examples that have acted as a lightning rod for protest include Robin Thicke's 'Blurred Lines' in which the creepy singer questions the concept of sexual consent ('I hate these blurred lines/I know you want it') while, in the video, sidling up to minimally dressed female models, and *Grand Theft Auto V* (where the player can choose to shoot a prostitute rather than paying for the services she has just provided). It is overly simplistic to argue that boys will be pushed into violence and abuse having encountered unsuitable content. The seeds of such behaviour are sown by a society that privileges male power – a form of dominance that may well be brutally reinforced at home and within peer groups. Yet the media is an ingredient in the cocktail of influences that shape boys' thinking, and it plays its part in structuring and sustaining the sexism and misogyny embedded in society.

Much media content aimed at young people, from music videos to fashion spreads, is informed by the grammar and aesthetics of pornography. One of the biggest worries for modern parents is the accessibility of porn. According to the international organisation Stop Porn Culture, a porn film is produced every thirty-nine minutes in the US, and internet porn in the UK receives more traffic than social media, online retail, news sites, email, gaming and travel. Pornhub, one of the major gateway porn sites, receives over 1.6 million visits per hour.[21] The once shocking content of lads' mags seems quaint in comparison to what is available for free with just a few stabs at a smartphone.

Porn has been produced and consumed since time immemorial – the word porn itself comes from the ancient Greek. But it is the ease with which children can now find it (or come across it) and the extremity of its content that troubles parents. Nadine, the mother of an eight-year-old son, comments, 'It is the omnipresence of porn that concerns me: the amount of it and how easily it can be accessed. I don't have moral objections to the representation of sex; I am not offended by nudity. But so much porn is violent, and racist and misogynistic.'

When I spoke to parents of primary-school-aged children for this book, they frequently expressed deep concerns about porn. It is tricky to come up with reliable statistics for the use of porn by children and young people. However, an extensive review of the existing research into the effect of pornography on the young commissioned by the Children's Commissioner for England suggests that between 83 per cent and 100 per cent of boys and young men have seen porn (compared to 45 to 80 per cent of girls and young women). The findings on the age at which children and young people first come across porn range from ten to seventeen, depending on the study, with some research suggesting it happens earlier for boys than girls.[22] It also seems that most viewing – for boys and young men as well as girls and young women – is due to unwanted exposure (for example, stumbling across it online) rather than deliberate access, though again the data on this varies significantly from one study to another.[23] If that is the case, then the account I heard from one of the fourteen-year-old boys at the Great Men workshop I attended at the east London secondary school may be quite typical. He recalled being locked in a stairwell and forced to watch porn on a smartphone by another, older boy when he was eleven. 'I didn't want to see it. I was on the way to playing football in the park.' As Indigo, the mother of two primary-school-aged sons says, 'Even if they don't access it, it only takes someone walking home with them to show it. I do trust my children. It's just other people's I'm not so sure about.' Boys are more likely than girls to both access and be exposed to pornography; boys' access and exposure is also more frequent, although the categorisation of 'frequent' varies. As an example, one report from Sweden found that although 99 per cent of the sixteen- to twenty-four-year-old men surveyed had seen pornography, only 16 per cent had seen it frequently, with 51 per cent having seen it occasionally and 33 per cent rarely.[24]

In my conversations with parents about pornography I was struck that there was far greater concern among those with primary-aged children – who were anticipating a wave of porn hitting their offspring – than those with older children, who were already negotiating the issue. 'I am sure they have used porn,' said Mel, the mother of three sons in their late teens and twenties, 'but it is not something that I worry about overly much.' Una, another mother of three boys in the same age group, is similarly unruffled: 'We have a wild child across the street. He's grown up now but when he and my oldest son were about ten, he came round and showed the boys a porn site. So they saw it fairly early. I imagine they do look at porn from time to time but it's not a big issue.' Parents with children who have already been through the porn-exposure years may well be more relaxed about it, but their children were unlikely to be using tablets and smartphones away from prying adult eyes to the extent younger children do now. As Una concedes, 'We only have one computer in our dining room, so when they were growing up I could see what they were doing. It must be much harder for parents of teenagers today, with their tablets and phones.' One such teenager, Kyle, a Birmingham-based A-level student whom I spoke to, is nonchalant about his porn use: 'I watch porn, and all my male friends do too. We haven't seen what the effects are. It's just speculation.'

So is there anything other than speculation? And if so, what is known about the effects of porn? In fact, there is very little sound evidence about what harm pornography may cause, and some of what is known may be surprising. For instance, Neil Malamuth, Professor of Communication, Psychology and Women's Studies at the University of California and one of the pioneers in testing the effects of pornography, has found that watching pornography does not increase the likelihood that most men will carry out a sexually aggressive act or feel more inclined to be violent against women. The exception is among men with personalities or backgrounds that would already count as risk factors for committing such acts – for example, having a narcissistic personality, sexually aggressive fantasies or a violent family background. For these men, if they consume a great deal of pornography, especially violent pornography, it is more likely that they will be sexually violent. In an interview on Radio 4, Professor Malamuth commented, 'The best summary I could give you is that for some people [pornography] appears to enhance their sex lives and may be viewed as a positive aspect of their life and does not lead them in anyway to engage in any form of antisocial behaviour. For some people who do have those several other risk factors, yes, it can add fuel to the fire and can lead to a greater likelihood of committing acts of sexual aggression.'[25]

The review for the Children's Commissioner for England reveals that although watching pornography is linked to a range of wholly undesirable opinions and beliefs – including unrealistic attitudes towards sex, less progressive attitudes about gender roles and a belief that women are sex objects – there is no evidence to show whether or not young people with these attitudes are more likely to seek out pornography – or whether the watching of pornography creates these attitudes.[26] (It should also be noted that an earlier literature review carried out for the UK media regulator Ofcom highlighted that these attitudinal effects in themselves have been found to be weak, accounting for just 1 to 2 per cent of the variance in teenagers' sexual attitudes.)[27] No one is going to set up an experiment in which children who have not seen porn are deliberately exposed to it in order to monitor the effects. But we may be able to gain a deeper understanding by other means. Miranda Horvath, Associate Professor in Forensic Psychology at Middlesex University, who carried out the review for the Children's Commissioner, explains to me, 'There will never be studies that set out to find if there is a causal link between young people using pornography and changes in attitudes and behaviours. The ethical implications of such studies prevent them from occurring. The closest we will ever get will be longitudinal studies that track changes in attitudes and behaviours over time.' She is also sceptical of the weak attitudinal effects noted by Ofcom: 'I don't think there is a clear enough evidence base to say definitely that this is the extent of the effect. There's a vast amount of literature where children and teenagers themselves are saying it has a marked effect on their attitudes.'

Dr Horvath makes the point in her review that, despite claims pornography has become more hardcore, degrading and violent, few studies have actually focused on content and the field is riven with varied and subjective definitions of pornography itself. In the autumn of 2015, Dr Kristina Massey at Canterbury Christ Church University, who also worked on the Children's Commissioner review, was about to embark on research with sixteen-year-old boys to find out what they are actually viewing when they say they are watching porn.[28] She will then analyse the content herself to find out whether it can be classified as porn (rather than, say, a crude music video) and if so what type of porn. Dr Massey told me that as far as she is aware this is the first time that such a piece of work has been undertaken, again largely because of ethical concerns about dealing with young people – and using university computers to access potentially pornographic content. As it stands, it is very difficult to get a grip on what is out there. The Children's Commissioner report is entitled 'Basically … Porn is everywhere' – a quote from one of the young people interviewed in the course of the commission's work. We are currently in the discomfiting position where porn is 'everywhere' and yet we have remarkably little firm evidence about its effects.

Sarah Perry, who was responsible for setting up the Great Men initiative, believes that the fears of many parents may be misplaced. 'The boys know it's not real life. They are more savvy than you think. And lots haven't even watched porn – they just say they have for bravado.' Her hunch was reflected in the comments that I heard from the schoolboys at the Great Men session in east London. 'Porn isn't even real, it's fake. It's their job to be doing that. They don't really want to,' one of the boys commented. It is true that young people begin to acquire media literacy from an early age and have a relatively sophisticated understanding of what they are watching.[29] Yet just because a young person – or anyone else – knows something is not real, it does not mean that it isn't influencing them on some level. We know that many of the adverts we see on television or online are fictional scenarios, yet businesses pump money into advertising because it works. Despite the media's souped-up outrage and titillated fascination with the porn habits of young people, watching porn does not lead, in the vast majority of cases, to sexually violent acts. However, there is still concern it causes damage at a more granular level that is harder to measure – encouraging a coarsening of attitudes towards girls and women. Examining a picture of a semi-naked woman during the Great Men session, the boys are asked what they think of her. 'Ho, whore, slag, sket,' comes the reply.

Neil Malamuth addresses this concern in one of his pieces of research. He writes: 'Beyond the dramatic popular notion that violent pornography spurs a minority of sexual deviants to criminal acts lies the far greyer and more complex but potentially far more pervasive area of indirect effects. Evidence suggests that a wide range of media affects the general population in a variety of ways. In particular, heavy exposure to sexual violence could affect thought patterns (e.g., attitudes, beliefs, perceptions, schemas) that are concurrently being shaped by family, peers, other media messages, and a host of other influences. If other risk factors exist in the person and in the environment, such thought patterns may contribute to acts such as stranger and date rape. In the absence of other factors that contribute to aggression or in the presence of forces that inhibit (e.g., fear of punishment) or are incompatible (e.g., empathy) with violence, there is still some likelihood that thought patterns will be expressed in other ways, such as a not-acted-upon desire to be sexually aggressive, a sanctioning of sexual aggression in others, or sexist, discriminatory, and/or harassing behaviour. Even when not translated into violent behaviour, such effects have wide social implications.'[30]

I am guided by the evidence and Professor Malamuth is careful to qualify his findings. He is clear that he is considering the effect of 'heavy exposure to sexual violence'. The frequency with which a young person views porn and the type of porn they watch must influence the effect it has. It is important to maintain a sense of proportion on this issue: a few viewings of non-violent pornography are unlikely to have a seriously detrimental effect in most cases. Yet it is difficult not to feel sympathy for Gail Dines, the prominent anti-pornography campaigner, when she tells the BBC, 'Let's think about this – my students, they tell me, for example, that their boyfriends want anal sex all the time. They also tell me that their boyfriends can't stand to look at any pubic hair. Now did something suddenly happen, drop from the sky, that a generation of women suddenly decided that pubic hair was unacceptable? Or did a generation of men suddenly get born and decided that anal sex was the thing? I mean, we are cultural beings. When you see cultural shifts you have to begin to ask what is causing these cultural shifts. So although in social science you obviously can't have 100 per cent causation studies, my question would be how are you going to explain these things? ... [Research] is the foundation of what I do but ... I am listening to women as well ... Research can only capture so much ... And what I am hearing over and over again are the same stories of how pornography is affecting behaviour.'[31] Isla, whose son is in his early twenties, is with Gail Dines: 'Parents who say their boys don't see or aren't affected by porn – well, how do they know? It is bound to have an effect on your sexual identity. How could it not? Hitting, choking, doing things that hurt people. My guess is that these things are happening more often. It has just got to be the case that this is linked to porn.'

The British National Surveys of Sexual Attitudes and Lifestyles are some of the largest and most detailed surveys of sexual behaviour in the world. The 2014 survey shows that anal sex is increasing, among both young men and women and older adults: 18 per cent of sixteen to twenty-four year olds had had anal sex with a member of the opposite sex in the past year, compared to 14 per cent of thirty-five to forty-four year olds.[32] A separate qualitative piece of research with 130 sixteen to eighteen year olds from diverse locations across England found that young people themselves say they have anal sex with someone of the opposite sex because of the influence of pornography. The research-ers involved argue this explanation is 'partial at best'. They discerned other reasons at play in what the young people were telling them, including the normalisation of coercion ('Sometimes you just keep going ... till they get fed up and let you do it anyway,' one young man told them) and competition between young men to try it.[33] Even if you were to argue that it is moralistic to disapprove of anal sex, the link with coercion should give pause for thought. The researchers view coercion and competition as distinct from the influence of pornog-raphy. Yet, although there is no explicit link between them, it seems reasonable to conclude that pornography might encourage both coercion and competition. Coercion is a common porn narrative and the competition between young men may derive in part between what they see in porn and then urge each other to try out.

Gail Dines' primary concern is for girls and women, but any harmful effects from pornography will extend to boys too. Focus group research with boys shows that pornography contributes to the pressure for them to conform to hypersexual, heterosexual and sexist behaviour. Once again the 'fag discourse' comes into play, with those failing to show the requisite interest in pornography dubbed 'gay'.[34] This echoes the 'competition' theme that came out of the qualitative research on anal sex. Laura, a researcher in her early twenties who lives in London, tells me, 'Part of the attraction of porn for guys is that they talk about it with each other – about the fact that they are watching it and how much they are watching and recommended viewing.' This social and communal aspect of pornography is described in vivid terms by masculinities researcher Michael Kimmel in his book *Guyland*. Kimmel has had the dubious privilege of sitting in on groups of male college students watching pornography together: 'They spent a good deal of time jiving with each other about what they'd like to do to the girl on screen, yelling at her, calling her a whore and a bitch and cheering on the several men who will proceed to penetrate her simultaneously.'[35] Laura has also been in the room when male fellow students were watching pornography. 'We were at one of the boys' houses, getting ready to go out. We were all drinking and listening to music and then someone switched on the TV and there was a naked woman on the screen. The boys were joking about it and some of the girls were joining in. Others were asking why they'd put it on. I felt really uncomfortable. I thought, If you see her like that then how do you view me? It can't be completely separate.'

As well as damaging the way they view women, porn may also influence what boys think sex involves, as Gail Dines claims. Barney, a student in Manchester, tells me, 'Boys objectify girls more, because they don't know how to relate to them. The first pair of boobs that they see is on a screen and by the time they are a teenager they are looking at hardcore pornography. Sex itself is definitely changed by that. In porn the guy's dominant, she walks in, she's a bit of a bimbo, she gets dealt with and then he gets what he wants. That's what guys think it's about.' This is no fun, and potentially very damaging, for both sexes. While talking up their sexual prowess and experience with each other, inside boys are often scared and daunted. Folarin, who volunteers with Great Men, tells me, 'These boys are made to feel that they are not whole, not complete, if they don't fit the masculine stereotype. They are made to believe that powerful masculinity is the only acceptable masculinity. It's about unpacking the myth that they must be up for sex all the time. You can see the relief on their faces when we talk about porn distorting sex in a workshop. They go, "Oh thank God, that's not what sex is like!" Someone asked me in one of the sessions, "Do men have to keep going for hours?" They are really relieved to hear that sex isn't about men dominating women, or hurting them or ejaculating on them.'

Just as girls are confronted with a plastic, hairless supposed ideal in pornography, boys too are bombarded with images of near-unobtainable physiques. Barney, speaking rather ruefully from personal experience, says: 'My girlfriend and her friend had not seen any porn so they asked me and my friend to show them some. Afterwards we joked that we wished we hadn't because the guys' penises were so big. Boys can't live up to what we see in porn.'

Barney also throws another interesting light on the potentially damaging effects of pornography. 'A lot of boys are not looking for long-lasting relationships as much. They can get off on what they see on screen. Now I am in a relationship I can see the difference between that and just sex. But you don't know that before you have it. It contributes to loneliness in adolescence.' Miranda Horvath identifies a significant social issue here: 'There is increasing evidence on the effect of porn on boys, in terms of the effect on their ability to make human connections as well as their attitudes towards girls, their own body image and anxieties about the ability to perform sexually. Many boys are learning abut sex through viewing porn on a screen instead of exploring and making connections with a real person.'

Research by the UK National Union of Students has found that 60 per cent of respondents watch porn to get information about sex. This is despite the fact that over 70 per cent say it creates unrealistic sexual expectations. A quarter said that sex education at school was either poor or terrible. Issues such as consent, relationships and LGBT issues were considered to be poorly covered. In the absence of statutory, high-quality sex and relationships education in schools, some children turn to pornography. Tellingly, young women were significantly more likely to rely on friends, family and magazines as sources of sex and relationships information. Young men were more reliant on sexual partners, pornography and the (often poor quality) school sex and relationships education.[36] As discussed in the last chapter, many boys find it difficult to speak to their friends about emotional and relationship issues. The masculine stereotype is of a man whose sexual performance is intuitive and expert. This is not an environment in which honest questions about the basics of sex are encouraged. Bravado is key.

Aside from friends, it is striking that boys do not regard family as a key source of information on sexual relationships. Perhaps many parents' embarrassment about discussing sex with their children is coupled with a belief that it is not necessary to do so when it comes to sons; boys can look after themselves, whereas girls are more vulnerable and so have to be protected with information. Lee, a father of two teenage boys from Manchester tells me, 'My mum and dad gave me a very stable upbringing. But they weren't people who talked about sex, girlfriends, contraception. None of that. We were a working-class, council-house family. Those things were just not talked about. It impacted on me massively. I felt a great deal of embarrassment about all those things. I tried with my eldest son to talk about this and that. It was a disaster. I came across as an idiot. Even now as I'm talking to you I'm saying "this and that" because I can't bring myself to say it. I feel they know more at sixteen than I need to know in my forties. At school they have much more sex education than we did when we were kids and at a much earlier age. And it's all over the TV. So it's there in the world around them all the time. Do we really need to add to it?'

Lee's mortification is heartfelt, and he also points out that his wife does speak to his children about sex. But if the majority of boys feel that discussing sex is discouraged within their families – and while provision in school remains non-statutory – we risk them acquiring a distorted view of sex if they turn to pornography as their main source of education. Fathers have a specific and significant role here. There are questions about the emotional and physical sides of relationships that boys may prefer to discuss with fathers. Sex and relationships will remain important to boys throughout their lives. This is an opportunity for fathers to influence their sons positively for the long term, helping them to forge healthy and fulfilling relationships based on respect. As Melissa Benn writes in her astute and wide-ranging book *What Should We Tell Our Daughters?*, 'Most articles, books or polemics looking at these issues put responsibility for the issue on women … Sons and their fathers do not seem to figure in this conversation at all, even though pornography is largely made by men, for men, and it is overwhelmingly men and boys who assault women … Where are the calls for a sex-education programme that encourages boys to look at pornography with a critical eye, or think about sexuality in more rounded, tender ways?'[37] Given that men are over twice as likely to have watched online pornography compared to women, with over three-quarters of men doing so,[38] many fathers will be expertly placed to discuss pornography's effects and its scant relation to real life with their sons.

'The pussy of the gang'

Using sexual prowess and dominance to secure power and status among peers predates the days of internet porn. So too does the belief among some young men that they have the right to sexual attention from women – and the right to express their own sexual interest in them – although it has taken the disturbing daily catalogue from inspired websites such as Everyday Sexism to bring this home.

Two recent reports demonstrate the results of the desire for sexual dominance, across the social spectrum. A devastating piece of qualitative research among gang members, carried out for the Children's Commissioner for England by the University of Bedfordshire, found that sexual violence is seen as normal and inevitable in gangs, with young women often blamed for their own abuse. Researchers spoke to 188 gang members in six different areas of England, most of which suffered from severe social deprivation. The report is aptly titled 'It's wrong … but you get used to it'.[39]

The vast majority of victims of sexual violence and exploitation in gang environments are girls and young women. Nevertheless, the boys and young men involved suffer too. For the boys concerned, brutal, non-consensual sex – perhaps in front of other gang members – is seen as a necessary means of proving their masculinity. Carlene Firmin, the director of MsUnderstood, who advised on the research, has said, 'You have leaders setting up the assault, getting a kick out of watching what their friends are doing, as well as abusing the girl they're abusing. But there are other boys who want to be able to say "no" and feel they can't.'[40] The Children's Commissioner research found that this pressure from other, powerful members of the gang was the most common form of sexual violence and exploitation of male gang members. Its report includes chilling testimonies, such as this from a boy all of sixteen years of age. 'I've done it to kids before,

I've been saying, "Go in there, what's up with him, here's a girl", you know what I'm saying? "I'm finished so you can go in." And he's like, "I'll go in there in a minute" and then you notice 'em, like you can see in their eyes that they don't want to go in … when I first like beat [had sex with] a girl and that, I got like not peer pressure but it was like, that was, that was how I ever lost mine.' The boy's use of the slang word 'beat' is revealing of the force and domination associated with having sex. A twenty-three-year-old woman also quoted in the study observes, 'I wouldn't say they're forced, but they're kind of egged on. Does that make sense? It's not like they're sat with a gun telling them, "You must do this", but if you're a member of a gang you've got to do it. They're not going to say "no" cos you're going to be the pussy of the gang, and because you're involved with that environment, you think fuck it and just do it.'[41]

In 2005 Michael Kimmel wrote that, 'A recent survey asked high school students what they were most afraid of. The girls answered that they were most afraid of being assaulted, raped or killed. The boys? They said they were afraid of "being laughed at".'[42] This says so much about the parallel worlds of girls and boys. The fears of girls objectively dwarf those of boys (whatever the chances of them actually happening), yet in boys' minds ridicule is the ultimate injury. In these traumatic accounts of gang sexual violence, the two fears collide disastrously. The girls involved suffer terribly at the hands of boys and young men. Yet, without detracting at all from this suffering, we must also recognise the trauma experienced by the boys who are coerced into gang life and sex. They may be gang members but many of them are children too. They were not born destined to sexually abuse other children. Poisonous forms of masculinity and peer pressure, together with deprivation, desperation and – perhaps – their own poor choices along the way, have brought them to this place. Difficult though it may be, they deserve compassion.

One of the lads

The desire among some young men to prove their masculinity, what-ever the costs to themselves or those around them, is also apparent in far more privileged social circumstances. So-called 'lad culture' in UK universities has been getting a great deal of publicity in recent years. The National Union of Students claims, based on a 2014 survey it commissioned, that 37 per cent of female students say they have faced 'unwelcome sexual advances' (such as inappropriate touching or groping). This compares with 12 per cent of male students. Over half of both male and female students think that women are more likely to feel unsafe or intimidated at university.[43] The survey did not record the sex of the person making the advances but it seems reasonable to assume the majority will be of the opposite sex. Academic research among German first-year students revealed broadly similar findings for 'sexual victimisation' (33 per cent for women and 17 per cent for men) where the perpetrator was a member of the opposite sex.[44] Unedifying examples of abuse that have caught the headlines include members of an Edinburgh University American-style 'fraternity' proposing a 'raping trip' to Montenegro;[45] the London School of Economics' Men's Rugby Club handing out a leaflet calling women 'slags' and 'mingers';[46] and freshers at Nottingham University chanting an obscene song ('Fuck her standing, fuck her lying/If she had wings I'd fuck her flying/Now she's dead, but not forgotten/Dig her up and fuck her rotten').[47] But, as an earlier 2013 NUS report picks up, much of the abuse and laddism is less eye-catching: the banality of misog-yny. Groping in night clubs, rape jokes in the pub, sexist comments on the way to lectures – all apparently so frequent this is accepted as the norm.[48] Excessive drinking is a core pastime of the university lad, along with sport, 'banter' (the modern-day get-out-of-jail-free card) and self-policing of a strictly heterosexual, sex-obsessed masculine identity. Aaron graduated last year from his university, where he says 'lad culture' was a prominent part of student life. 'It's all part of the drinking culture that starts in Freshers' Week. It's very laddy, right from the beginning. It's about going out drinking, taking home as many girls as possible. It's something people aspire to.' Barney, who is still a student, agrees, 'Boys try to compare themselves and compete all the time. How many girls have you slept with? How much have you had to drink? The only thing they are not boasting about is the grades they are getting.' So keen are some boys to get started in their lad career that they don't wait until university. A-level students Annie, Clare and Liam tell me it's in full swing in their sixth form. 'On nights out the rugby team use Sharpies to mark out the "easy" women,' says Clare. 'They spike girls' drinks and take photos of themselves groping them. They hold competitions to see who can make out with the ugliest girl. "Pork is pork" – that's their slogan.'

Although Barney is upfront about the objectionable aspects of 'lad culture', it does not stop him from joining in occasionally. A keen rugby player, he tells me, 'I've been on a university rugby social. You have to go to a certain amount of club nights. The rugby lads wear suits. It's thought of as the wankers' night – pumped-up guys trying to get into fights. I'm aware it's a cliché, but it doesn't stop you being a cliché.' As Laura, who was at university until recently herself, says, '"Lad culture" is a set of behaviours that people dip in and out of. It is not necessarily a constant thing or who you are all the time. There's a lot that's positive about it: they are a great group of friends, they can be very funny and they have a great time. There's nothing wrong with that but the downside is it's very loud and it takes up space.'

When talking to young people about their experiences of 'lad culture', the involvement of members of sports teams comes up often, particularly those in rugby teams (although not every rugby player is a paid-up lad. 'There are a couple of lovely guys on the team,' Annie assures me). So who are these 'lads'? Aaron, who both saw lad culture up close at university and studied the history of the lad phenomenon as part of his degree, tells me, 'In the past, a definition of a lad would have been a football and working-class thing, but it's a lot more of a middle-class, private-school thing now. It is a very white, straight thing. Laddism is about all things manly and to a lot of people being gay isn't being manly.' For young men who are not straight, it is alienating. 'I felt they didn't know how to include someone who wasn't sexually interested in women,' says Lewis of the other male students around him during his undergraduate days. 'Some of them would occasionally recognise that they were not including me in what they were saying and they fumbled desperately to make the conversation accessible to me. But it's not just about who you want to have sex with. It's about how you view sex. Just switching the pronouns doesn't work.'

NUS research into 'lad culture' in England and Scotland notes that, 'The context for "lad culture" includes a discourse of women's success and a linked "crisis of masculinity"'. It can be seen at least to a degree as a renewed form of sexism which is part of a defensive response (although, as the report adds, this 'discourse of women's success' is inaccurate and simplistic).[49] Lewis agrees, 'There tends to be a ramping up of stereotypical masculine behaviour when men feel under threat. "Lad culture" is another form of that. It's to show girls that what really matters is strength. It comes from a feeling of disempowerment. So you exert the power in the way that you can.'

There is clearly a problem with the behaviour of some young men at university. Yet the debate about 'lad culture' is frustratingly simplistic. It is framed – by both the media and some campaigners – as a battle between marauding young men and young women at bay, when the situation is more complex. Young women are being proactive and powerful in challenging the laddish behaviour they come across. As one local example, Laura pushed for her student union to take drink-fuelled, sexist behaviour more seriously and also set up an alternative freshers' week, organising daytime events that did not involve drinking alcohol. 'It was important to do,' she says, 'otherwise starting at university can feel very excluding and overwhelming.' Even the researchers commissioned for the 2013 NUS report, found that female students' 'objections to laddish behaviours did not support contemporary models of "sexual panic"', within which young women are portrayed as passive victims under siege from rampantly libidinous men.[50] Likewise, young male students are not one 'down-in-one' homogeneous mob. The comments from Lewis, Barney and Aaron are proof that male students are capable of being intelligent, empathic and questioning of what they observe (and on occasion are a part of). Many male students are allies in the fight for equality.

'Lad culture' seems to be a new name for a long-established way of behaving. Look at old university drinking clubs. I remember very similar behaviour among a distinct subset of male students when I was at university many years ago. Undoubtedly a culture of cheap booze and online 'banter' has encouraged regressive attitudes (or at least made them more prominent). But this type of young man existed in the pre-Facebook dark ages too. Indeed, women are capable of laddish behaviour. As the NUS survey and research among German students found, young men suffer 'unwelcome sexual advances' from young women as well as vice versa. And the one age group for which female heavy drinking outweighs that of men is among sixteen to twenty-four year olds.[51] 'Girls are very keen on sleeping with rugby boys. Boys can get pinned up against the wall by girls,' says Barney. 'And the girls' football team is more laddy than the boys'. They try to out-lad them, with excessive drinking.' He then draws a distinction between male and female laddishness: 'The girls are not intimidating and objectifying boys, though.' But it seems to me that girls and women are capable of objectifying boys and men, and there is a strand of film and television catering for just that phenomenon, as I showed in the previous chapter. Yet the power dynamics are different. These hard-drinking, perhaps objectifying, young women are seemingly being indulged in their behaviour because they are not in charge. Like tomboys, they are aspiring to heights they can never reach.

The media covers the 'lad culture' phenomenon assiduously. Stories of bad behaviour among the privileged classes always make good copy. In 2015, within the space of three months, a serious case review was published into the systematic sexual exploitation of girls and boys living in deprived areas of Oxfordshire,[52] and the principal of a university college a few miles down the road spoke out about laddism among male students.[53] While the sexual exploitation had been ignored across the board for years, the sexist culture debated in junior common rooms received instant, extensive coverage. This is not to belittle the harm that culture causes, but double standards are at play. Social class really does seep into everything.

Although the sexual exploitation of children in poor parts of UK cities and the harassment of gilded youth in our universities appear poles apart, there is a link. As Sam pointed out at the beginning of this chapter, it is about male power. Within universities, it is specifically about white, straight, middle-class male power – a breed of boys who have been raised to believe that they are entitled to do as they wish. Their behaviour is not as new as we might think but it is still deeply distasteful.

In the wake of the press attention on 'lad culture', and pressure from female students themselves, some universities are setting up consent and Good Lad workshops. The government has also got in on the act, asking universities to establish a 'task force' on tackling the issue. In a world where students might arrive at university having had inadequate sex and relationships education at school and armed with tips from porn sites, workshops may provide an important corrective. But a number of the young men I spoke to objected to what they saw as a group ticking-off, which doesn't reflect the disquiet many themselves feel about laddish behaviour. They also questioned the effectiveness of a relatively late and short intervention. 'It's not taken seriously,' says Barney of the workshops being run at his university. 'You can't just teach people how to be a good person in a day. There's got to be a cultural shift. It's more to do with how people are brought up. If you are a rugby geezer who thinks it's all right to slap a girl's arse on a night out it's not going to make any difference. It's just covering the backs of the university authorities and the student union president.'

'How do I want my kids to find out about sex?'

Whatever the truth behind the motives for laying on these courses, or their lack of effectiveness, discussing consent and harassment should be part of an ongoing conversation with both sexes that starts much earlier in their lives. The seeds of sexism and misogyny go right back to boys' early days. They are sown in the pecking orders that boys establish in primary-school playgrounds, their alienation from and contempt for the opposite sex, and their desire to prove themselves as stoic, domineering playmates and sons. Parents alone cannot change this, though their role in socialising boys is the primary one. This is why it is vital that sex and relationships education (or, better put, relationships and sex education) in schools is made statutory – and from an early age.

The need for education on healthy relationships and sex is a common finding of the reports mentioned in this chapter, which range across domestic violence and abuse in teenage relationships, gang violence, 'lad culture' and what is known about the effects of pornography on young people. In 2015 Nicky Morgan, the Westminster education secretary, urged schools to teach a 'curriculum for life' including Personal, Social, Health and Economic education (PSHE), with the aim of producing 'rounded, resilient young people' able to see off everything from bullying via sexting to revenge porn.[54] PSHE incorporates sex and relationships education. But at the time of writing the Conservative government still refuses to make the subject statutory, unwilling to impose new duties on schools and fearful of a backlash from social conservatives.

Those campaigning to eradicate violence against women and girls stress the importance of early, high-quality sex and relationships education in schools, which doesn't just deal with the biology but also with notions of respect, equality and consent. It is in these early years that we can most effectively influence boys' (and girls') thinking and encourage them to interrogate and reject the notions of opposition and power that prop up patriarchy, make girls and young women vulnerable and poison relations between the sexes. As Miranda Horvath says when I speak to her, this should go hand in hand with guidance from parents. 'What parents can do, from birth really, is teach their children about equality and respect and create open communication with them. Parents can talk to children about bodies and what is appropriate in public and what should be private – so that at the age when porn does become an issue they feel comfortable talking to their children about it. Many adults find talking about sex to other adults difficult, never mind children. So it is a big ask, but it is crucial. Compulsory relationships and sex education has to be there too – as a backstop almost – so it's not left to chance as to whether or not children are given that information.'

A 2013 Ofsted report on the state of PSHE in English schools found that 40 per cent of teaching required improvement or was inadequate. This chimes with the discontent expressed by students in the NUS research. Ofsted said this poor provision leaves children open to inappropriate sexual behaviours and sexual exploitation. Lack of expertise among teaching staff meant that sensitive issues such as sexuality and domestic violence were missing from the curriculum in too many places and in the weaker schools homophobic and disablist language was commonplace.[55] (Lewis, for instance, recalls a teacher at his secondary school telling the students that she 'didn't feel comfortable around gay people'.) The PSHE Association argues that one of the reasons why it is hard to establish consistent, high standards of teaching in this subject is because it is not statutory.[56]

Some educators are tackling this challenge in radical and inspiring ways. Lynnette Smith runs an organisation called Big Talk Education, which teaches sex education in North Lincolnshire and East Yorkshire. Having started out running classes in secondary schools, three years ago she adapted the content in order to take it into primary schools too. 'We moved into primary education because we were getting the children in secondary school and seeing that it was too late. The seeds of misinformation had already been sown. We'd go into these secondary schools and boys who had been watching pornography would ask, "Is it okay for me to ejaculate over my girlfriend's face?" or, "If you force a girl to have sex and she doesn't want to but then enjoys it, is that all right?" They are not asking these questions to shock. It is genuine. If you can reach them early in primary school you do not have to undo the damage that has been done.' In their primary school sessions, Lynnette and her team use cards featuring engagingly drawn, cheery cartoons displaying a range of situations from kissing to masturbation to adults watching pornography on the television. Lynnette encourages the children to talk about the body parts that others should not touch, who they would talk to if they felt uncomfortable about what someone else was asking them to do, and welcome and unwelcome physical contact. She gives a presentation to parents before she speaks to the children, emphasising the importance of talking to children early and stressing the need for parents and the school to work together. 'Parents need to ask themselves: How do I want my kids to find out about sex and puberty and their body changing? From me and the school or from the internet? Sometimes I feel like saying, "Why are you not taking this seriously?"' Helen, a secondary school teacher in Sheffield, is similarly frustrated: 'I wish parents would have the conversations we have with kids about sex and relationships, citizenship and the safe use of the internet. Schools should play a role, but so should parents.' Drawing parents into the conversation in the way that Lynnette describes may encourage them to do so, by stressing the importance of talking to children and giving fathers and mothers the confidence to do it. Parents themselves may even find that they pick up some useful information along the way.

However, Lynnette offers a word of caution on the push for statutory relationships and sex education: 'I am usually very adamant about things. But this is one thing that I am very scared about. If the government suddenly decides to make it statutory, what would be delivered, how and by whom? At one secondary school where we delivered sessions, they said they would use some of their own teachers to cut down costs. They ended up asking a supply teacher who had come in that day to deliver the workshop on consent. He was mortified but wanted to work at the school. We discovered he was divulging personal information, telling the students about his own sex life. We took him to one side at the break and told him he mustn't do that. He said, "But that's the only thing I know about sexual consent – through my own experience." That would be my concern. Statutory education has to be planned and well resourced so that there are enough specialists to go into schools and deliver it.' Miranda Horvath agrees: 'Relationships and sex education has to be delivered by appropriately trained teachers and other providers.'

Get real

Education in this area that engages with the reality of young people's lives would be welcomed by Kyle, who at seventeen feels he has endured enough irrelevant sex ed. 'We've done the biological ins and outs but we would rather mess around than learn in those lessons. I didn't think teachers are in a position to comment on what is going on with us. You are being taught by people who don't understand the context in which we are growing up. When they were growing up, if they liked someone they'd ask them to go out. For my generation, you've got all the pre-tension: the texting, the sexting, the build-up. People teaching us don't know anything about that. We are creating the whole thing ourselves, it's completely new.' Kyle's view is shared by a majority of young people his age. Sixty-one per cent think that adults are out of touch with the relationships and friendships of their age group.[57] Lynnette laughs when I tell her about Kyle's concerns: 'As I get older, and the people in the team are in their forties and fifties now, when you walk in to a secondary-school class you do get a reaction just like that young lad. But within fifteen minutes they are sat there with their mouths open. It's really quite hilarious. We ask them a series of multiple-choice questions at the start and from that they learn how much they don't know. It really brings it home to them. They think they know everything. In fact, they may know about marginalised sex acts but they know very little about the body parts and functions. We work in everything from very nice private schools to residential pupil referral units and it's the same across the range.'

But Kyle is on to something with the adult panic around practices such as sexting. Surely we would have been sexting had the means been available when we were at school? It is simply the latest iteration of flirting and half of young people think it is part of everyday life.[58] Forty-four per cent of girls aged fourteen to seventeen in England and 32 per cent of boys of the same age have sent a sexual image or text to their partner.[59] A quarter of a century ago teenagers were also exchanging sexual messages – they just did it face to face, or in a phone conversation, or by actual hand-written letter. As Kyle says, sexting is all part of the sexually charged build-up. The problem is when images sent by phone are misused. The journalist Rhiannon Lucy Cosslett astutely points out, 'An unsolicited picture of a disembodied penis is not sexting – it's harassment. Blackmailing a child into performing sexual favours by dangling an explicit image over their head is not sexting – it's abuse. The pressure young people feel to send these images is no different to that which teenagers have always experienced as far as sexual activity is concerned.'[60] Forty-two per cent of fourteen- to seventeen-year-old girls who have sent a sexual image or text say their boyfriend then shared it with other people.[61] The best way – in fact, the only realistic way –to encourage young people to think twice before sending and disseminating these images is to talk to them about what makes for a healthy, equal relationship and for schools to do the same.

While holding back on statutory sex and relationships education, the Conservative government puts its faith in ISP filters and age-restriction controls on pornography websites to protect young people. But we cannot build a fortress against the modern world and nor should we. Even if the seamier side of the internet can be switched off in our homes, it is better to equip children with the knowledge and wisdom to negotiate what they see, render girls and boys less vulnerable to abuse and educate boys to respect and recognise the common ground with girls.

Making change happen

Frank, a teacher and father of a nine- and a twelve-year-old son, comments, 'My wife and I are pretty relaxed about the internet and pretty trusting that the right messages are getting through to them. We talk to them about what is right and wrong and instil our own values. They will try things and make mistakes. But learning in that way seems more sensible than trying to lock things down – that's a Herculean task that is destined to fail.' Rosalind Wiseman is the author of the excellent *Ringleaders and Sidekicks: How to help your son cope with classroom politics, bullying, girls and growing up.* As on other matters, she gives candid, sensible advice about dealing with the perils of the internet: 'if we're really clear with our sons about our ethical standards and how to treat people, then they will apply these standards to their online lives … Sure they'll make mistakes … But that's what you do when you're fifteen. You make mistakes and you learn from them – so you don't do the same thing as an adult and lose your job.'[62] Given the reckless things people do at fifteen, the UK's iRights campaign for a 'right to wipe' for young people – that is, the right to remove content about themselves that they have posted online – sounds sensible and humane: if the technological means can be found to deliver it.

The internet, and specifically the proliferation of online porn, has focused parents' minds on the need to discuss sex and the treatment of women with their sons. As Nadine, who lives in London with her husband and eight-year-old son says, 'We need to tackle this issue by talking to our boys ahead of when they are exposed to it, so they can defend themselves. I hope that when my son sees violent and misogynistic content he will already be the sort of person who can say, "That's wrong and I know that's wrong." I feel that there is a dislike of brutality and unkindness within him that we have cultivated. But we mustn't shy away from talking to him. You just have to believe that will work.'

It is a good thing that parents are now more actively thinking through how they will talk to their children about sex and relationships, even if they are motivated by a fear of porn. We need to step up to our responsibilities in guiding our children. And we need to push to enable schools to do their part by calling for the government to face down critics and make sex and relationships education a statutory – and properly funded – part of the curriculum. Academics have been recommending this for years to no effect. It is a concerted parent voice that has the best chance of changing the government's mind. As parents and schools working together we stand a chance of equipping our children with the ability to negotiate their world and stay true to their beliefs. For all the attention they generate, internet pornography and 'lad culture' are modern twists on an age-old misogyny. We must teach young people to recognise this misogyny for what it is and resist it. It does great harm to girls and young women and it brutalises boys and young men. It will be hugely beneficial to our children (and to those they interact with) if we desist from peddling a 'Mars and Venus' line about the sexes and, rather, focus on our commonalities and the need for boys and girls and men and women to treat each other with respect – whether that's in school corridors, out on the street, or on our screens.

4. HERE COMES TROUBLE

Angry Young Men

Falling from favour

'The lower you go down the food chain, the more male advantage disappears – poverty is a great leveller.' So says Shane Ryan, writer and Chief Executive of Working With Men, a charity that aims to improve the lives of marginalised young men. When equality between the sexes is debated, the conversation usually starts with the premise that boys do better in later life than girls, based on such measures as earnings and career trajectory in adulthood.[1] In Chapter 5 I will examine the hidden costs of living up to a rigid form of manliness for those men who apparently do well for themselves professionally and materially – and the price paid by those around them. But before I turn to them, what of the men who are left behind – those about whom Shane Ryan is concerned?

Through his life course, the average man enjoys greater privilege and career success than the average woman, but those men who do not 'make it' in the modern world fall further than women. The statistics speak for themselves. Men make up 70 per cent of the long-term youth unemployed in the UK,[2] around 88 per cent of rough sleepers in London,[3] and 95 per cent of prison inmates in England and Wales.[4] Young men are three times more likely to be long-term, 'hard-core' members of a gang than young women,[5] and 69 per cent of murder victims are male, as are 90 per cent of those tried for murder.[6] Males in England and Wales commit around 90 per cent of violent crime,[7] driving offences[8] and drug offences.[9] Those in their twenties make up the largest single age cohort in the prison population.[10] The fall can be swift and steep for young men.

The recession at the end of the last decade hit young people in the UK – men and women – particularly hard, due to falls in the employment rate and a steep decline in real-pay levels.[11] The slowdown in male-dominated sectors such as manufacturing and construction was especially marked.[12] By 2015 youth unemployment was still almost three times higher than the overall rate.[13] Recent years have also seen a £259 million reduction in money spent on youth services, with youth workers reporting that these cuts unsurprisingly hit the poorest young people the hardest.[14] Alongside this, since 2010 the Future Jobs Fund, Connexions (the careers service) and the Educational Maintenance Allowance have all been axed. The abolition of housing benefit for eighteen to twenty-one year olds is also in the pipeline at the time of writing. All this contributes to a sense of hopelessness among young working-class men who have seen both older men around them lose their jobs and their own prospects of gaining decent work decline. For many of them this is happening in already de-industrialised areas suffering from decades of large-scale joblessness. Shane Ryan comments, 'Life itself is changing for young men in the twenty-first century. But we aren't supporting them through it. We've had the first recession in which male sectors have been hardest hit along with young people who are also at the bottom of the pile – so young men are at the very bottom of the pile in terms of those affected. Most of the young men we work with are really struggling. They are not the Bullingdon boys of this world. They have very low expectations.'

Much has been made of the fact that since the early 2000s there has been a larger number of young women compared to young men not in education, employment or training (NEETs in the jargon).[15] However, the reason for the disparity is very specific and blindingly obvious. It comes down to domestic responsibilities: these young women, like others of their sex, do most of the caring in their families. The majority is economically inactive rather than unemployed. They are not looking for work or are unable to start work immediately.[16] An enquiry by the Young Women's Trust reported that 60 per cent of economically inactive young women are 'looking after family'. The inquiry report suggests that caring for their own children plays an important part in the job search for twice as many NEET young women as young men. These young women often want to work, and are frustrated that they are unable to do so.[17] Becoming a mother at a relatively young age is hard work and comes with a harsh financial and social penalty. Greater involvement from some young fathers would often help, for a start, but they are frequently discouraged from playing a full parenting role, and occasionally do not want to. Yet beyond the social disapproval encountered in the early years as a young mother, raising children often affords these women a place in the social hierarchy and a greater purpose in life than many marginalised young men will ever feel. These young men sense people have given up on them. Consequently, they give up on themselves and those around them too.

While in recent years teenagers have become less inclined to risky behaviour (such as heavy under-age drinking and drug use)[18] and youth crime has declined,[19] for some the pull of criminality remains strong. Young men who are rejected by their schools and other sites of authority believe that already – in their late teens and twenties – they are deemed failures with no legitimate place in the world. Many of these young men will have done things they should not have done but rather than be given the space to express regret and start again, they are cast out. The options that do appear still open to them are the potentially easy gains and subversive excitement of criminal activity, and the sense of belonging and high status that come with being part of a gang. For these young men there seems no other way to prove your worth as a man than to cause trouble, wield a weapon and dare others to have a go at you.

'You are The Man'

I meet JV in the Fitzroy Lodge, a boxing club in south London, housed under the railway arches where the track runs between Waterloo and Vauxhall. An anonymous black front door opens onto a room where young men and older coaches are training in the ring or working out with punchbags and weights. JV and I head to the upstairs office to talk above the barely muffled sound of eighties rock that is belting out from the speakers below. He vividly describes his own self-destructive trajectory to me, looking back at his alienation from education and time in a gang. 'I am fairly intelligent, as maybe you can tell. So I would come to school a little bit, do the bare minimum, miss a lot of school and I'd still get my grades. So I kind of thought I was cool. "Oh, JV's still getting his grades; JV's still getting his grades." I liked all that. But after school and getting my GCSEs they said I couldn't come to sixth form. Now that's the worst thing they did. I got the grades to go but they said, "We are not letting you come. You are a bad example." That really upset me. I am not saying it was to do with race. But that whole image about being the young black man, everyone against you, life is hard, for the first time I felt it. So I thought, Forget everyone. I don't love anyone. I am going to do what I want. I don't care. I tried little apprenticeships here and there but I was really angry by then. So I'm on apprenticeships and I'm getting stabbed and I'm getting arrested and missing work. I was getting into trouble: being a young man, so to speak, if you are from where I'm from. Exploring what it is like to be a bad man and discovering if it's for you, being a naughty guy.'

In his perceptive account of 'being a naughty guy' JV is lucid about the 'push' factor – that is, the sense of rejection that repelled him from a constructive focus on his education – but also the 'pull' factor that attracted him to gang life. 'Looking back on it now, it sounds nuts, but do you know what? I can explain it in one word: thrill. The thrill of getting into fights, altercations, street stuff, gang stuff. That intensity of the police are after you and if they catch you they are going to lock you up and you are going to be in trouble. I'm going to be honest with you, being a street guy, known for being a bad boy, is an amazing feeling. It's an amazing buzz. You are The Man. All the girls in your area want you. People are scared of you. You can kind of do pretty much what you want. You are the king. You are amazing.'

JV is clear-eyed enough to admit that he messed up at school, rue-fully acknowledging that at the time he thought it was 'cool' not to try. But he was in his mid-teens and studying for his GCSEs. Not every child of that age is going to approach such a task with the serious-ness and sense of import that their teachers might want. Wouldn't it have been better to allow him into his sixth form on condition that he knuckled down, than to throw him out without a chance? JV was interested in the subjects he was studying – he wanted to carry on at school – but instead he was forced into a situation where his lively mind and desire to prove himself found a far less positive focus.

'If you are not a bad boy … you are a victim'

The Labour politician Rt Hon David Lammy MP represents the London constituency of Tottenham. It is where he and his siblings were raised by their mother before he went on to an impressive career as a barrister and then a front-bench politician. In recent years he has become known, and gained respect for, his writing and thinking about 'profoundly alienated young men'[20] – in particular, his leadership during the 2011 England riots, which began in his constituency after the police shot and killed a local man, Mark Duggan. He draws a line of alienation through from gang members to English Defence League recruits and all the way on to the young men raised and educated in Britain who then committed acts such as the 7/7 London bombings and the murder of Lee Rigby. He has written, 'It is not unreasonable to ask why British males of a certain age and demographic but from all backgrounds almost exclusively provide the talent pool for our legions of racists, football hooligans, rioters, gang members and terrorists.'[21]

I met David Lammy in the run-up to the 2015 general election in which many from the Labour Party lost their seats but he was returned with an increased majority. He described to me the 'powerful, seductive force with a masculine edge' that draws boys and young men into criminality and violence. 'It could be the gangster selling drugs or selling knives and if you get involved with it you can get the girls and the consumer goods that make you feel powerful and cool. Or it could be a gang leader preaching hate about immigrants – "that Asian guy took what is yours" – so you join the EDL, or go out to football games and drink and shout and create trouble and beat the crap out of people. Or it could be in a silo, in your bedroom or in the recess of a mosque. Into this silo comes an idea from the other side of the world, that is well resourced, attractive and seductive. In all these cases behind it is another man or older boy peddling something seductive or powerful.'

David himself grew up in a community where young men were alienated and became involved in crime. He explains that as a young boy, in Tottenham, 'I was very aware of older boys on the street who were in prison or in trouble with the police. I grew up with a fear of prison. Prison was a reality for other – largely older – kids on the block. But it was also to do with my mother. My mother had a very Christian, upstanding, almost Calvinistic attitude towards things. Her outlook on the world made a great impression on me. I could hear my mother's voice warning me of what would happen if I strayed. It was very powerful. So I was very aware of prison as a possibility.' In economically constrained circumstances, ambitions were limited. 'It was a time of high unemployment and I associated aspiration with "the hustle", with selling something in order to get money. It was about petty criminals, sharp suits, being a bit of a rogue – that was as ambitious as it got for me at that time.'

Ashley Walters well understands this desire for material goods. Now an actor who has earned praise in a range of television and film roles, and formerly a member of the garage group So Solid Crew, he has had a number of brushes with the law. When we meet he had recently returned from Morocco where he had filmed *The Ark* for the BBC, playing an angel alongside David Threlfall's Noah. 'Whatever people imagine an angel to be like, it's probably not Ashley Walters,' he remarks drily. Reflecting on his teenage years, he says, 'My next-door neighbour was a huge figure in my life and he was heavily involved in drugs and stuff. I didn't realise it at the time. I just saw the money he had, the lifestyle he had, whatever. And the respect he had from everyone. And he took me under his wing because I was quite a shy boy. I'd be walking to school and he'd pull up in his new Mercedes to offer me a lift. People would see me with him and it'd be like they wouldn't mess with me because they knew that I knew him. Slowly you start aspiring to those things.'

Like JV, Ashley's peers offered him both the status and the camaraderie that he craved. 'So Solid for me was about more than music. It was having protection and a family, about being a part of something. Because either you are a part of something or you are not – and if you are not you become a target. So in order to protect yourself you surround yourself with these people. When I felt I had the protection of my peers at the time, I became very arrogant, very aggressive. I was doing a lot of silly things. I'd been bullied a lot before, I'd been mugged by people round the area, I'd been beaten up and kidnapped even at one point: there was a phase that older kids were going through where they'd take young kids and force them to commit crimes: stealing old ladies' bags or whatever. I was always worried that something was going to happen to me.' JV too speaks of this need to be part of a gang as a means of self-protection: 'In a lot of areas if you are not a bad boy, a street guy, doing illegal stuff, you are a victim,' he says simply.

JV's search for social standing and a sense of belonging by means of a marginalised sub-culture brings to mind the brilliantly sharp and brutal poem 'We Real Cool' by Gwendolyn Brooks. An anthology favourite in classrooms throughout America, it describes the strutting antics of a group of boys who reject school in favour of hanging out in pool halls and courting trouble. The poem ends with a shocking premonition of their early deaths. The American feminist writer bell hooks took the title of the poem for her own book, *We Real Cool: Black Men and Masculinity*.[22] In it she deals elegantly and insightfully with problematic masculinity as manifested in criminality and the abuse of women. Her critique of 'imperialist white-supremacist capitalist patriarchy' is refreshingly uncompromising, yet coupled with compassion in her assessment of men. However, over ten years on from its publication – and from a UK perspective – its focus on an alienated class of black young men now seems too narrow. When bell hooks writes of 'demoralized black males who could not gain the types of employment that would affirm their patriarchal manhood' her words might today be applied to 'demoralized' young men from a range of ethnic backgrounds, not just those who are black, although it is often black young men who struggle the most.

The data on boys' educational achievement analysed in Chapter 2 indicates marginalisation across a number of ethnic groups. The proportion of black young men who are unemployed is certainly higher than for other groups, at 26 per cent, but the rates for white and Asian young men are appalling too, at 16 per cent each.[23] Similarly, the information on those who took part in the 2011 riots in England shows they were drawn from a range of ethnicities. It has rightly been pointed out that the numbers of people involved were actually relatively small and that the disturbances have been exploited to pursue a punitive, stigmatising and ill-defined attack on 'troubled families'.[24] Nonetheless, the demographic make-up of those arrested is still of interest. Across England, 89 per cent of arrestees were male, with just under half aged eighteen to twenty-four and just over a quarter ten to seventeen years of age. Overall, 40 per cent were white, 39 per cent were black, 11 per cent were mixed race, 8 per cent were Asian and 2 per cent were from another ethnic background. But regional statistics varied significantly according to the ethnic make-up of the area in question, so for example in Greater Manchester 77 per cent of those arrested were white, whereas in London it was 32 per cent.[25] Findings from the joint *Guardian*/London School of Economics' Reading the Riots project where the team interviewed 270 rioters (as distinct from the arrested or accused), reflect this variety, revealing that in Manchester, Salford and Liverpool the rioters were overwhelmingly white, while in London the majority were black or mixed race. One-third had no qualifications higher than GCSE.[26] As David Lammy observes when we meet, 'There was a big racial dimension, because a young black man was shot on the streets of Tottenham by the police. But the rioting took place across the country. It ricocheted across very different towns and cities and areas in four days of unrest. And what united those that rioted is that they felt they did not have a stake in society.' JV endorses this view of an alienated population of young people: 'The kids, even adults, things are tight for them, there's no money. We don't love the government. They are not showing us any reason to respect them or to care. They don't care about us. So why wouldn't people go out and try to steal a television and try to make money? Why wouldn't they have a go? Not that it's all right. They shouldn't. But that's a lot of people's rationale.' David Lammy notes, 'Young men's rights are not a dominant theme on the left or right in politics. Nor are young people generally because they don't vote. There was the debate about university fees and that's about it.'

Young people lose out to older voters in public policy. And young men – in particular young working-class men, whatever their ethnicity – are not just ignored; they are problematised. As Ashley Walters says, 'The boys that aren't taken care of become these boys that people complain about so much. I don't want to just put it down to them being black kids with hoodies or whatever, because it goes across the board. It's not just black children, it's white children, it's Turkish, it's all over.' For Zane, growing up on an estate in Wandsworth (like so many places in London, an area where run-down tower blocks stand cheek by jowl with immaculate Edwardian terraces), society's lack of respect for working-class young men such as him was palpable. 'The media used to say bad things about us – calling us thugs and hoodies, saying we all had guns and were committing knife crime. People on the street called us "gypsies" and "pikeys". Or they would cross over the road to avoid us. You do feel anger and frustration that no one wants to have anything to do with you.'

Not only do young men like Zane feel alienated from neighbours, the government and other representatives of authority (school and the police, for example), they also feel alienated from each other. As Niobe Way, Professor of Applied Psychology at New York University, who has studied young male friendships observes, 'The hundreds of adolescent boys in my research over the past twenty years make the direct link between not having close friendships – friendships in which "deep secrets" are shared – and … "taking it out on others". Isolation, the boys report, makes them feel inadequate, envious of others with better connections and angry. This, in turn, leads them to thoughts of self- and other-directed violence.'[27]

This late-teenage sense of isolation and alienation coincides with a significant neurological stage, which may also contribute to the drive to create trouble. Having previously thought that most important brain development happens in early childhood, over the past fifteen years neurologists have discovered that human brains continue to develop right into our twenties and thirties, with mid- to late-adolescence a time in which we are particularly disposed to risk-taking and influence from peer pressure.[28] Whilst there are huge creative and educational advantages to such an extended period of brain development, for some young people it may well propel them into risky behaviour. For marginalised young men, this leaning towards potentially damaging actions and the desire to go with the crowd – when combined with a lack of stake in society and the wish for macho status – risks causing great harm to them and those they come into contact with.

It is not inevitable that young men raised in challenging circumstances, or who find it difficult to secure their place in the world, will go off the rails for good. As Raewyn Connell has written, masculinity is live and dynamic: it changes from one era, location and group of friends to the next, with complexities and contradictions apparent even within individual men themselves.[29] Ruben was brought up in a series of foster homes, moving around the UK and separated from his siblings. He points out, 'The role of men varies across cultures. I saw this with the football friends that I used to hang out with and the way they behaved compared to my other friends in the area. They were very different. If there was a confrontation, my football friends would take it on the chin and walk away. My other friends couldn't do that. They would rise to it. When I first moved to Birmingham I noticed I was a lot angrier than the other boys I was with. I began to see that you do not need to be so angry and that it is possible to be a man in a different way. Many people who are in care take the destructive route. There was a point where that might have happened to me but I came through it. I think, considering my background, I could have done a lot worse.' Ruben, who had a son at the age of twenty-two, now mentors young fathers himself, advises children and family services on working with young fathers and hopes to go back to college and train as a social worker.

As Ruben observes, the prospects for so-called 'looked-after-children' are not good. A quarter of the prison population is made up of those who were fostered or in care;[30] and only 16 per cent of these children get an A* to C grade in maths and English GCSE, compared to 59 per cent of their peers.[31] Likewise, other young men grow up in relatively stable families but still take wrong turns in their lives. JV told me, 'My mum is a school teacher. The women in my family are professionals and very intelligent. I had that advantage. Yet it still took me until my late twenties to figure out who I was. I put her through a lot, man. She knew, to a degree, what was happening. But the stereotype of, if your kid's bad, you are going to know he's bad, that's just not true. I've got a little brother – really polite, really quiet, even a shy boy. And Mum is really happy and thinks he's so good. And I don't want to burst her bubble but – you know what? – I was still good at that age. He reminds me of myself a lot. Don't take your eye off him. We are not a family that has been brought up to be rude. So he's not going to be rude in the house or to you, you are not going to see in that way.' The same is true for Ashley Walters, so often portrayed as an archetypal bad boy from the troubled streets of Peckham. He too grew up in a family of educated women: 'My mum's been brilliant. She's a well-to-do black woman and my education and the academic side of life was of utmost importance for her. When I got into trouble, I remember thinking, My mum didn't bring me up to be like this. What have I done? I can't believe this.

Male role models – a miracle cure?

In current debates about supporting young people much store is set by 'role models', and in particular the place of fathers in boys' lives. Both Ashley Walters and JV spoke to me about the effect of growing up without their fathers. Ashley talked of the destructive fury this bred within him: 'I look back now and I realise my behaviour was because my dad wasn't around a lot of the time and the anger about that had to come out in some way.' A father of six, including two sons, Ashley adds, 'So I'm really keen on being in my boys' lives and being a consistent role model.' David Lammy, too, stresses the absence of fathers as a contributory factor in young men's alienation and criminality and the importance of male role models. 'The absence of men and of powerful role models really matters. Some men can't be about for their children because they are working all hours in multiple jobs. Others are just not there at all.' Speaking of his own childhood, after his father left the family when David was twelve, he says, 'As a boy, I fretted about not having a dad to show me how to shave or to put on a tie, or to give me advice about girls, as well as how to stop me getting into unnecessary fights.' Yet I wonder if, in these powerful accounts, the trauma caused when fathers desert their children is conflated with abstract notions of 'male role models'.

The term 'male role model' is used frequently by politicians, commentators and the wider public, usually when proffering it as the answer to social ills. It is seen as a 'common sense' need – and solution – and has been the driving force behind a range of government policies at Westminster, such as the last Labour government's 'Playing for Success' programme that promoted footballers as role models for boys and the Coalition government's 'Troops to Teachers' initiative to encourage ex-service personnel into teaching.[32] The term has been deployed in such a loose way that it appears to cover everyone from Jay Z to Bear Grylls, and on to male teachers and fathers generally – men with a variety of roles that they are supposedly modelling. It implies a simplistic relationship in which one person demonstrates how to be and another seamlessly adopts it. The team from the Open University's Beyond Male Role Models research project spoke to young men around the UK in order to find out what being a role model really means to them and the types of support and guidance they value.[33] It found that so-called 'celebrity role models' are considered too distant to be helpful guides on how to behave. What young men value is active engagement from those closer to home. Although they used the term 'male role model', there was a lack of clarity about what it meant. Rather, the support that the young people say they appreciate might be more accurately and meaningfully described as that of a mentor. This includes not just look-ing to youth workers and other older people in the area but also to each other for guidance. Whilst friends can be a 'bad influence' they can also be a source of positive support. As one of the young men interviewed in Scotland commented about a friend, 'He's away to the army, and he's lived a chaotic life, so I believe you look at people and say, "My God, man, how much he's changed, if he's done it then, aye, I'll be able to do it." '[34]

The researchers also found that both men and women are capa-ble of being effective mentors to the young men they interviewed.[35] When I spoke to David Lammy he paid testimony not only to the influence of his older brother, 'who took it upon himself to be a father figure to me', but also to that of his brother's first wife: 'She was an older woman, bohemian, talented, professional. She was a wonder-ful mentor. She was the first slightly alternative person I met in my life. She was powerfully interesting and interested in me.' At the same time, he also reminisced about, 'Two phenomenally impressive "uncles" who were friends of my father, Uncle Mike and Uncle Berys, who took me under their wing when my father left. I felt loved by those two uncles: they cared for me and they didn't have to.' In a cor-rective to the notion that young people need to be able to recognise something of themselves in the people they seek guidance from he says, 'Sometimes difference is important. It challenges your percep-tions and your parochialism. Great teachers played that role for me too – and professors at university. They made me feel intelligent, curi-ous and interested in worlds beyond my own.' While David Lammy talks movingly about the effect of his father's absence on his life, he is also heartfelt in acknowledging that others (teachers, the local vicar, relatives, family friends and of course his mother), both men and women, can provide guiding support – and did so in his case.

However they are labelled, family members and others in the com-munity play a significant part in shaping the behaviour and moral code of young men – for good or ill. JV remarks, 'A lot of young men like myself at the time are just a bit misguided and they've got a good heart and the scary thing is that a lot of these guys sitting in prison and doing these crimes are probably good people that have been taken off the right path. They don't even see it as bad. Their peers, their family around them, even their uncles, say, "Yeah, you've got to do what you've got to do. If the kid does wrong, you've got to stab him."' Some young men do not have positive family and community resources to call on. Ashley observes, 'I have seen a lot of fifteen year olds around [north London] and where I grew up in Peckham, even from the age of thirteen, they are involved in gang crime, already carrying guns and knives and doing a lot of silly things. It is these kids trying to find their way in life and once you go down the wrong path if there is not someone there to grab you and say you are going the wrong way you are pretty much gone.'

Boys behind bars

I met JV and Zane through George Turner, a former local authority youth worker who is now the Chief Executive of Carney's Community, a London-based charity that works with disadvantaged and excluded young people, including ex-offenders. He tells me about another of the young men he has worked with. 'Dave comes from a family where his mum is the victim of sustained domestic abuse from his dad. His dad has got a reputation as a real bad boy; he's attacked people with knives and all that sort of stuff. Dave's first offence was when he was eight, trying to steal a car with some older boys. He's been in and out of prison. A year ago he left prison desperate to sort himself out. Couldn't get housed by anyone. Probation were meant to link him in with a bail hostel and they didn't. I complained and eventually they gave him an appointment with housing. The appointment they gave him was the day after his licence finished. So when he turned up they said, "Your licence has finished so we've got no responsibility for you now." So he had nowhere else to stay. His dad's a street drinker. His mum's now left the country. All his friends are negative influences. All his family is negative influences. So when you come across that sort of family, to get yourself out of that, that's really something.'

George estimates that over £1 million has been spent on Dave as he's been bounced from social workers to prison to parole officers and hostels. But despite all this money, there has been no consistency in the support that he has received and no one that he can turn to and rely on, in lieu of caring family members. He has dealt with upwards of five people within each service he has come into contact with. George says, 'Some people ask, "Why should these kids, who've been offending, expect support? That's unfair. Why should they get that when my kids get nothing?" Well, my answer to them is: it's unfair that your kid has parents who care for them and support them and the kids I work with have parents who don't give a shit. So we are just trying to even up the balance.'

George tells me it is common for the boys and young men that he works with to suffer mental health issues. The Centre for Mental Health in the UK states that under-eighteens in custody are three times more likely to suffer from mental illness than other children of their age. Very often, they have multiple mental health issues, as well as a learning disability and drug and alcohol dependency.[36] The failure to identify and treat their illnesses effectively means that they cause harm to themselves and to others and are drawn into a system from which it is very hard to extricate themselves. The number of young offenders in custody is declining but this leaves a hard-core of very troubled young people – almost 70 per cent of young offenders released from custody go on to reoffend within twelve months.[37]

*

These mental health trends are reflected in the adult prison population. One prisoner in ten has a severe mental illness such as schizophrenia. Nearly half have depression and anxiety and half are also dependent on alcohol or drugs. Overall, 90 per cent have a diagnosable mental health issue and 70 per cent have two or more such problems.[38] Antisocial and criminal behaviour can be a symptom of mental distress.[39] When I speak to Jane Powell, Director of the Campaign Against Living Miserably, she tells me, 'When men are depressed, they take risks – get drunk, drive fast, start fights, do something stupid. Health professionals wring their hands at how hard it is to reach these men. Yet here they are in the streets, getting drunk and arrested or having a big row with their partner, leaving home and ending up homeless. Our prisons are filled with guys with mental health problems.' It may at first sight appear that prison is the best place for these men, but they need treatment rather than punishment: or perhaps both. As the Centre for Mental Health points out, prison is a high-cost, inappropriate and ineffective means of treating these people.[40] It would be far better for these prisoners, and those they have harmed or risk harming, if their mental health issues were spotted and treated earlier.

Feltham Young Offender Institution, one of the toughest youth custody institutions in England and Wales with boys and young men from forty-eight different gangs among its inmates,[41] has a waiting list for those requiring psychological treatment. Despite initial doubts from prison officers that they would be interested, inmates are voluntarily signing up for counselling. The governor of Feltham, Glenn Knight, told a meeting of the London Assembly's police and crime committee that, 'Some young people in our care have probably gone through more trauma than soldiers in Afghanistan … If you say, "Okay, have you seen anybody stabbed?" everyone puts their hand up.'[42] Having been socialised by family and peers to behave in an aggressive and unempathic way, the most damaged among them – whether they have been brought up in severely dysfunctional homes or have mental health problems or learning difficulties or all three of these things – inflict their pain on others and are then thrown into jail to fight it out among themselves.

Isaac, another young man helped by George Turner, is now in his twenties but was sentenced to a term in Feltham at the age of fifteen. He was the youngest prisoner there at the time. Isaac was excluded from school in Year 8 and then sent to a pupil referral unit: 'I was slower to learn than everybody else. I was embarrassed by that and it made me not work as hard, because I didn't believe that I could do it. I thought I was the dumbest guy in the classroom. I wasn't a bad child but I was naughty. I wish I could turn the clock back on my education. I wish I could read better. I can't think of one thing I learned at school.' Like JV, Isaac began to seek belonging and status through involvement in gangs: 'I used to be involved in street life to feel cool. But it's not really cool. You want to be The Man. It's all about the life-style. You want to have a reputation where you live. You want people to think about you and be scared. So you need to put down dirt.' (This, he informs me, means getting your hands dirty – in crime.) Putting down dirt led to his first arrest at thirteen before serving time in Feltham. 'I was gobsmacked when I first arrived,' he says, in what must be an understatement. 'It was a horrible experience. The others took advantage of me because I didn't know the ropes. I had to stand my ground the best way I could, at fifteen. Two kids tried to rush me in the shower. I fought back and I got respect from that day on.' Having proved himself by a forced show of brute strength, things changed for Isaac: 'After that it was nice,' he comments – although given the context I imagine 'nice' means 'not completely shit' rather than 'pleasant'. 'From that day on people talked to me and would do stuff for me. It changed overnight. You have to do what you have to do. There is nowhere to run.' Isaac now hopes to stay out of trouble, although he says, 'It is never behind you. I've moved from where I grew up because I wanted to feel free. But I could always come across someone from way back who wants to stab me up.'

Isaac praises the officers at Feltham who, he says, 'always had time for me. They would check up on me because I was the youngest.' In Feltham, as elsewhere, there will be well-intentioned and compassionate people among the officers and other staff (although, at the last official inspection of Feltham, recorded use of force was found to be up[43]). But with a quarter of inmates there locked up in their rooms for twenty-three hours a day (effectively solitary confinement, according to the inspection report[44]) what level of therapeutic and rehabilitative work is realistically achievable? At the time of writing, Michael Gove, who David Cameron appointed as Justice Secretary in 2015, has signalled a focus on rehabilitation and education for offenders. His department is also reviewing the youth justice system.[45] This approach stands in contrast to the punitive ways of his predecessor, Chris Grayling. The shift in tone was welcomed, but cautiously so as campaigners, prison officers and opposition spokespeople pointed to the need to tackle problems such as overcrowding and violence in prison, as well as effective treatment for mental illness, in order for educational and other progressive programmes to stand a chance.[46]

The stakes are high. Without effective therapy and rehabilitation young offenders risk continuing to live tortured lives themselves and to damage the lives of others. Some may not even make it out of custody. Between 2007 and 2013, eighty-seven young people committed suicide while in prison or a young offender institution in England and Wales. All but two were male. This included four children – boys aged fifteen to seventeen. In his review of suicides in custody, published in 2015, Lord Toby Harris noted, 'No one should be under any illusions: prisons and young offender institutions are grim environments, bleak and demoralising to the spirit.' Lord Harris and his panel learned of many occasions on which mental health appointments were missed because staff shortages meant there was no one available to escort prisoners to these appointments. He also noted that the cases they looked at 'demonstrated that many of the young people's problems and vulnerabilities, including mental health issues, had been evident from an early age. We had to ask the question, why were so many of these young adults in custody in the first place?'[47] Despite recognition that there was a grave problem, which led to the Harris review being commissioned by the government, suicide rates remain high. At the beginning of 2015, the Howard League for Penal Reform reported that the overall prison suicide rate in 2014 was the highest in seven years, with eighty-two prisoners taking their own lives. This included fourteen young offenders.[48]

In the American city of Chicago, there has been some success with a behavioural therapy programme called Being a Man, which is delivered to small groups of boys in high school. The programme attempts to teach boys to think and act differently in situations they find challenging or threatening, in the hope that this will lead to less confrontation and violence. Randomised control trials have reportedly found that participants in the programme are less likely to be arrested for a crime than other students and that their educational outcomes also improve.[49] There is much scepticism about such Cognitive Behavioural Therapy quick-fixes and the degree to which they have any long-term beneficial effects. But this project does at the very least point to the potential role of preventative strategies, even if those strategies have to go deeper than CBT to produce lasting results.

Crime – a male problem

The other lesson that we might learn from the approach in Chicago is that it explicitly identifies and engages boys and young men. It acknowledges that crime is a male problem. Given the statistics on the proportion of crimes committed by the male population, this may seem an obvious and uncontroversial observation. However, it is in fact surprisingly unusual for crime to be viewed through such a lens. The academics Ann Oakley and Cynthia Cockburn set out to uncover the extent and cost of male criminality in the UK. They found that unearthing this information took some digging. As they put it, 'antisocial acts that harm well-being – from speed driving to calculated murder – are overwhelmingly performed by men'. Yet although government data on crime goes into great detail on the type of offence and even the victim, you have to go some layers down to find information on the sex of the offender. This is despite, in the words of Oakley and Cockburn, the figures being 'startling'. They point out that, 'of the one-third of a million people in England and Wales found guilty of an indictable offence in the twelve months ending June 2012, 85 per cent were men. The more violent the crime, the more men predominate. From a unique table deep in the quarterly Ministry of Justice Criminal Justice Statistics Bulletin for England and Wales, we learn that males were 88 per cent of those found guilty of violence against the person, and more than 98 per cent of those committing sexual offences.'[50] But men's domination of crime is not just confined to the most serious offences. The academics note that theft, disorder and antisocial behaviour are all overwhelmingly perpetuated by men.[51] They also make the significant point that the 'gendering of indiscipline' starts from a relatively young age, with boys receiving the majority of exclusion orders, as we've seen.[52] Crime is gendered and its roots lie in childhood.

Despite this mass of evidence that crime is an overwhelmingly male problem, Ann Oakley and Cynthia Cockburn found barely a mention of the sex of offenders in the official documents that they scrutinised. I too noticed this when reading a Centre for Mental Health briefing on criminal justice 'liaison and diversion' services, in which offenders were referred to as 'children', 'young people' and 'people'.[53] This absence of references to offenders as male even occurs in the section on what can be done to divert 'people' from prison – surely an area in which it would be useful to take account of sex and gender.[54] Oakley and Cockburn contrast the omission of references to men with government documents that explicitly focus on women in the criminal justice system, a direct result of the 'equality' provision in the 1991 Criminal Justice Act. As they point out, these documents are worthwhile and revealing, yet they beg the question of why the same analysis is not carried out with regards to men, particularly as men make up the vast majority of those who commit crime. The writers state, 'where "gender" is interpreted as "women", men remain in the shadows'. Oakley and Cockburn very effectively ram home the point that the sex of offenders matters by putting a price tag on it. They estimate that the cost of male crime (from the funding of police investigations through to paying for prison places) works out at about £30 billion per year.[55] To put this in context, in the 2015 UK general election the Conservatives promised to increase NHS spending by £8 billion a year, in a bid to show irrefutably that they would protect it.[56]

It is only a minority of men that commit crime, but the majority of criminals are men. Why? Beginning to ask questions about why men are responsible for most crimes and how this might be addressed would save a great deal of money. It would also save a great deal of suffering and even people's lives – including the lives of women. Indeed, it is by joining the dots between apparently isolated incidents of male violence against women that the link between sometimes murderous aggression, masculinity and gender is slowly beginning to get the necessary attention. Karen Ingala Smith runs the London-based charity Nia Project, which works to end male violence against women and girls. She began her Counting Dead Women project on her personal blog in 2012. It calculates the number of women killed through male violence in the UK each year. In the first year she recorded 126 deaths, then 144 in 2013 and 149 in 2014.[57]

The stark statistics make an inarguable point about male perpetration of violence. Karen Ingala Smith says, 'People are falling for the line that women can be violent too … But nearly always when a woman kills a man, the woman herself has been a victim of his violence or abuse. When men kill women they tend to have been perpetrators of violence against that woman and other women for years.'[58]

Ingala Smith acknowledges that – according to official statistics – men are more likely to be the victims of male violence than women but, as she says, 'when we're talking about fatal violence, we are almost always talking about men's violence'.[59] Such is the impact of the project that Ingala Smith has now joined forces with Women's Aid and two blue-chip law firms to launch an online database, Femicide Census: Profiles of Women Killed by Men, which will draw on police statistics and court reports, with the aim of making it easier for researchers to carry out robust studies on the issue. This more formalised data collection stands as a rebuke to the Home Office, which does not collect and publish such information itself.

In a powerful presentation at an International Women's Day event I attended, Karen Ingala Smith made the point that, 'the basic concepts of masculinity and femininity are poisonous'.[60] The division of boys and girls in playgrounds and classrooms, the opposition that is encouraged by parents and others, the antagonism that is played out in deeply destructive ways in the teen years; all this culminates for a minority of men in such an extreme sense of entitlement and violent hostility that they kill women. Our misogynistic and patriarchal culture alone is not solely to blame for these men's actions – the vast majority of men raised within the same culture do not commit such crimes. Nor is coming from an environment where physical, sexual and emotional abuse occurred. As adults, these men are capable of making choices and they must take responsibility for what they do. But these factors do form a part of the explanation, if not a defence, and we must also take collective responsibility for a society that defines boys and girls in opposition to each other, that regards women as inferior to men at a systemic level and encourages male aggression.

New Zealand's independent Glenn Inquiry into Child Abuse and Domestic Violence, which reported in 2014, found that stereotypical concepts of masculinity propped up the belief that violence against women was acceptable. These concepts reinforced patriarchal views of women as subservient to men, and so male perpetrators took the view that they had the right to intimidate and attack a female partner.[61] A wide-ranging study of self-reported perpetration of sexual violence in five countries found that men who espouse notions of male privilege and entitlement are consistently more likely to perpetrate rape. It also found that sexual violence overlaps with physical violence against a partner. Men who are physically violent are significantly more likely to be sexually violent. As discussed in Chapter 3, this is linked to childhood experiences. Sexual aggression and rape are more likely among men who witnessed or experienced physical or sexual violence as children, or experienced neglect while growing up.[62] Research and fieldwork carried out by the United Nations Population Fund has shown that challenging gender norms is vital in order to combat male violence and abuse against women.[63] When the United Nations special rapporteur Rashida Manjoo visited the UK in 2014 she spoke of 'a sexist culture that exists in the country'.[64] She also expressed concern about the drive in UK policy-making to frame violence as gender-neutral.

Intimate terrorism

Men's rights activists have for some years argued that women are as likely, if not more likely, to perpetrate domestic violence and abuse as men.[65] 'Domestic violence … is not a male-on-female issue, but is non-"gendered". That is, it's perpetrated by both sexes. In fact, it's pre-dominantly a *female*-on-male phenomenon. If it is "gendered", then it's not a male crime but a female one,' says Steve Moxon in his book *The Woman Racket*.[66] 'Female perpetrators are more likely than male,' stated the Justice for Men and Boys Party in its 2015 UK General Election Manifesto, while also insisting that domestic violence and abuse was 'not a gendered problem'.[67] Such claims are frequently based on data drawn from skewed samples or a conflation of different types of violence.[68] The American academic Michael Johnson has written of the distinction between 'intimate terrorism' – which is brutal and controlling, involves living in fear and is what most of us would associate with the term 'domestic violence and abuse' – and 'situational couple violence' – that is, incidents of violence that arise when a specific conflict escalates. Such incidents, though deeply upsetting and more common, are not part of a bigger pattern of control. The former is overwhelmingly inflicted by men on women. The latter is inflicted by men and women in almost equal numbers – although, among young people, women are more likely to be perpetrators than men.[69] Importantly, the men who perpetrate 'intimate terrorism' have significantly more misogynistic attitudes than non-violent men, whereas perpetrators of 'situational couple violence' do not.[70]

For those men who do suffer violence – of one kind or another – at the hands of women, it is an indictment of our rigid and stereotypical notions of masculinity that they are often ridiculed. Perhaps the most high-profile example in recent decades of society's unwillingness to treat such men compassionately and respectfully was the mocking reaction to the violence allegedly suffered by the actor Ross Kemp at the hands of his then wife Rebekah Wade (later Brooks), at that time the editor of the *Sun*.[71] Even more recently, television presenter Jeremy Kyle – not usually a man associated with upholding high standards of decency – rebuked his studio audience for laughing at a male guest when they heard of the violence reportedly meted out to him by his girlfriend.[72] Our inability, as a society, to feel sympathy and concern for men in such situations is wrong (and we seem to ignore the issue of violence within same-sex relationships completely). Indeed, at an institutional level a blind eye is turned to male victims of domestic violence and abuse, as well as other forms of violence – such as sexual abuse. The Crown Prosecution Service in 2015 folded data on the number of male victims, including of domestic violence and abuse and sexual abuse, into a publication entitled 'Violence against Women and Girls Crime Report'.[73] To give the report this title is not only, clearly, factually incorrect but denies those men and boys concerned explicit and official recognition of what they have been through. The percentage of female victims recorded in the report vastly outweighs that of male victims, but nonetheless this latter group exists and should be given the simple respect of acknowledgement. To do so does not detract from the need to address the specific, gendered power relations at play in the majority of cases, involving a male perpetrator and female victim. Following well-argued protests led by the journalist Ally Fogg,[74] Alison Saunders, the Director of Public Prosecutions, agreed to amend the report and ensure those published in future were clearer about the inclusion of men and boys in their data. However, she still planned to retain the misleading main title.[75] It will be interesting to see how this contorted position plays out.

Yet the fact remains that most domestic violence and abuse is perpetrated by men, even when we take into account the likelihood that some men will not come forward as victims for fear of being disbelieved or being perceived as unmanly. Ben Jamal, Chief Executive of the Domestic Violence Intervention Project, says, 'There is more than an element of truth in the belief that some men don't report being a victim because of the stigma. But if we solved that problem would we find there is a 50/50 split between male and female victims? No, we wouldn't. There wouldn't suddenly be a flood of male victims emerging. The danger with the argument about stigma is that there is another agenda at play.' The agenda is that of the men's rights lobby. To buckle to their pressure and view violence through a gender-neutral prism (or even as more likely to be perpetrated by women) risks overlooking the central role that domineering, aggressive masculinity plays in violence. And if this form of masculinity is not tackled then the lives of women and men targeted by violent and abusive men remain at risk. Such gender-based violence and abuse includes the majority of those crimes that are mis-labelled as 'honour killings', as well as polygamy, forced marriage and female genital mutilation: practices upheld by claims of, and deference to, religious authority or cultural authenticity. As Pragna Patel from Southall Black Sisters writes, for the women suffering in these cases, 'Their experience of violence is in fact part of a continuum of violence against women but it is increasingly perceived as a cultural practice in debates where we are witness to an extraordinary loose use of the term "honour-based violence". If we are to take the matter seriously, it is vital to unpack the term to reveal the underlying patriarchal dynamics of control and patterns of gender inequality ... in the vast majority of domestic violence cases in South Asian communities, the honour principle operates as a silencing factor. Here the violence or abuse is not motivated by the need to maintain honour, but honour is invoked to silence women in the face of such violence and abuse. Such cases should not be termed "honour crimes".'[76]

At the same time as there is a shift in UK policy towards gender-neutral approaches to domestic violence and abuse, there is a growing body of evidence showing that working with male perpetrators, alongside support for women, is having an effect. Historically, in the cash-strapped world of organisations fighting to end violence and abuse against women, the notion of spending some of those resources on perpetrators has drawn suspicion and hostility. Some would still take that view, or believe that the only answer is to send offenders to prison rather than on a course. Feminists with progressive views on most things can hit a blind spot when it comes to treatment of domestic violence perpetrators. But overall there has been a wide-spread shift in attitudes in the field. Liz Kelly, Professor of Sexualised Violence at London Metropolitan University, and co-chair of the End Violence Against Women coalition, is a veteran of the sector, having worked in it for thirty years. In 2015 she published the results of Project Mirabal, an extensive five-year study evaluating accredited programmes that engage with male perpetrators of domestic violence and abuse. Her reason for leading the research, she explained, is that 'domestic violence shows no sign of abating ... It has become clear that in order to reduce and prevent domestic violence, the spotlight must be placed on men and their behaviour, alongside the interventions for women and children.'[77] With an average of two women a week being killed as a result of such violence and abuse it is imperative to put enmity to one side and concentrate on what works.[78]

Men who participate in these programmes either seek out help themselves or are referred by the family courts or other legal proceedings, often as a condition of contact with their children. The Domestic Violence Intervention Project, one of the accredited programmes, involves the men coming to weekly sessions over twenty-six weeks, with the aim of getting them to question their self-justification for the violence and abuse that they have inflicted in the past and to think before they act in the future. It also attempts to re-educate them on the importance of equality in relationships. Ben Jamal told me, 'The work we do involves giving the men an understanding of gender: what it is to be a man; how this plays out in relationships, power and control; and how this is embedded by family and society. Gender is not the only factor in their behaviour. It is also about childhood experiences and other aspects of their personal psychology. But how could gender not be there, because it's there in the whole of society?' It is the intensity of the sessions – requiring deep self-reflection over a sustained period of time – as well as the discussion and critique within the peer group that marks out such projects from other approaches.

In an echo of the Open University research on role models, 'peer mentors' hold significant sway: those who have travelled further in re-assessing their attitudes can encourage and challenge others who have some way to go. Ben says, 'The men learn from each other. The group dynamic is very important. At the heart of our model is the belief that men can change – though not all of them do.' Alongside this work with men, accredited courses work with the partners and ex-partners suffering abuse and, sometimes, children.

In the Project Mirabal evaluation programme researchers spoke to the perpetrators about what it meant to them to be a man. The question often flummoxed them but, nonetheless, the answer came out in other responses. Although most of the men paid lip service to equality between the sexes, they also spoke of adhering to a traditional view of masculinity in which they were the protector, provider and 'legitimate' head of the household. 'This fed into a sense that they should, and did, "know best" about what was good for the family, the standards by which they lived, which simultaneously positioned women as deficient or in need of "help" or "guidance". The notion of provider served to legitimise a sense of entitlement to decide on relationship and parenting norms. It was women challenging and contesting these unwritten rules which sat at the heart of men's perceived need to control, which when manifested through violence and abuse destroyed the very safety and security they were supposed to ensure. Men who made the most steps towards change had spent considerable time rethinking and remaking themselves as men within their relationships and in terms of their parenting. The changes women reported making were similarly a rejection of the diminished femininity they had been coerced into adopting.'[79] It is worth quoting this extract from the evaluation report in full because it makes it so startlingly clear that gender, and the 'poisonous' notions of masculinity and femininity that Karen Ingala Smith invokes, are central to men's violent behaviour.

The evaluation found some significant changes following on from the programme, particularly in women and children's sense of safety and freedom from domestic violence and abuse (for instance, before the programme 30 per cent of women reported their partner making them do something sexually that they did not want to, and this reduced to 0 per cent after the programme; instances where men slapped, punched or threw something at women reduced from 87 per cent to 7 per cent; the number of women reporting physical injuries reduced from 61 per cent to 2 per cent; and the extent to which children witnessed or heard violence fell from 80 per cent to 8 per cent). However, other changes were much less significant, such as the 3 per cent reduction in men using money and finances as a means of control or the 2 per cent increase in men being more considerate in their treatment of partners or ex-partners. Most troublingly, a high proportion of women reported that their partners were still attempting to justify or excuse their violent and abusive behaviour after the programme (71 per cent down from 91 per cent).[80] Ben says, 'Some of the findings from the evaluation have prompted us to make changes. For instance, we are looking at how we can improve outcomes relating to financial abuse. We know that we can impact from an early point of the process on the use of physical violence but a fundamental shift in attitudes that underpin other controlling and coercive behaviours takes longer. This is why the programme lasts for twenty-six weeks. With many men we would like to work for longer. The reality is that we are fighting a battle to work with these men for twenty-six weeks. There is no will out there to fund anything longer than that and in fact there is pressure to accomplish what we do in less time.'

Nonetheless, the results show that something positive is happening in these sessions that is beginning to improve – to varying degrees – the behaviour of the majority of men involved, to the benefit of those around them. Liz Kelly and her co-author Nicole Westmarland are admirably honest in their report when they state, 'As feminists, with most of our policy and practice work firmly located in the women's sector we began this programme of research with a healthy scepticism about the extent to which men choose to change … we are convinced that our data shows steps towards change do start to happen for most.'[81] Ben recognises this shift: 'When perpetrator work started in the UK there was real suspicion in the women's sector. Those anxieties largely dissolved, partly because of the evidence that these programmes work and also because we support the partners as well as working with the men. But, probably because everyone is now scrabbling for money again, the fault lines are re-emerging a bit. I'd say, look at what women are telling us. Women say their lives are better than they were before because of these programmes. Are we creating perfect relationships and perfect men? No of course not. But we are often creating safer relationships.' As Ben indicates, and as is so often depressingly the case in the UK, the availability of these valuable programmes is compromised by funding. At present just one in ten local authorities in Britain runs accredited prevention projects.[82] In the meantime, in other areas, whilst women and children may possibly (although by no means certainly) be able to receive help and support, the behaviour of the men from whom they need protection – rooted in a warped masculinity – is not being addressed.

The fight to be free

Tackling the specific notions of control and power that form the breeding ground for domestic violence and abuse requires a very specific approach. But what about the more aimless, often self-destructive sense of alienation and frustrated masculinity that defines life for those in gangs or crime, those who are NEET or in some other way have begun to lose their way in life?

We met JV at the beginning of this chapter. Like many of the men that David Lammy referred to, he felt a combination of a sense of rejection and frustration as well as a desire to belong and be respected, which led him into gang life. Fortunately for him, he decided one day to walk through the doors of Fitzroy Lodge, the amateur boxing club in south London where I met him. For JV boxing changed everything. The training gave him a focus and discipline that had been missing from his life, but there were other aspects to joining the lodge that were arguably more important. It gave him the necessary cover to retreat from gang life. 'Boxing is a way out. It's a way out when a guy can say, "I can't get involved, I've got training." And I think [the other members of the gang] respect that – more than they would anything else. Because you are a boxer and you are dangerous. So you are doing something hard. So you get respect and you don't have to risk your freedom. It's probably the perfect – some would say the only – way out.' As he extricated himself from the gang, JV also found that boxing provided a replacement – in fact, a better – community and source of support. 'These guys helping the kids – they want to help. They are not getting paid much. They have a passion and a love for it. From the street, you are not used to guys who care for you. No one cares about you. [The coach] would turn up at my house at six o'clock in the morning to take me running. And I started to feel, like, Wow, these people care. Your whole perspective on life changes – I've got an obligation. Even the juniors know what you've been doing. You don't want to let them down. Your coach has put a lot of time into you. You don't want to let him down. You can't let anyone down. It's a good pressure.' The coaches at Fitzroy Lodge demonstrated their belief in JV, and he lived up to and repaid that belief.

JV is visibly moved as he talks about the late head coach of the lodge, Mick Carney, who first mentored him. Mick was the embodiment of the idea that mentors do not necessarily need to be cut from the same cloth as those they support. 'As a young man growing up you kinda have your stereotypes, y'know? I'm a black man. He's an old white guy, really strait-laced. He started dropping me home, and sitting in the car I realised – I'm not saying white guys ain't cool – but this guy's really cool. The jazz music would start coming on, he'd start dancing in the car. We'd have a chat and he wears his fancy suits and all that. I'd get home and I'd be like, "Mum, this white guy's just dropped me home and he's really cool." Mick is probably the coolest guy I've known. Even at seventy-five years old he was really cool. He'd be in the office, he'd put his leg up on the table, quite like at an angle. You'd think, Ooh, be careful there, and he'd be talking and just relaxed. He was wicked, man, wicked. And we'd talk. And first, with an older guy you say certain things, think he's only gonna understand certain things, but the truth is he understood everything. He'd say things that related to my street life. He was an amazing man. I've got young children. He even helped me to be a better father. He taught me what was wrong and what was right and to do the right thing.'

It is through Fitzroy Lodge that JV met George Turner, who went on to name Carney's Community in honour of Mick Carney, who died in 2011. George says: 'Eleven years ago I was working in Lambeth and Wandsworth Youth Offending teams doing the Intensive Supervision and Surveillance Project. So it would be the last chance before someone went to prison. They'd have to spend fifteen, twenty hours with me. Or they'd get out of prison early and have to spend that time with me. Mick heard about it and he let me bring young people down and he didn't charge us. It was brilliant. Hardly anyone became a boxer out of it but just the training, the discipline, the honour code and the benefits too of being surrounded by other people demonstrating their masculinity in a good way.' It is this approach that then enabled George to help Isaac and Zane; Zane, like Isaac, was excluded from school, had special educational needs that went unmet and wound up behind bars.

When you speak to JV and George, the reverence and love that they feel for Mick Carney is immediately evident. Zane and Isaac in turn speak of George in similar terms, having finally found someone who respects and believes in them and is a constant, reliable presence in their lives. 'When I met George he was not like a normal youth worker. He actually cares for you and goes out of his way for you. Others come and go but he is always there,' Zane tells me. 'George has got a brilliant heart,' says Isaac. 'He would always have my back. He really cares for us and that is why I love him so much. What he has is real. He's my guiding angel.'

Boxing, this toughest of sports, gives rise to the most tender of emotions. The macho, bloody battles of the ring are something many people feel antipathy towards. As George says, 'You always get, "You are teaching young people to fight." Well, no, young people know how to fight. We are teaching them to box and control their aggression. Because if you can't control your aggression you are going to lose the match.' To my mind, ideally, we would live in a world where we did not need to identify controlled channels for male aggression. But we do not live in that world. We have to meet young men where they are and then work with what we have got. Boxing is a violent sport and some people have suffered terrible injuries in the world of money-driven professional boxing where seeing through the fight is what counts. But it is arguably less risky than being out on the streets looking for trouble, and comes with particular benefits attached. Boxing connects with the young men whom the rest of society needs to reach out to. A Pilates class isn't going to get them through the door.

With Carney's Community, George Turner is attempting to integrate the discipline and support that comes with boxing, with wider community connections and networks. 'What we are trying to do is copy a lot of the stuff that Mick did. He worked with boxers but he also had links to local businesses. So a boxer would come in and if he felt they were ready he'd then refer them on to a local employer. So we are trying to do the same thing, working with the young people that come to the club, and giving a personal development plan to the ones that do want to turn themselves around.' Zane tells me, 'I thought it would be just like a gym. But the sense of family surprised me. I've met good people with normal jobs. I had isolated myself. I had no contact with those sorts of people. It made me realise what is possible.' After meeting George, Zane trained as an electrician and now works for a local authority.

What struck me, in addition to the valuable, if very labour intensive, work that Carney's Community is doing to support young men and help them into work, is how it also opens up their emotional lives – allowing and encouraging them to talk about the care and love they receive and reciprocate, and then pass this down from one generation to the next. This, combined with the boundary setting, discipline and status that JV and George identified, is a powerful package. In seeking a sense of belonging and purpose through an outwardly very stereotypical show of macho behaviour, the boxers that I met through Carney's Community are creating an altogether more nuanced and interesting form of manhood for themselves.

The need to tackle a destructive masculinity, bound up with displays of aggression and domination, is not only an issue for those in the most disadvantaged communities. Even families that believe their sons are too well supported or educated to fall into criminal or other harmful behaviour would benefit from society losing fewer boys to criminal machismo. They would see these benefits through greater neighbourhood stability, less gang activity and a reduced chance that they or their sons would fall victim to assault, mugging or other crime. George Turner makes a point of opening up the boxing sessions he arranges to a wide range of young people. 'We get young offenders come in, kids from the local estate come in and recently we've had a couple of lads from a private school come in as well. And it's really nice. It's funny because you see one of our persistent offenders, looks like a real thug, and this guy Miles and they're training and having a laugh together. Where else would you see those two side by side? Miles is mixing with people that he used to fear and seeing that actually they are all right. And the young people that go out and do the robberies, they are mixing with people they are robbing, and realising they are real people as well with feelings. I have lots of the middle classes saying, "Why should we volunteer to mentor them? It's not going to affect us. We are in our bubble, they are in their bubble." And my response to that is, well when they are going out robbing wealthier kids, that's your kids. Those worlds do merge. You need to look at the wider picture. If you want your kids to walk down the street safely then there needs to be some work done to help the kids that are doing the offending.'

Listening to the experiences of the boys and men I spoke to, there seems to be an awful lot of luck involved in putting them out of harm's way. JV was lucky to walk into Fitzroy Lodge and encounter Mick Carney – a move that has now led him to pursue boxing professionally. 'I believe they saved my life. My life has been saved through boxing, through what I've accomplished at the Fitzroy Lodge. If it wasn't for this place I'd have stayed in trouble, been in prison, or got killed. It saved me by setting me on a straight path.' Ashley Walters was lucky that his bad-boy image was alluring enough to lead to the central role in the film *Bullet Boy* (playing a young man just released from prison). He has been canny and talented enough to exploit to the full the television and film industry hunger for gritty reality, and has built a successful and varied acting career off the back of it. He has also been able to do some deep thinking along the way: 'It's taken me a long time to come round to understanding what a man should be. Allow yourself to be vulnerable. It doesn't matter if you cry. I have my head held high. I've got my kids, my family, I've got a wife who loves me and I love dearly. That's all I need. But it can take a man a long time to realise that.'

Yet boxing or acting can only be a way out for a small minority of young men. George Turner comments, 'We try to get the lads we work with to widen their horizons. Not just boxer, rap star, footballer. You need to be realistic.' Charities such as Carney's Community do hugely valuable work turning around young men's lives in their local area. But it is very labour intensive, long term and necessarily small-scale. For the handful of young men they are able to reach, there will be hundreds who continue to wreak havoc because they haven't been helped. They deserve society's support and care, rather than to be left behind. Their aspirations matter too.

5. GREATER GAINS

Family Men

In the lead

'These boys who people think are a handful,' declares Mandy, 'will go on to be successful. The boisterous ones will be the men who stand up and lead in later life.' Mandy is speaking as the mother of a son who has found it difficult to settle down at school, yet she points to a wider truth. Men enjoy greater success at work than women. On the face of it men come into their own as they get older. Those who live troubled lives are a minority. Most men grow up to feel comfortable about where they are in life, certainly in the workplace.

Across Europe men rate their life satisfaction highly, at just over 7 out of 10.[1] Despite on average lower school attainment than girls, most men manage to pull ahead in the jobs market. In the UK the pay gap between the sexes for full-time workers, though narrowing, is still over 9 per cent[2] (and some put this narrowing down to a reduction in men's wages rather than an increase in those of women[3]). The Office for National Statistics (ONS), in its analysis of the UK pay gap, points out that over-all the gap is 'relatively small' until women reach their forties. Indeed, women narrowly overtake men in earnings from their early twenties until their late thirties, before slipping behind, as men begin to out-earn women significantly. 'This is likely to be connected with the fact that many women have children and take time out of the labour market,' states the ONS briefing paper, mildly.[4] Established in their work, men forge ahead in their thirties and forties, while women's progress and earnings nosedive – or at least come to an abrupt halt. The fact that the pay gap kicks in after women have had children rather than before gives the lie to the belief that the division of cash and care roles is all down to earning power – with the first child at least. A range of gendered cultural assumptions comes into play when making decisions about family life.

The roll-call of statistics on male domination of top jobs is very familiar, if still striking. Globally, men occupy around 80 per cent of board positions and parliamentary seats and are 95 per cent of CEOs of the largest international corporations.[5] In the UK over 85 per cent of police chief constables are men,[6] as are 60 per cent of secondary school heads (in a profession dominated by women[7]) and 88 per cent of council leaders.[8] Overall, men occupy two-thirds of managerial positions and make up the majority of the top 10 per cent of earners – their proportion increasing past the age of thirty.[9] While there are equal numbers of men and women in the lowest skilled positions in the UK, 37 per cent of men are employed in 'upper middle' skilled roles (perhaps a skilled trade or technical role), compared to 18 per cent of women, whereas 46 per cent of women are employed in 'lower middle skilled roles' (such as admin or customer service roles) compared to 24 per cent of men.[10]

It has become fashionable in some circles to declare – in the words of Hanna Rosin's own book on the issue – the 'end of men'. Their outmoded skills and ill-educated minds have done for them, the argument goes, while clever, adaptable women steal a march. 'Yes, the United States and many other countries still have a gender wage gap. Yes, women do most of the childcare. And yes, the upper reaches of power are still dominated by men,' Rosin writes breezily, as if by giving these points the nod they can be written off.[11] But these three sentences alone are argument enough against the notion of the 'end of men'. Women have become adaptable and compliant – perfect material to staff the booming service industry – but out of necessity, as they attempt to earn a living while covering all the bases at home. They aren't rising to the top and getting rich on it. That is reserved for the men running the giant service-sector corporations in which they work.

I meet Hugh, a father of one, at The Dadly Arts, a 'fatherhood fiesta' run by Josh Lee at a children's centre in Bristol. In the garden, fathers and their children watch an ice-cream-making demonstration or play in the sand pit, while inside they cut out model cars from cardboard or join in a ukulele workshop. Sitting on a sofa as his daughter sleeps in her pram, Hugh reflects on men of his demographic. 'If you are white, male and live in England, you have it made from a material perspective,' he says. 'But these men are like logs floating in a river, because they can be. They go to university, get on the job ladder and think they are a great success. They put it down to their own abilities and hard work. But they didn't do anything to make it happen. Being white, male and living in England made that happen. These men are vacuous and closed off.' As Hugh indicates, while women take on most responsibility for home life, professional and job-focused men pay an emotional price, despite their material advantages. Although the life satisfaction of European men is marginally higher than for women,[12] well-being research for the OECD indicates that high male life-satisfaction ratings are linked to jobs and income, whereas female life satisfaction is focused on health, education and community.[13] While men are forging ahead in their careers, they are missing out on greater fulfilment closer to home.

'I want to live a full life for my kids'

Men's work patterns change very little if they become fathers. The great majority continues to work full time; only 6 per cent of men with dependent children work part time.[14] In fact, fathers work longer hours than other men.[15] Various explanations have been put forward for this. Some argue that men may feel the need to be 'good providers' when they become fathers.[16] Others say becoming a father often happens to coincide with a time in life when careers are more demanding.[17] Cynics suggest that men work longer hours to minimise their time at home with tiring children, something fathers will occasionally say themselves.[18] Mothers spend just over double the time spent by fathers on housework and looking after family members,[19] even in couples where the wife is a high earner.[20] In contrast to fathers, many mothers are employed part time[21] or not at all[22] in order to also look after their children and the home. Those men working part time are more than twice as likely as part-time women to do so because they cannot find full-time work.[23]

In her landmark book *Fatherhood Reclaimed*, Adrienne Burgess provides an important historical perspective on these divisions of time. The cash versus care split that has dogged parental roles is a modern-day phenomenon. Far from being the remote figures of popular imagination, in previous centuries fathers were present and active in the daily lives of their children. It wasn't until the turn of the twentieth century that long working hours and commutes propelled families into 'role specialisation'.[24] However, it now looks as if trends are shifting again. As we shall see, there have been changes in men's work and care patterns in recent years, and there are now encouraging signs that men want to be more closely involved in the lives of their children and are making this happen.

When surveyed, men say they believe in sharing childcare equally and that they want to spend more time with their children.[25] Becoming a father, just like becoming a mother, is a watershed moment. The acerbic comedian and journalist Charlie Brooker, not usually one for sentimentality, wrote a sincere and touching piece about his experience of becoming a father. 'So it turns out the birth of your first child is perhaps the most emotionally charged experience you'll ever have,' he wrote, '… your universe momentarily pauses while a fundamental shift in perspective takes place.'[26] One aspect of this fundamental shift that comes through in many conversations with fathers is the wish to be a 'better' father than they consider their own to have been; 'better' meaning being more physically and emotionally present in their children's lives. This chimes with wider findings. In research conducted for the UK's Fatherhood Institute, half the men questioned said they wished their fathers had spent more time with them when they were growing up and over a third thought that their fathers had had little or no positive influence on their upbringing. Almost 40 per cent said they were trying to be closer to their own children.[27] Isaac, whom I met at Carney's Community, became a father when he was twenty years old. He said to me, 'I have got no respect for my dad. He hasn't done anything for me … You have to be a dad and show children that you love them.'

When I speak to David, a researcher in the south-west of England who adopted two brothers with his male partner, he tells me, 'I was raised by my mum.' I assume this means that she was a single parent until, later in the conversation, he says that, 'My father was always out working. He worked long hours during the week and then was on call at the weekends. He didn't feature very prominently in my childhood. I try to be around more than my father was for me.' He is at pains to point out that, 'He was a very loving father and that was largely the culture of the time, so it is not an accusation against him, at all. And my relationship with him improved enormously when I went to university. I think he felt that we had more in common at that point.' Nevertheless, he says, 'I do a lot more things with my boys. I want that relationship with them now, rather than deferring it to later as happened between my dad and me.' Likewise, Isaac credits becoming a father as the catalyst for fundamental change in his life: 'I decided to get out of my gangster phase and to change my ways. I don't want to die knowing my kids are without me. I want to live a full life for my kids.' His friend Zane had just come out of prison when he became a father: 'The last time I was inside I promised myself I would give it a shot and stay out of trouble for a year once I got out. Having my son made me stick at it. I wanted to be a good example for him and someone he could respect.'

Men's desire to be actively involved in the upbringing of their children is resulting in some small yet concrete shifts in behaviour. Research published in 2014 shows that the time fathers in the UK spend with children increased from ten minutes a day in 1974 to an hour a day in 2005 (although this is part of a bigger trend: mothers' time with children also rose, from forty-five to 115 minutes a day over the same period).[28]

Men are able to devote more time to their family because women are spending more time earning. As writer and researcher Nikki van der Gaag points out in her impressively global book *Feminism and Men,* the 'fatherhood revolution' has chiefly been propelled by women. 'Men are changing (slowly) because women have been changing (fast),' she observes.[29] Since the early 2000s British mothers in couples have upped their own paid work hours: between 2001 and 2011 there was a slight increase in the hours worked by those in part-time jobs as well as in the number of mothers in full-time jobs. Given the economic turbulence within that period, some of these changes will have been driven primarily by the need for mothers to earn more money. However, over the same time, although they still work longer hours than other men, the number of hours worked by British fathers in couples declined.[30] Greater equality and fathers spending more time with their children are beneficial side effects of the increase in mothers' paid work.

The changing role of fathers is reflected in the wider culture. High-profile men from Jamie Oliver to Barack Obama are keen to portray themselves as regular family guys. Businesses and their advertisers are getting in on the act. Whilst there is still sexism aplenty in advertising, some companies are latching on to this social shift, with recent campaigns from Dove, Halifax and SMA depicting fathers doing everyday care: no heroics, no supervisory mother, no comedy incompetence. A Cheerios advert in Canada in 2014 took the – for the world of advertising – radical step of depicting a gay couple talking about becoming dads to their young daughter. The following year saw a number of ads during the American Super Bowl hailed for their depictions of largely positive (if schmaltzy) images of fatherhood and male childcare.[31]

Involved fatherhood – why care?

The masculinities researcher Michael Kimmel credits a friend with coming up with the inspired phrase 'premature self-congratulation' for those men who believe they have liberated themselves from masculinity's confines.[32] Although the changes of recent decades give some cause for optimism, fatherhood has not been transformed. If fathers and mothers both want fulfilment at home and in the workplace, this will take ongoing, determined effort from each, as well as from employers and those delivering family services and formulating family policy. The rewards will be worth it, for parents and children. A significant raft of research links close father involvement with a range of positive outcomes for children, including higher academic attainment, diminished psychological and behavioural problems, a greater sense of self-worth and lower levels of delinquency in adolescence, and, in adulthood, more satisfactory relationships, lower levels of depression and better self-reported parenting skills.[33] Young people who have a strong, positive relationship with their fathers are more resilient to knock-backs later in life such as unemployment.[34] Looking after children from early on encourages fathers to be more nurturing, developing their sensitivity towards, and attachment to, their children.[35] It eases a man's adjustment to fatherhood, improves fathers' satisfaction with family life and is even thought to reduce aggression.[36] Heterosexual married fathers who share childcare and domestic work tend to have better relationships with their wives than those men who fail to do so, irrespective of whether or not their wife is in paid work.[37] Happy and engaged fathers are more likely to do things with their children, to praise them and to talk to them daily about important things,[38] creating a virtuous circle. In summary, fathers who play a full part in home life are happier, more fulfilled in their relationships and less likely to end up divorced.

Being involved means much more than being a 'hands-on' father. 'Hands-on' implies that you can also be 'hands-off', and so conveys the impression that these fathers have, beneficently, elected to join in with the care of their own children. The phrase is routinely used to describe the sort of father who shares the school and nursery drop-offs and pick-ups, and, when required, can get his children dressed, or cook them dinner, read to them and supervise homework, or escort them to a party or a swimming session. Very occasionally he might take his children out alone for the day or even overnight some-where. But it falls short of denoting the truly involved, daily care that brings joint responsibility: arranging parents' evening slots, booking holiday club sessions and dental appointments, requesting repeat prescriptions and keeping track of PE kit and borrowed library books, not to mention chatting to children about their day, hearing about their triumphs and concerns, tending their scratched knees, cutting their nails and simply hanging out in the same room, aware of each other's company while getting on with separate activities. This would truly be the equal parenting that opens up the emotional lives of men.

So why are many fathers failing to reach this higher level of involvement, despite their professed wishes? In her fascinating and meticulous books on early motherhood and fatherhood, the sociologist Professor Tina Miller shows that the best intentions of new parents – their commitment to sharing care equally – soon give way in most cases to a split between a female primary carer and male primary earner within the household. One year on from the birth of their children men talked of having to 'fit fathering in' around their paid work.[39]

'Parental Leave Dad!'

The reasons for this distinction between fathers' and mothers' roles in the UK are numerous and interlinked. They range across the social, cultural and structural context within which fathers and mothers are bringing up their children, as well as the character and preferences of individual parents themselves. In part it is because fathers are not encouraged in their caring and nurturing role by the institutions and services that they come into contact with, from the moment they become expectant parents. Unlike mothers, they are not entitled to paid time off from work for scans and antenatal appointments. Of course, unlike the mother, they are not carrying the fetus, so their own physical health is not a primary issue but, at this time when men are often excited about what is to come, curious to know more and ready to be engaged as fathers, their interest is not encouraged. As Ruben, who co-parents his three-year-old son with his former girlfriend, tells me, 'If dads can't make it to an appointment, that's seen as okay. They say it doesn't matter, so you feel disinclined to be involved. I felt that my input wasn't needed. I didn't put myself forward or ask anything.' Even when a father is able to come along to such appointments, often he is simply ignored by the medical staff. Josh Lee is father to one daughter and set up the group Bristol Dads, in part to improve social networks for male carers in the city. He says, 'A lot of men talk about how they were ignored – if not by the midwife, then by the health visitor or someone else. Even minimum eye contact would help: that would be grand. It says you are here and your role is important because fathers are important.' Ruben, who in his work advises services on how better to engage men, comments, 'These services are completely unaware of how to go about including dads. They don't think about dads by default. The biggest mistake they make is unintentionally to ignore dads.'

The Royal College of Midwives acknowledges that there is a problem with the attitude of midwives and other medical staff towards fathers. It recently produced a document on engaging fathers, acknowledging that the 'twin perceptions of being both uninformed and unwelcomed/excluded are recurring themes in studies relating to expectant fathers' relationship with maternity services'.[40] The document sets out guidance for maternity services on how to include fathers but the press release accompanying it declared, 'Guidance urges fathers-to-be to get involved', as if it is fathers' reluctance to do so that is the issue, rather than the attitude of medical staff towards them – a neat bit of victim-blaming.[41] John Adams, a 'dad blogger' and primary carer for his two daughters, recalls his experience when his wife was expecting their second daughter: 'At every scan I attended, without fail, the sonographer didn't introduce themselves to me, didn't say hello, didn't offer me a chair. The problem of exclusion starts before the child arrives.' David Lammy, who has developed fatherhood policy for the Labour Party during his time in Westminster, is adamant that this culture must change: 'We have to examine our public services and challenge the fact that we've got midwives and hospital staff who ignore dads.' Ruben, charitably, describes the way that staff do this as 'unintentional'. But I wonder if he is too generous. There appears to be a systemic and institutional hostility to fathers. While acknowledging that 'men need to be more outspoken about being engaged,' Josh Lee also says, 'Midwives feel protective of their mothers but it breeds an "us and them" attitude. The last thing you want fathers to feel is that they are getting in the way. They are about to start on the most important job of their lives.'

The exclusion of fathers manifests itself in stark, physical terms once the baby is born. The vast majority of mothers (eleven out of twelve) who give birth in the UK do so in a standard hospital maternity ward, rather than in a birthing centre or at home.[42] In such cases fathers are usually unable to stay overnight on the ward with their partners. Hugh's daughter is nine weeks old when I meet him. 'The dads all share their horror stories of treatment in the hospital,' he says. 'For me it was shit. The midwives on the wards are not in favour of dads at all. My partner had a complicated birth and it was the worst time of our lives but I didn't feel welcome or supported. After the birth I had to leave her every evening even though our baby was in intensive care. It was like, you have a penis, so you shouldn't be here. One evening I was still there after visiting time had ended and when the midwife found me she chucked me out saying, "We don't want strange men wandering the corridors." Men are treated with suspicion. It's a shoot first, ask questions later culture.'

In flagship birthing centres in hospitals around the country fathers do stay overnight, proving safety concerns can be overcome. Establishing these centres is costly but farsighted hospitals such as the Royal United Hospital in Bath have come up with economical solutions: allowing partners to stay overnight on standard maternity wards, providing them with a reclining chair and requesting that they go home to shower. This rough-and-ready solution has been greatly welcomed by fathers and mothers.[43] If more fathers were able to share the care of their children from the off in this way, it would set appropriately high expectations for their role in the child's life to come. It would also take some of the pressure off mothers in those first hours and days, allow babies to bond with both parents and provide an extra pair of hands so that midwives and other staff need not attend to all the mother's needs. As it is, the 'women-centred care' trumpeted by the NHS can be so hostile to men that it has the perverse effect of making life harder for mothers who are left to cope on their own. The exclusion of fathers during pregnancy and after birth takes its toll. A qualitative study of first-time fathers carried out at Oxford University found that of the fifteen men involved, five showed signs of mild to moderate depression a fortnight after the birth and one displayed symptoms of moderately severe depression at six months. This coincided with occasions where the men reported the lowest levels of support from health workers.[44]

Once home from hospital the separation of the father from his child and partner continues. Men are entitled to a miserly two weeks' paid paternity leave in the UK, paid at the statutory rate of £139.58 per week, or 90 per cent of pay, whichever is lower (though individual employers may pay more). Half of all fathers do not take the full fortnight of formal leave[45] and this increases to three-quarters among those in low-paid jobs.[46] Mothers are entitled to up to fifty-two weeks' maternity leave, one of the longest maternity leave periods in the world. The first thirty-nine weeks are paid (at 90 per cent of pay for the first six weeks and £139.50 per week or 90 per cent of pay – whichever is lower – thereafter; and again employers may top this up). As deputy prime minister, in 2014 Nick Clegg claimed he was kick-starting 'a revolution'[47] in family life with the introduction of shared parental leave in England and Wales (Northern Ireland and Scotland also followed suit). The new regulations mean couples can now convert maternity leave into shared parental leave after the first two weeks and divide the care of infants between them from then on as they wish, thus disrupting the main carer mother and main earner father model. Both same-sex couples and those who adopt also benefit from the changes. This will 'transform outdated attitudes and systems in Britain', asserted the deputy PM.[48] However, in reality, two out of five fathers are not eligible for this new shared parental leave (in the main, because their partner is not entitled to maternity leave and pay),[49] and the effect among those who are eligible is underwhelming. Behind the bold public statements, the official paperwork on the policy put together at the planning stage reveals that the government itself estimated just 2 to 8 per cent of eligible fathers would take up any of the shared leave period, and the majority of those who might would take just one or two weeks and leave the rest for the mother.[50] Six months on from the introduction of the new policy, a poll of seventy companies found that only 2 per cent of them had seen a significant take-up of shared leave. Fear of disapproval from bosses, low levels of parental leave pay and confusion over the policy were cited as the key obstacles.[51] The policy has the potential to make a great difference for a small number of eligible fathers who opt to take significant amounts of leave. Yet, it is hardly the 'radical change' Clegg promised.[52]

As the government's analysis clearly shows, offering shared parental leave alone is not enough to reform care arrangements. What is required is ring-fenced, non-transferable paternity leave of significant length, paid at a level that enables men to afford to take it. Non-transferable paternity leave sends fathers (and their employers) a clear message that this is their leave and they are expected to take it. Paying paternity and maternity leave at a high rate of wage remuneration further encourages them to do so. Again, as the government's analysis notes, it is the lack of these elements in their own policy that means it will have only a limited effect.[53] John Adams takes an optimistic view on the reforms: 'It's a positive step in the right direction. It helps.' John is right that at least the policy acknowledges the benefits of more equal leave entitlements. But it is frustrating that the government has introduced measures it knows will not deliver this for the vast majority.

The Nordic countries tried just this approach from the 1970s onwards, and it didn't increase the amount of time that new fathers took off with their children.[54] So they changed tack. Today in Norway, nine weeks of leave are reserved for mothers and six weeks are reserved for fathers – on a non-transferable 'use it or lose it' basis – with the remaining thirty-nine weeks divided as the couple chooses.[55] Leave is paid at 80 per cent of earnings (or 100 per cent if parents take just forty-four weeks). In Sweden, parents have a generous 480 days' leave. Until recently two months of this were reserved for the mother and two for the father. Leave is paid at 80 per cent of salary for 390 days, and at a flat rate thereafter.[56] In January 2016 the government increased these two ring-fenced periods to three months each.[57] In Iceland, mothers have three months of leave, fathers three months and then there are a further three months that they can divide as they please, all paid at 80 per cent of salary. The results of these policies are instructive. In all three countries 90 per cent or more of fathers take up their quota.[58] It should be noted that male take-up rates of the shared element of leave are much lower, even in these countries with their strong egalitarian ethos and high leave remuneration rates, which serves to underline the importance of reserving and labelling significant periods of leave specifically for fathers. Fathers need to be explicitly invited *and* expected to care for their children. Family policy, as the Nordics have shown, can change parenting norms.[59]

Getting these policies right is not just crucial for influencing the behaviour of individual men but also for changing wider cultural notions of masculinity and fatherhood. In the 1970s, when just a handful of Swedish dads were taking up parental leave, they were mockingly referred to as 'Velvet Dads'. Various tactics were employed by the government to increase take-up rates, including a renowned 1978 advertising campaign featuring Swedish weightlifter Lennart Dahlgren (sporting very seventies big ginger hair) cradling a baby in his arms. 'Barnledig Pappa!' announced the advert ('Parental Leave Dad!'). The message was not a subtle one but it was clear: you can be a 'real man' and look after children. Thirty years later and Swedish fathers are more comfortable being primary carers. Nathan Hegedus, an American who lived in Sweden for eight years, including a stint of parental leave, says, 'The guys on parental leave, it's not like they are super sensitive. You've just got a lot of dudes hanging out and there are still all these male codes. And yet they are taking really good care of their twelve month old, *really* good care, they are great with them. The men are still men but they are able to take care of children too. And that's the new nurturing sensibility.'

The Swedish politician Birgitta Ohlsson points to another upside for fathers. 'Machos with dinosaur values don't make the top-10 lists of attractive men in women's magazines any more ... Now men can have it all — a successful career and being a responsible daddy ... It's a new kind of manly. It's more wholesome.'[60] Of course it is not a smooth transition from Scandi elk-hunter to toddler-soother; the work of the Norwegian writer Karl Ove Knausgaard is proof of that. His lauded books chart his attempts to reconcile work and domestic life while retaining a sense of self – territory very familiar to most women. Similarly the witty and unsettling film *Force Majeure* lifts the lid on Swedish manhood, interrogating the fall-out after alpha male Tomas flees, deserting his wife and children, during a ski holiday avalanche. Here are cultural signs that the Scandinavian father is still wrestling with what it means to be a man, and is not wholly reconciled to life as an equal domestic partner.

But it is not just in the Nordic states where real change is happening. Other European countries are following suit. In Germany the system is more complex than the Scandinavian model but, essentially, since 2007 fathers have been entitled to two months' ring-fenced leave at two-thirds of earnings, in addition to any of the twelve months' shared parental leave they opt to take (there is also fourteen weeks of ring-fenced maternity leave for the mother).[61] As a result the percentage of fathers taking some leave in Germany has risen from 3 per cent in 2006 to 32 per cent in 2013.[62]

Even within countries with less enlightened parental leave policies, individual companies and organisations are making a difference. So in the USA, which astonishingly has no national statutory paid maternity or paternity leave provision, Netflix announced in 2015 that it was offering female and male employees in the 'streaming side' of its business up to a year each of fully paid parental leave. IBM came in shortly afterwards with a competing maternity leave offer to entice the Silicon Valley talent pool. In the UK, Virgin Management, a (small) branch of Richard Branson's empire, now offers full pay for any shared parental leave taken by male and female staff members who have been there for four years or more. The company credited the introduction of the UK's new shared parental leave legislation as prompting this change, showing that even quite limited policy moves can have knock-on beneficial effects. Perhaps it was also no coincidence that Branson himself had recently once again been exposed to the rigours of caring for infants: 'As a father and now a granddad to three wonderful grandchildren, I know how magical the first year of a child's life is but also how much hard work it takes.'[63]

These are all welcome examples of individual employers taking the lead in offering staff benefits that improve family life, as well as strengthen employee loyalty. The next step should be for such initiatives to be extended across a range of sectors and throughout every branch of a company, so it becomes standard rather than a perk designed to attract and retain those at the top of the tree. This push need not be confined to big business. Smaller enterprises too could offer more generous paternity leave. They may baulk at the red tape and expense, but as an acquaintance and small business owner remarked to me, entrepreneurs should be able to cope with staff taking time off to care for their children: it is all part of their role as employers, and supportive organisations earn goodwill in return. Male business owners themselves would also benefit from taking leave. Hampus Jakobsson, a Swedish CEO, has written that his time on paternity leave gave him a chance to step back and ask himself fundamental questions about how he ran his business, as well as bringing him into contact with a range of parents and others who he would ordinarily not have had the opportunity to meet – in effect, free, on-the-hoof market research.[64]

Well-remunerated, ring-fenced paternity leave weaves men into the seam of family life, with all the benefits that brings. A study using longitudinal data from Australia, Denmark, the United Kingdom and United States reveals a significant association between fathers taking two weeks' leave or more and their ongoing care for their children, including changing nappies, getting up in the night, supervising bath times and reading them books.[65] Discussing the adoption leave that he took with his partner, David says, 'When we had the boys placed with us first of all we both took a load of time off work and we split everything as equally as possible. We wanted to both be properly bonded with them and for the children to know that we were both there for all aspects of their upbringing. As far as possible we try to maintain that now.' As one study among heterosexual couples in Canada and the United States found, extended leave for fathers means they make the transition to parenthood in a 'structurally comparable' way to mothers, thus promoting their role as 'active co-parent' rather than helper.[66] All this benefits parents' relationships. In Norway, the fact that fathers take longer leave has been linked to lower levels of conflict about division of household chores and more equal distribution of those chores.[67] Swedish research has found that fathers' take-up of leave correlates with lower rates of separation and divorce.[68] Even among Swedish couples who do separate, leave is linked to fathers' greater levels of contact with children after separation.[69] Taking leave has long-lasting, positive effects. In Iceland, men who take three or more months of leave to look after a baby are still more likely to be involved in the day-to-day care when their child is three years old.[70] Research among Swedish fathers in large private companies found that those who took long leave to care for infants were more involved with their care twelve years later.[71] With fathers playing a greater part at home, mothers can play a greater role in wage earning. Women with young children in Norway, Sweden and Iceland have high employment rates compared to other countries.[72] Swedish research shows that for every month of leave the father takes, the mother's earnings increase by 7 per cent.[73]

Children also grow up less constrained by gender stereotypes and reap the subsequent rewards. A major international study carried out by Harvard Business School has found that daughters of women who do paid work go on to have better careers, higher earnings and more equal relationships themselves, compared to daughters of mothers who are not in employment. The same study found that sons of mothers in paid employment go on to spend more time caring for family members than their male peers with mothers who do not do paid work. That their mother worked outside the home has no effect on sons' or daughters' self-reported happiness.[74] This research chimes with an intriguing study of adolescent Norwegian girls whose fathers were in the first cohort to take paternity leave. Most research shows that girls do more housework than boys. However, this study found that, in families where fathers took paternity leave, their daughters did less housework than girls in other families. Enabling fathers to take leave encourages them to do more at home and establishes important patterns of domestic equality among children.[75] Add to this that maternal employment is linked to lower levels of child poverty[76] – and that young children of employed mothers do better at school and have fewer behavioural problems (especially those in lower socio-economic groups)[77] – and the importance of fathers playing an active role in raising children so that mothers are able to maintain a life outside the home, becomes even more clear.

The fact that same-sex parents, who are not constrained by polarised gender norms, share family roles more equally than heterosexual couples serves to underline what can be achieved if gendered expectations are cast aside.[78] Equality between parents, from day one, results in beneficial waves across the family and down the generations. David says that he and his partner 'try to treat looking after the children as an equally shared task between us, though of course that's not always successful. When I think of my friends within mixed-sex couples, in all instances the man is out at work and the woman does more around the house, even when they do try to balance the childcare.' Diane, who has a son and daughter with her female partner, agrees their set-up is different to those of straight couples: 'Most families in the area are quite traditional, the women are either stay-at-home mums or work part time. We both work full time and split the school drop-offs and pick-ups. We agreed that we both wanted to be there for the kids but we wanted to work too. Sometimes it feels like it would be easier for one of us to be the main earner and the other the main carer but it wouldn't suit us in the long run.' Charlie Condou shares the care of his two children with their mother and his husband, Cameron. 'The three of us are all freelance, which gives us the flexibility to help make it work. Cameron and I pretty much divide everything. Neither one of us tends to do more cooking or money earning.' However, he does caution against the idea that every household headed by gay parents splits tasks 50/50: 'I know another gay couple with kids where one works long hours in an office and the other has given up work and is now doing a clothes-making course. Very 1950s!' he says.

Charlie credits his freelance career for enabling him to better fit his work around his children. Other fathers in the UK often do not have that flexibility. As we've seen, part-time working among fathers in the UK is low. Men who ask to work flexibly are more likely to have their requests turned down than mothers,[79] and many fear that asking for such working arrangements would be taken as a sign of lack of commitment by their employer.[80] In other countries, the progressive attitude to care for newborns carries through to flexible working practices. In Sweden and Germany, for example, parents have the right to work part time, not just the weak right to request flexible working that exists in the UK. The Netherlands has the highest part-time working rate for both men and women among member states in the EU and the OECD.[81] There parents are actively encouraged to practise a 1.5 model of working (that is, both parents doing the equivalent of three-quarters of a full-time job) in order to share childcare between them. As in some other countries, Dutch employees have a right to both decrease and increase their work hours, meaning that parents can respond flexibly to the changing needs of their children. There are some safeguards for employers. Small companies are exempt and the arrangement can be refused if it seriously harms business interests. Importantly, this right to vary their hours exists for both parents and non-parents, preventing barriers and resentments that might otherwise build up between these two groups of workers. In the UK, the right to request also applies to all workers and all types of flexible working, not just part-time work, which is positive, but the right itself should be made much stronger.

Rather than considering how to enable fathers to combine work and family life in such a way so they can spend more time with their children, the Westminster government sets most store by formal childcare. The political parties got into a bidding war on the issue at the 2015 general election, with the Conservatives promising a doubling of free nursery education hours to working parents in England. Affordable, high-quality childcare is undoubtedly a central plank in enabling mothers and fathers to reconcile work and home commitments, and it can also make a positive contribution to the development of children. However, the focus on formal childcare has reinforced the notion that the choice is either for mothers or for external providers to look after children, with the father figure hovering uncertainly in the background. This was vividly illustrated by the Labour Party's general election pink bus tour, designed to engage female voters 'around the kitchen table', with childcare at the top of the agenda.[82] Politicians should put more emphasis on enabling fathers and mothers to have a rewarding family life, allowing them both to spend time with their children, as well as ensuring there is high-quality care provision available when parents are at work.

Mystical motherhood

From antenatal services to baby leave and beyond, fathers would benefit from a secure place within the childcare ecology, as primary carers alongside mothers. Indeed, this should be expected of them. But the exclusion of men from the family does not just happen in public institutions or the law. Women also exclude men. At a recent event on fatherhood that I attended in Westminster, the room was filled mainly with women from the parenting and related sectors who expressed deep concern about equality between the sexes, pursued this concern in their professional lives and yet poured scorn on the efforts of fathers to care for their children. 'If my husband had been at home after I had my baby,' one woman mused, 'it would have just been another person to look after.' Smirks and sniggers of agreement travelled across the room. 'I wouldn't have wanted to give up a day of my maternity leave to my partner,' remarked another, 'I was so exhausted I needed all the time off I could get.' Perhaps her exhaustion was connected to the fact that her partner was not around to share the care of her baby – although that idea did not appear to occur to her. 'I don't think anyone's suggesting that the mother shouldn't be the primary carer, are they?' another asked rhetorically – sure in herself at the absurdity of such a notion.

Given what we know about the significant positive effect that sharing care can have on the lives of women, it is perverse that those purportedly working for women's rights can be so resistant to the involvement of fathers. Policies that enable fathers to spend more time with their children are central to delivering equality for women, in the early years of family life and beyond. For women who believe themselves to be on a par with their partner, this is the time to be vigilant. It is on having children that the power dynamics within a relationship begin to shift. Patterns of care, habits, relationships and family dynamics are established in those first months that are then very difficult to change. Mothers break their link with work for a sustained period, fathers get used to the main-earner role, and children look to their mothers first for their needs. Louise, a mother of four from Kent who gave up work as a lawyer and re-trained as a yoga teacher, reflects on what happened to her and her husband after she had their first child: 'I don't think we understood then the impact on my career. We didn't look far enough ahead and didn't know we would end up having four kids. If I had my time again I would balance it differently. My husband wouldn't say he has regrets but he has felt under pressure to earn. Kids get more expensive to provide for as they grow up and there's a limit to what I can earn in the job I'm in now.' Separate roles may make life logistically easier for parents in the early years, but this can bring long-term stresses, turning up the heat on fathers to bring in money.

Mothers do not have some mystical skill in caring for their children that is passed from one generation of women to the next, like a battered heirloom. Motherhood is learned on the job, just like fatherhood. The more you do it, the better you are at it. The act of nurturing makes a person more nurturing and research shows that this happens for men just as much as for women.[83] Even breastfeeding, that totem of content and able motherhood, is more likely to happen if the father is free to support the mother – as the breastfeeding rates in countries with long periods of paternity leave indicate.[84] In the 1970s, when the Nordic countries brought in shared parental leave, exactly the same female resistance arose to male involvement there as we now see among some in the UK. Then, as now, this included women who saw it as a move to take 'their' leave from them and failed to appreciate the greater benefits to mothers and families of a shared-leave system. Yet we now look at the Nordic record on sex equality with envy, and progressive parties within those countries want to build on their policies rather than retrench from them. It should give any feminists wary of father involvement pause for thought that, in the UK, it is the new Women's Equality Party that has the most radical and forward-thinking agenda on improving fathers' leave rights.[85]

The exclusion of fathers also operates on a personal level within relationships. Women can be quick to criticise men's efforts in the home and with their children, or to declare that only they are sufficiently capable or knowledgeable to perform certain tasks, all the while re-enforcing the notion that the mother is the expert and the father is the (often inept) sidekick. Mothers' feelings can be contradictory. They can both want and resist the full involvement of fathers. Often bewildered at having their place and status outside the home stripped from them whilst their partner remains secure – and with their mood and judgement perhaps skewed by the 360-degree exhaustion brought on by broken sleep – some new mothers jealously guard the power that they now have within the home. There is also, no doubt, a deep-seated and unacknowledged, perhaps even unconscious, assumption about appropriate roles within the family. All this pulls against the competing wish to join forces with the father as equal parents. How could there not be this internal conflict given the mother-centric culture within which we live, even among those who consider themselves progressive? Evidence of mothers' own prejudices appears in research by the Department of Business, Innovation and Skills, which found women are less likely to support the idea of shared parenting and shared parental leave than men.[86] Research shows that 'maternal gatekeeping' – a recognised, if controversial phenomenon – has the effect of entrenching divisions as mothers push fathers out of domestic life.[87]

Rather than siphoning off specific areas of responsibility, fathers and mothers could do with taking a leaf out of Charlie Condou's book. His family set-up might be relatively unusual but there is much that we can all learn from its model of sharing time with the children, money earning and other obligations and activities. 'There's a lot to be said for getting a break from looking after children. Generally we don't get to that point where the kids start to drive you nuts. And when the children are with us we really enjoy spending time with them,' he says. Variety in what we do and the roles we perform benefits fathers, mothers and children. Families and relationships are better off when mothers and fathers work together. David Lammy observes, 'I find myself, when I make the case for shared parenting, saying it's good for women. But why can't we talk about fathers as well and why it would be good for them? I am a feminist and I am not trying to roll things back. But I am also interested in the whole family and looking holistically at these issues.'

Missing men

The argument for fathers to be equal partners in bringing up children would undeniably be strengthened if more individual fathers themselves were making the case for it. As Beatrix Campbell astutely points out in her book *End of Equality* (a bracing rejoinder to the argument that women are moving inexorably towards equality with men), 'Nowhere have men reciprocated women's paid work and unpaid care by initiating mass movements for men's equal parental leave or working time that synchronises with children and women; nowhere have men en-masse shared the costs – in time and money – of childhood.'[88] Just as women have deep-seated assumptions about the role they should play, so too do men. Men are not helped by family policy, workplace culture or sometimes their own partners, but too many settle for the way they see things being done around them, rather than thinking more imaginatively about how they might fully exploit the options that are available – or even campaign for something more. And their denial is part of the problem. Louise says, 'My husband has pretty old-fashioned views, though he wouldn't want me to say that. He wanted me to stay at home and to bring up the kids. He says he would like to be with them more than he can be. But sometimes I wonder if that could happen – I don't think he would want to do it really. His career path is too important for him.' Lee, whose two sons are now in their teens and 'much less hassle now', thinks back to when they were younger: 'At that time in my life I was so ensconced in work. I had a new job and was trying to build something up from scratch. When I was at home my mind was on work. I think subconsciously I was trying to avoid facing up to the fact I had a family. I really was the man who wasn't there.'

The male career path is afforded more significance than childcare within families. Fathers enjoy more leisure time than mothers,[89] the implication being that couples think men deserve time off away from the family and from the rigours of their job in a way that mothers do not. Men's employment is viewed as more gruelling and their childcare more burdensome compared to women, for whom looking after children supposedly comes naturally. Employer expectations reinforce the male focus on career. Just as some employers dismiss women with children as on the 'mummy track', they expect fathers to play the provider role and redouble their commitment to work. As we've seen, men's applications for flexible working are looked on less favourably than those submitted by women. Men are likely to be paid more if they are fathers specifically because of biased and gendered views of them as warm, devoted family men, although the devotion of mothers appears to count against women in the workplace. American research has found that, even when other factors such as work hours and education levels are taken into account, fathers earn more money (a 'daddy bonus') in comparison to mothers and men and women without children.[90]

Even at the more enlightened end of the spectrum, the view of family roles is restrictive. At a Government Equalities Office event that I attended on 'men as change agents for gender equality', the discussion was largely focused on how male managers and other employers could support women in the workplace rather than on how those men might change their own lives and working patterns to further equality closer to home. Men are capable of more than cheerleading for equality: their personal choices and actions can deliver greater change. A senior male manager who switches to working four days a week once he has children is making more of a statement about equality, and thus having a greater impact on the local work culture (not to mention his own home life), than if he agrees to a female staff member's part-time working arrangement. But men are reluctant to take such steps, fearful of the negative effect it may have on their career and their status as a 'player' in the world of work. Such a move risks attracting derision rather than respect.[91] James, one half of the Twitter account @GenderDiary, works part time in order to look after his children during the week. He says, 'Some people do react as if they think I have a lack of ambition, whereas for a woman it would be seen as normal.' Andrew Moravcsik is a Princeton academic and the husband of Anne-Marie Slaughter, now an American think tank director and formerly an adviser to Hillary Clinton at the US State Department in Washington. Throughout their careers Moravcsik has often been the main carer to their children. In 2012 Slaughter caused a great stir when she wrote an article explaining that she had left the State Department because she felt she needed to spend more time with her children. The article was headlined, 'Why Women Still Can't Have It All'.[92] Moravcsik has written of attending a festival where his wife was being interviewed about work/family balance. During the questions and answers session a woman in the audience asked him to stand up so she could check if, 'he really still is an alpha male'.[93] It is not just other men who judge such fathers against rigid male rules.

Women too can be complicit in the mockery of men who immerse themselves in family life.

A minority of men, like James and Andrew Moravcsik, are prepared to sacrifice significant time at work in order to play a more equal role in raising their families. Joe, a father of two boys from London, is self-employed and cut down his work to three days a week when he became a father. 'I'm lucky in some ways to decide my own hours, though I also don't earn as much now,' he says. 'But I feel in control this way. No one is telling me what to do. And I think being at home pays off, rather than chasing the dollar. I want to be there while my kids are growing up. Time goes so quickly. It's "whoosh" and they are gone. Most men's focus is on work, which is the wrong way of looking at things.' Dan, who has a young daughter and son with his wife, tells me, 'We do things fifty/fifty. I earn significantly more than my wife but we both work the same hours and see it as hours not money. My parents, when I was growing up, had pink jobs and blue jobs – that's what they would call them – down to who took out the bins. But we share all the chores in the house. It feels natural to do it that way. Maybe we fuss around our children too much these days. I was completely left alone as a kid: it was the 1970s, there were four children and two working parents so there wasn't much parental intervention. But I'm definitely emotionally closer to my children than my parents were.' These men have realised that it is good for their own sense of well-being, and beneficial for their children and partners, to cultivate balance in their lives and strong emotional connections within their family.

Andrew Moravcsik writes: 'At the end of life, we know that a top regret of most men is that they did not lead the caring and connected life they wanted, but rather the career-oriented life that was expected of them. I will not have that regret.'[94] Regret was a recurring theme in my interviews with fathers of older children. These men had set out wishing to be fully present in the lives of their children, but had lost that focus along the way and were now rueful about what had happened. Joel is the father of two sons, now in their twenties. Throughout their childhood he worked full time outside the home while his wife gave up her job to bring up the children. He told me, 'I was running a successful business, doing quite long hours. I usually got home by seven o'clock in the evening, but it could be ten. The time goes so fast: those years when the kids are shaping their lives. We were doing lots of house moves at the time and doing up places. The boys would want me to do stuff with them and I'd be too busy. I'd be up to my eyes in brick dust and paint and I'd say "Sorry, boys, I can't do it." I regret that badly, not being able to be there with them, having too much to do. That's time that I could have spent with them.'

Children see all too clearly where their parents' priorities lie. Liam, Clare and Annie, the three teenagers I met in Cambridge, articulated this forcefully. Annie recalls, 'My mum and dad earned about the same amount, in fact when my dad was studying my mum earned more. But she would do most of the work in the home. At one point she was so concerned about spending time with us that she quit her job, but she hated it so much that she went back to work. Even now she feels guilty about not spending more time with us. Dad has never apologised for going to work and not being around.' Liam agrees: 'My mum switched her shifts so she could be with us during the day. Dad wouldn't have been able to do that in his job, but there was a feeling that even if it were possible, he wouldn't have done the same.' In talking of this 'feeling', Liam's comment brings to mind the words of Adrienne Rich, who in her still astounding and deeply relevant book from the seventies, *Of Woman Born*, writes, 'As for male figures, the child's experience is that they are less physical, less cherishing, more intermittent in their presence, more remote, more judgmental, more for-themselves, than the women who are around him.'[95] Children pick up on the behaviour and choices of their parents, just as Liam has done.

This insight into the dynamics between mothers and fathers remains with children even in adulthood. Fathers are remembered as out at work or fixing things in the home, rather than being with their children. 'My dad was preoccupied with work and emotionally withdrawn,' recalls Ian, now a dad himself. 'This was the Home Counties in the 1970s. Nearly all the men worked in the City and the women were housewives: that's how they would describe themselves. By the time I was entering puberty I realised that the women in my area were unhappy. They were in awful marriages with men who were absent and doing something untoward.' The feminine mystique was alive and kicking in seventies Britain.

'Daddy duty'

Wider society is strikingly conservative and gendered on the issue of family roles. There is a firm view that mothers should be the main carers. The British Social Attitudes survey shows that people favour mothers of young children working part time and fathers full time, or mothers staying at home and fathers working full time, far above any other model (such as both parents working part time or fathers staying at home while mothers work full time).[96] Resistance to fathers sharing care can come from surprising quarters. I recall a conversation with a woman in her sixties, a successful academic who has always been the main earner in her household and would describe herself as a feminist. As we were catching up on her family news, she detailed the latest impressive achievements of her high-flying son. She mused that it was an excellent thing that he had married a young woman who was happy to stay at home with their children and who was used to moving around for a man's career (her father had been in the army), rather than ending up hitched to one of the 'career-focused' girlfriends he had had at university. For this second-generation feminist, part of a cohort who fought so fiercely and achieved so much for women, all bets are off when it comes to her own son's advancement. This mirrors a wider trend. Attitudes to gender roles are more conservative among older age groups, even among a baby-boomer generation that itself lived through, and campaigned for, significant social change.[97]

This conservatism clings on elsewhere. Frustratingly, it crops up in programmes and books for children – showcasing outdated family roles for the impressionable young consumer. The flagship CBeebies drama *Topsy and Tim* is notable for its teeth-achingly 1950s representation of family life, with its stay-at-home mum and working father. One week he's fixing the roof while she sorts out the laundry, the next it's their wedding anniversary and he arrives home from a hard day in the office with a bunch of forecourt flowers for her to stick in her special vase. Here the BBC has pulled off the trick of producing a drama that is more culturally retrograde than the books created fifty years ago on which it is based. Among children's books themselves, a 2005 analysis of popular titles found that fathers were either absent or idle in many storylines. There was no father present in over half of the books. Among those in which they did feature, they appeared in about half the number of scenes as mothers and were less likely to interact with the children.[98] This view of fathers as semi-detached does then seep into public perceptions. Hugh tells me: 'You get that all the time. If I'm out with my daughter, someone will say, "Are you on daddy duty?" No, I'm just being a parent.'

Within some hyper-masculine sports cultures, it is not just the role of fathers but the act of caring itself that is belittled. In 2015, newly signed-up members of the Los Angeles Lakers basketball team were made to push around dolls in toy buggies as a hazing ritual endorsed by the coach. What could be more embarrassing then being forced to act like a girl role-playing parenthood? The Lakers' head coach, Byron

Scott, explained the apparently hilarious rules in a radio interview: 'They are in charge of bringing them to every home game, making sure they are right by their locker, that the baby is not crying or anything like that, then after the game take them home.'[99] Happily, more progressive attitudes do exist within sport. The rugby player and father-of-two Ben Foden fronted the Westminster government's promotional campaign on parental leave changes: a contemporary, English take on 'Barnledig Pappa'.

The new pioneers

High-profile fathers are helping to change the view of childcare as emasculation, which the American academic and writer Stephen S. Holden has termed 'the other glass ceiling'.[100] Its effect is to cow men and make them feel uncomfortable in their own fathering. Josh Lee tells me, 'If you come across dads at a baby clinic they look mortified. It's as if they are having their nails painted pink. One dad told me that when he sees a man pushing a pushchair it makes him feel sick. He's a really blokey guy. Men like him feel feminised.' Ian, a father of two who shares the care of his children equally with his wife, has been on the receiving end of such unenlightened attitudes, although he thinks times are changing: 'When my son was born, eight years ago, I remember being with another dad both with our children in push-chairs walking down the street. We passed an old man and he said, "Poofs!" as we went past. But now I see loads of men with their kids. It's happened in the last decade.'

I had my son around the same time as Ian and I agree with him that men with kids on the street, in playgrounds and supermarkets are a more common sight now. Change has certainly happened, even if much of it is out of standard work hours. Recently I have also noticed more gay male couples with children and official figures show that, for example, adoption by gay men is on the rise.[101] Perhaps one knock-on effect of the greater acceptance and rights of same-sex couples is an increase in those starting families, in a variety of ways, with a subsequent rise in the number of men out and about with their children during the week. Again, the wider cultural environment, as well as legislation, plays its part. Charlie Condou agreed to write a column for the *Guardian* about his family life largely in order to contribute to the positive image of gay men as fathers. 'There were no gay male parents in the public eye when I was growing up. In the past many gay men would have ruled out having kids. They would have thought it wasn't possible. Whereas now, it's part of the conversation for a gay couple. That's a big change. Being gay is irrelevant to being a parent. Parenting is parenting, whatever your sexuality,' he says. He rejects the criticism from some in the gay community that gay men who marry or have children are conforming to a hetero-normative, conservative world view. 'We are just people, who are married and have kids. I am not saying that it is for everyone. But we are not aping heterosexual couples. It is being a person.'

For those men who are actively involved in their children's day-to-day lives, the impact is profound. Fatherhood is one route to greater fulfilment, with more aspects of one's humanity acknowledged and nurtured. David Lammy, already a father to two sons, has recently adopted a daughter with his wife: 'It has brought out a side in me that I had forgotten was there. I can't stop kissing my daughter and I am not a very kissy person. West Indian families are not very tactile. It has given me an opportunity to be a different me.' Still being with the other parent is not a pre-requisite for involved fatherhood, although it probably makes it less of a challenge. This is something Ashley Walters has personal experience of and, when I met him, he was developing a drama about a father who takes in his estranged son, as well as a documentary about young, single dads. 'I want to show positive fathers, because you rarely see that in the media, but they are out there – the good single dads who want to maintain a relationship with their kids.' Reflecting on his relationship with his own children, he says, 'My oldest son when he is at home with me, he will lie with his head on my chest. You know he's in his late teens, he's nearly as tall as me, but he snuggles. He just loves his dad; he loves his family, his sisters. I am just so glad that we are that way.'

When David Lammy describes fatherhood as 'an opportunity to be a different me' he puts his finger on something fundamental. Men come to fatherhood with assumptions about family roles, often based on what they observed in their own parents when growing up. But becoming a father gives them the chance to rethink the life they want for themselves, as well as what they want for their children. Charlie Condou says, 'I am a lot more grown up and responsible now than I once was, because I have to put other people first. And I love that change in myself.' Fatherhood holds the key to greater satisfaction and happiness not only through the changes it can bring, but also through what those fathers can teach their own sons about love, emotional truth and equality. Ruben tells me, 'I am from an African background, where men are seen as the leader of the house, disciplinarian, work focused, don't do anything around the home. To show affection is not natural. A man has to play a role – to be a leader, macho, showing feelings is not welcomed. It is seen as a weakness. I want my son to be smart, strong and able to say, "This is who I am." I say to my son, "Be happy with who you are."' Phil, who has adopted a brother and sister with his wife, has also made the conscious decision to do things differently: 'My mum brought me up alone. She did an amazing job but she didn't have much money and her focus had to be on basic survival, rather than nurturing me. I am trying to provide the complete opposite to what I had with our children. I spend a lot of time with them and show them lots of affection. Being able to express and understand their own feelings will give them a chance to get more out of life. It will help give them the all-round skills they need to become balanced, responsible adults and to do the same for their own children one day.' Here Phil perfectly illustrates the virtuous cycle that involved and emotionally open fatherhood can set in train.

Even fathers who have missed the boat in the early years can do so much to become more involved in the lives of their children, from committing to leaving work early so they can spend time together a couple of days a week, to taking unpaid parental leave so they can have the summer off with their children or help them settle into secondary school. Men such as Phil hope to instil quiet self-confidence in their sons, enabling their boys to reject male posturing and to lead worthwhile lives built on respect for themselves and others. These men, through their personal actions, demonstrate that nurturing children and having a life out in the world are both the rightful jobs of mothers and fathers. In this way we might really begin to transform the lives of men and women across the generations.

6. LONE MALES

Friends, Love and Later Life

What do men want from friendship?

'Men like to think of themselves as romantic Lone Rangers,' says Hugh. 'It's a self-fulfilling prophecy. We say, "I don't need anyone because I am Clint Eastwood", and then we push people away. It deadens the senses a bit.' Hugh's description may be rather dramatic – and cinematic – but it casts a light on the stoical behaviours cultivated in boys and how these affect their later friendships. For most people, happy and secure friendships and family life are the bedrock of well-being. Yet for many men supportive, close friendships remain out of reach, as the emotional constraints laid down in boyhood continue to reverberate throughout life.

A number of the men I spoke to for this book described feeling semi-detached from their friends, perhaps because friendships had been squeezed out between the demands of work and home, or because they had lost the will to maintain weak connections. As we will see, loneliness is a feature of many men's lives, whether revealed in an underlying sense of alienation from their friends or work colleagues, or manifest more acutely in deep despair.

Professor Lisa Wade, an American sociologist who has studied male friendships, notes that men are as likely as women to say they want intimacy with friends and to define that intimacy as emotional support, disclosure and having someone to take care of them. But despite wanting the same things as women, 'they aren't getting it'. Instead, men develop 'shoulder to shoulder' friendships focused on communal activity, which may provide some camaraderie but do not involve the emotional closeness and authenticity men say is important to them.[1] Similarly, research among Australian men shows they are less likely than women to have social contact, yet regard such contact as essential.[2] Barney, a student in Manchester, explains this focus on 'shoulder to shoulder' activity, although the activities he references are hardly the hearty kind that this phrase conjures up. 'It's easier to go to a party and be intimidating and get into a fight than to go there and make friends. It's the same with rolling a joint together – it's a filler to take up the time, rather than talking.' 'All the talk men do about football and politics is a distraction,' says Hugh. 'They are incapable of having a sustained, emotionally honest conversation.'

Loneliness is distinct from social isolation. The latter is isolation from others, perhaps due to geographical location or physical impairment. Loneliness is a psychological isolation whereby even those who are surrounded by others fail to make a meaningful connection with them. For the lonely there is a painful gap between the quality of social interaction they desire and that which they achieve. Loneliness is not synonymous with being alone, although it may be a consequence of it. In 2014 research by Relate, the counselling service for couples, found that 9 per cent of people in the UK say they have no close friends, an increase on the figure of 6 per cent from the survey the organisation conducted in 2010.[3] The numbers are not huge, but the suffering from loneliness can be significant. Human beings are profoundly social creatures. We have always felt safety in numbers. A sense of discomfort and unhappiness when alone – loneliness – derives from man's earliest days on the planet. For our first ancestors loneliness was a survival impulse, an urgent, evolutionary signal to seek out company and forge alliances the better to build shelter or ward off attacks. Although we can now lead far more autonomous lives, our deep desire for company remains. Rather than looking out fellow shelter builders, it is companionship, acceptance and inclusion that we crave.

In recent years there has been more research on loneliness and social isolation, with a particular focus on links to health outcomes. Social isolation, specifically, is strongly associated with mortality – independent of factors such as a person's previous health record. Researchers believe that the socially isolated are more prone to smoking, inactivity and a poor diet because they do not have family and friends around them to monitor their behaviour and encourage them to make healthy choices – or to pick up on signs of acute health deterioration.[4]

Looming loneliness

Historically, loneliness and social isolation have been more prevalent among women than men, partly because women tend to outlive male partners. But there are signs that this is changing. The 2014 Relate research found that men in the UK are more likely than women to say they have no close friends (11 per cent compared to 7 per cent).[5] Likewise, research by the Samaritans reveals that men gain less support than women from their networks and have fewer meaningful relationships. Thus they tend to experience greater loneliness than women, even in cases where they are not socially isolated.[6]

It has been suggested that male rates of loneliness may be underreported as men often find it more difficult to admit to such feelings than women, or perhaps do not see themselves as lonely to the same extent as women, particularly if they have a partner.[7] I wonder if gendered expectations come into it too. It is possible that many women, as mothers and carers with all the social contact that implies (other mothers, shopkeepers, schools, GP surgeries), expect to feel part of a local community and so suffer if they find that their local toddlers' play session is not the vehicle for meeting like-minded women as they had hoped. In contrast men, from boyhood, have been taught that independence and emotional distance are expected of them. For many, their friendship groups have always focused on action, rather than interaction, so perhaps they do not feel disappointed about the lack of interpersonal connections to the same degree. This self-reliance has been learned, however, rather than being present from birth, so it will take an emotional toll on men, even though they may not admit to it – or even recognise it, so used are they to this way of being.

But some men do recognise their feelings of loneliness for what they are. A number of the fathers that I interviewed, for example, spoke of experiencing loneliness. Ruben told me, 'When a woman has a baby, if she has down times she has someone to turn to. Men don't have that. When my son was born and the mother was down or tired she could talk to me or to her own mother. Whereas I had no one to go to. You have to weather the storm.' Ruben has no contact with his biological parents, which may account in part for feeling he had no one to turn to. He may also have felt that he could not seek help from the mother of his son if she was feeling down herself. But he also suggests that men are simply expected to cope, 'to weather the storm', as he puts it. Hugh offers a further explanation: 'Men don't know what to say to each other. If I go to a drop-in session with my baby and other dads are there, they all zone in on their kids to avoid talking to each other. Mums will put their babies down on the play mat and sit with a coffee having a conversation. Men don't know how to interact. Trying to make a connection with each other is difficult.'

At one of the schools I visited while researching this book, I spoke to a gregarious and sharp-witted male humanities teacher. Most of our conversation was about his observations of the pupils whom he taught. We got on to the subject of friendships and I asked, in passing, whether or not he felt emotionally close to any of his friends. He stared at me blankly for a short while, before saying that he couldn't think of one conversation that he had ever had with a friend that strayed into discussion of feelings. He then recalled that a mate had recently spoken to him about difficulties in his relationship. 'But funnily enough,' he told me, 'we ended the conversation by making a joke of it.' So who would you discuss problems with? I asked him. My wife, he replied. But what if the problem related to your wife? He was stuck for an answer. I do not want to pathologise male friendships – and this teacher was keen to point out that he believes those friendships operate in a different way to those between girls or women and so should not be judged by the same measures – but, objectively, it cannot be good to have no one to talk to beyond your partner about the emotional challenges of life.

'As a bloke, I need clubs'

The risk of male loneliness and social isolation as an adult has its roots in childhood. As I explored in Chapter 2, the close friendships that boys establish at a young age weaken as they grow older. Teenage boys worry that their wish to be close to male friends will be ridiculed and they start to lose trust in each other as loyal confidants. Ben, who is in his twenties, reflects on his schooldays: 'As we got older my friendship group definitely became more distant from each other, especially in front of other people. I began to realise that other boys were treating me differently when we were in a group and that I was guilty of doing that too.'

'By the time I was eighteen,' says Aaron, a student, 'if it wasn't for alcohol we wouldn't have talked at all.' As Hugh articulated at the beginning of the chapter, boys also begin to internalise messages about self-reliance as a manly characteristic.[8] This, combined with the fear of mockery, means that many male friendships become more superficial. The actor Ashley Walters tells me, 'I don't have friends. I have one friend but he is a business associate. Other than that I keep it close – close family. I've got no friends that I would say to my wife, "I'm going to so-and-so's house to chill." I just don't have friends like that. With male friendships it's all about: What have you done? How much money have you made? What's your girlfriend like? Rather than things I will talk about with my wife. But if I let my defences down like that with men, they would automatically see me as weak, so I'd become prey.' Reflecting this view of intimacy as a perceived weakness, Hugh tells me, 'I have one good friend. We go on holiday together once a year, cycling, drinking, smoking a bit of weed. But he's not one of my usual mates. I wouldn't tell my friends down the pub about him. It's like a dirty little secret.'

As Hugh's description of time spent with his good friend demonstrates, some men do have warm friendships that they value. Andy recently left school to take up an apprenticeship. He still has a large group of friends from his schooldays: 'There's a lot of soft hearts in the group. They put a front on but you can talk to them about anything.' Lee, who is now in his late forties, considers the friendships he has developed over the years: 'As a bloke, I need clubs, to get out and escape from work and family. I've got two mates that I go to football with every other Saturday and have done for twenty-two years. That's one club. My second club is the gym and the third is my allotment. It's all ages and backgrounds there. No one knows anything about me and the conversations are about vegetables. At the gym if I talk to anyone it's about the facilities. With my football mates, we've grown older together and we talk about everything – music, getting older, stuff at home, relationships. It is the only time I feel that bonding with other blokes.'

Yet despite the closeness and fellow-feeling described here, as we have seen, men themselves identify a lack of intimacy and emotional support in their friendships with other men. Lee says he can talk to his football friends about 'everything', but the evidence suggests that he is unusual. The former Archbishop of Canterbury, Rowan Williams, has written that 'most men need to discover or rediscover friendship – not the semi-competitive jostling of colleagues, but conversation, shared leisure, exploration of the world without the edge of anxious rivalry or obsessions with power'.[9] Lisa Wade notes that the frenzied but hollow model of friendship that Rowan Williams describes appears to be a feature of heterosexual male friendships specifically.[10] Larry, a man in his forties who has had relationships with both men and women, says, 'Speaking very generally I see fewer friendships between straight men that are full, rounded, warm, loving and caring – though I see lots of blokey relationships – than I do among gay men. In some respects being gay in our society at the moment enables you to reclaim parts of yourself that other men lose. Being gay is still a bit transgressive, you are a bit of a rebel. And being a rebel allows you, or can do, sometimes, to pick and choose which bits you are going to conform to and which you leave behind.'

Family are the new friends

Beyond the retreat from close friendships in adolescence, the other point at which many men find their friendships seizing up is once they are settled with a partner. 'When men find their life partner, their friendships end,' Hugh says matter-of-factly. 'You think, I can just chill out now.' A comparison of male and female friendships carried out by the Samaritans in the UK found that, whereas women maintain close friendships throughout their lives, men's friendships tend to drop away from about the age of thirty and heterosexual men become more dependent on a female partner for emotional support.[11] Lee is typical of many of the men I spoke to in observing, 'As I've got older and got married and had kids, my best friends have become my family: my wife and the boys.' Alan, from Kent, who is married with two young children, tells me, 'Work and family dominate really. Trying to tie down the time to catch up with friends is difficult. A friend of mine from secondary school, someone I have known for thirty years, is passing through the area next week so I will see him and his family very briefly. But I don't have much time at all for friends. Just existing takes all the time.' Dan, also a dad of two, offers an interesting insight into this rationale: 'I spend less and less time with friends. I think I probably use the kids as an excuse for not being available, rather than that being the reality. I've got less energy for it. I spent thirty years talking nonsense in pubs. I don't want to do it any more.' Instead, men's social circles become ever more closely connected to their partner and children. And the building of those local networks falls mainly to women, by way of care for their children and their management of the house, which means they become the keeper of the household diary. Male socialising is frequently mediated by female partners who arrange meet-ups with the parents of their children's friends or 'couple get-togethers' with their own good friends and their partners.

At the same time as being over-reliant on their partners for company and emotional support, men are also more reluctant than women to talk about their emotions and are significantly less open to the idea of seeking out counselling and other forms of formal support when they do experience relationship problems.[12] In 2013, research by Relate found that over half of men believe there is a stigma attached to getting professional relationship help.[13] This mirrors findings among American men, particularly white, heterosexual men.[14] Many men are setting huge store by their partner relationships – in terms of the support they expect from them – yet also potentially putting these relationships at greater risk by avoiding seeking help if they hit a rocky patch.

Given that men are less likely than women to build up wider support networks, those who have never had a partner, have been through a relationship breakdown or are widowed can feel the lack of close friends particularly acutely.[15] Australian research has found that for men who are no longer in a couple, loneliness is a more serious problem than for women in the same situation. So, for example, while separated women are twice as likely as married women to experience serious loneliness, separated men are thirteen times more likely to do so, compared to married men.[16] Heterosexual men in these situations are estranged from the woman they relied on for company, and who connected them to a wider social circle. Edward, who lives in Bath, went through a divorce, followed by a drawn-out legal process to agree contact arrangements with his two children. 'You can be matey with a guy but not get close; you won't talk about personal problems. When I was getting divorced it was very difficult. I had a couple of friends, but no one wants to hear this stuff. My ex-wife had fallen out with her best friend, so I'd talk to her. We'd bitch and moan for fifteen minutes, and then have a nice meal and a couple of drinks. It was a highly stressful period.' It was eventually agreed that Edward's son would live with him, and his daughter would move between his home and that of his ex-wife. However, his relationship with his son has since soured after they fell out over his schooling, contributing to Edward's sense of loneliness. 'I had hoped we would be pals,' he says. 'I imagined us going to matches together, going fishing, later on perhaps going on holiday with his family. I can't really see how we will become close again. It is tragic what happened.'

Edward's case is an unusual one in that he was the main carer for his children before his divorce, and then afterwards lived with his son and had shared custody of his daughter. Just 8 per cent of lone parents with dependent children in the UK are men.[17] Almost 60 per cent of fathers in Britain who do not live with their dependent children are in touch with them once a week or more. Although not at dizzy Scandinavian levels, this is a fairly high percentage of frequent contact and is another sign of the shift in attitudes about fatherhood and of men's increasing desire to be involved in the lives of their children, including after separation. Yet 13 per cent of men have no contact with dependent children with whom they do not live.[18] This lack of contact could be for a number of reasons, including difficulties in agreeing contact arrangements or concerns about the safety of children. Bluntly, however, some estranged fathers will be reaping what they sowed in terms of the lack of time they spent with their children before separation. The ties that they have with their children are too fragile to sustain a connection after separating from the mother. It can be a great sadness for their children never to have had the opportunity to develop a nurturing, supportive and loving relationship with their father. And it is a great sadness for these men themselves. Hugh did not see his father for many years after his parents split up, although they had just renewed contact before he died. 'I did spend time with him at the end, even though he was a cantankerous git. By then he was just a shrivelled-up little old guy with false teeth. We got drunk and had it out. He was very selfish. He didn't think about us when we were growing up and he was busy finding himself. He could have found meaning through caring for his kids and others round him. He died the loneliest man in the world.'

Low-income loneliness

Another group of men who are disproportionately affected by loneliness and social isolation are those on low incomes. For these men, going for a coffee or down the pub, to a football match or to visit friends and family in another part of the country (or, for low-paid immigrants, elsewhere in the world), is unaffordable. On paper, these men appear unattractive life companions. Low-skilled working-class men have seen their job prospects and pay levels plummet.[19] Women may have children with these men but, ultimately, do not choose to settle down with them. The Pew Research Center in America has found that women place greater importance than men on potential spouses having steady employment.[20] The birth rate outside of marriage, to the extent that marriage can be taken as a proxy for a stable relationship, is notably higher among non-professional and non-degree-educated women.[21] The small pay gap – in women's favour – that has opened up prior to having children is making women more picky and today's low-skilled men are not making the cut. Books such as Susan Faludi's *Stiffed* and *Angry White Men* by Michael Kimmel have charted the emergence of a band of washed-up, embittered men.[22] As Kimmel observes, they are caught up in their 'aggrieved entitlement', railing against women for stealing their place in the jobs market or denying them their seat at the head of the household. The ire of these men would be better directed at the employers screwing down their wages, shipping their jobs overseas and in turn exploiting workers in the global south. These men are outraged because the scales are not tipped so steeply in the male favour as in the past and their class has lost out the most. They have not been schooled in the skills that might make them more attractive partners and workers in the exploding care and service sectors: empathy, flexibility and nurturing. As a consequence, many struggle for a place in the post-industrial world, leading resentful, lonely lives.

Lonely old men

Although loneliness affects people of all ages, it is often associated with old age. Older men have less contact with their friends than older women. Those older men who live alone are slightly more likely to say that they are lonely compared to women of their age in the same situation (76 per cent, compared to 71 per cent).[23] Just as with separation and divorce, men who are widowed can suffer a freezing over of their social lives, dependent as they were on their wives to make these arrangements. Widowers, facing life alone, usually in advanced years, are even less likely than younger men to have friends who are still alive or with whom they have maintained close relationships. The charity Independent Age, using data from the English Longitudinal Study of Ageing, estimates that there will be one and a half million men in England and Wales aged sixty-five and older living alone by 2030. This male population is growing at a faster rate than its female equivalent, largely due to a greater improvement in male life expectancy as fewer men work in heavy industry. This suggests that male rates of social isolation and loneliness may soon see sharp hikes.[24] These trends are likely to be exacerbated given the links between both old age and poverty and social exclusion.

Many old people regard their family as a buffer against loneliness and social isolation but the rate of contact between older men and their children is lower than that for women, with 23 per cent of older men having less than monthly contact with children, compared to 15 per cent for women.[25] Not all men have children, in any case: it is estimated that 20 to 25 per cent of people now in their forties in the UK will age without having children – more than ever before.[26] Although in Larry's experience, friendships between gay men tend to be closer than those between straight men, loneliness is a worry for older gay men. Perhaps this is connected to the greater stigma associated with homosexuality historically. Research by Stonewall shows that gay and bisexual men over fifty-five have a greater concern than straight men about loneliness in old age due to a combination of being less likely to have children, more likely to be estranged from other family members and almost three times more likely to be single than heterosexual men.[27] Likewise, striking qualitative research among older, involuntarily childless men (a tellingly under-studied group) by Robin

Hadley at Keele University has revealed the intense loneliness felt by some of them. Not only are children in themselves a social 'safety net' if other contacts fall away, they also bring rituals, structure and social entrees (through their school community, sports teams, choirs and drama clubs, before going off into the world and eventually perhaps producing grandchildren to start the cycle over again). Men without children feel conspicuous – fear of being taken for a paedophile was a recurrent theme among the men Robin Hadley spoke to – and they feel deserted, as friends with children drift away into their own kids-orientated social circle. As Russell, one of Robin Hadley's interviewees, commented: 'People have no conception of just how isolated someone who hasn't got kids in middle age is. That's point number one to get through in your bloody Ph.D.'[28] The men that Robin Hadley interviewed also spoke of their fears about who would care for them if their health deteriorated. Stonewall too identified the need for greater reliance on formal care services among gay and bisexual men (as well as lesbians), given their sometimes smaller informal support networks. Many were not confident that their social care and physical and mental health needs would be understood or met.

The strong man myth

When it comes to mental health needs, men are in a double bind. They are less likely than women to seek out help for mental health issues.[29] And their reluctance to seek help is matched by a reluctance to offer it on the part of mental health services. Shockingly, there is evidence that even among mental health professionals the myth that men are mentally as well as physically stronger than women and therefore in less need of support persists, as does the belief that it would be emasculating for men to encourage them to talk about their anxieties.[30]

Men often fail to ask for help because of rigid views about appropriately masculine behaviour – they suffer from 'self-stigma', stopping themselves from seeking support because of the shame they might feel in doing so.[31] Yet it is precisely the burden of acting 'like a man' that causes many mental health problems for men in the first place.[32]

As in every other aspect of their being, the way in which men manifest mental health issues is gendered, often showing up as anger, excessive drinking or drug abuse. These signs of mental distress may go unrecognised (by the men themselves as well as by others) or be regarded unsympathetically by doctors, the police or their employers due to a lack of awareness of the gendered needs and symptoms of men.[33] Men in prison are fourteen times more likely than men in general to have two or more mental health disorders.[34] The high rate and complexity of mental health issues suffered by prisoners are not simply due to their experience of being incarcerated; they may also go some way to explaining the criminal actions that land them in prison in the first place. Aggression, dangerous driving, excessive drinking and drug use can all be symptoms of depression as well as risky or illegal acts. Charities have set some store by the suggestion that friends and family might act as advocates for men who are reluctant to ask for help, but scope for this may be limited among the many men with a restricted social circle.[35] And, sadly, the lack of close friends and family may act as a barrier to seeking help in another way: reducing the motivation to get better, because there is no one there to cheer you on or show that there is light at the end of the tunnel.

Those men who do turn to mental health services often find treatment is compromised by the lack of funds. Despite promises by the former Coalition Government to deliver 'parity of esteem' between mental and physical health services, when it comes to hard cash there is none. Mental health conditions make up 23 per cent of illnesses dealt with by the NHS, yet in England 13 per cent of the annual budget is spent on diagnosing and treating mental illness.[36] In late 2015 over two hundred public figures launched the Equality for Mental Health campaign calling for greater investment in mental health services.[37] As it is, a third of those with common mental health issues receive no treatment at all. 'For most mental disorders it is still the exception not the rule to be recognised, detected and treated,' says Professor Simon Wessely, the President of the Royal College of Psychiatrists.[38]

The man killer

The problems men experience do not go away but often fester within. The Samaritans calls this a 'big-build', in which men don't deal with – or perhaps even recognise – their distress.[39] But it has to come out somehow. Tragically, one of the consequences of this process is male suicide. Rather than talk about or seek help for their problems, men take themselves off to die – and they do so in alarming numbers. Over 4,000 men kill themselves each year in the UK, accounting for more than three quarters of all suicides.[40] The number of men killing themselves annually in England and Wales is almost three times the number of all deaths due to road accidents.[41] Across the UK, suicide is the primary source of death for men aged twenty to forty-five.[42] Suicide rates are highest among men aged forty-five to fifty-nine.[43] Each one of these statistics is a horrific indictment of the way in which boys are raised and socialised into being men. It is a tragedy for the men involved, and the others whose lives it affects. And the UK is not alone. In Australia men are three times more likely to commit suicide than women and four times more likely in America, with similar ratios in European countries such as France, Germany and Spain.[44]

Women are more likely to suffer from depression than men[45] and are also more likely to have suicidal thoughts, but they are less likely to go through with it.[46] It is commonly said that the male suicide rate is higher because men use more 'successful' means when they attempt to kill themselves – hanging themselves rather than taking an overdose, for instance. It is true that there are more male suicides by hanging, strangulation and suffocation than female suicides by the same methods but given the huge disparity between the male and female suicide rates this alone cannot account for the difference.[47] When I speak to Jane Powell, the redoubtable Chief Executive of the Campaign Against Living Miserably (CALM), she is disparaging about such theories: 'Is the higher suicide rate among men because women can't tie knots or is it because women feel able to ask for help and unload? Women can talk out problems and have the cultural permission to do so. There is also the clichéd explanation that men have a higher suicide rate because they are just bigger risk takers and more impulsive. What? They've suddenly become so in the last twenty years, as the male suicide rate has gone up? I think such arguments are fatuous.'

CALM is a charity that works to prevent male suicide, using innovative methods and teaming up with sports, music and entertainment partners to reach and support men in need. Its position on the reasons for the high male suicide rate is clear from the title of one of its recent reports, 'A Crisis in Modern Masculinity: Understanding the causes of male suicide'.[48] Jane Powell tells me, 'As a society we tell boys they shouldn't talk or can't talk. I know that being told how to be "as a woman" is awful and destructive, so let's not do the same with guys.' Three out of four people who end their own lives have no contact with mental health services.[49] In a survey carried out by YouGov for CALM in 2012, three-quarters of women who had suffered from depression said they had spoken to someone about it, compared to only half of men. 'Our idea of a suicide as a loner is wrong,' says Jane. 'Often these men have lots of friends but they don't feel able to talk to them. Men feel that they can't and shouldn't talk about the things that affect them. If I was pissed off or upset or crying no one would say,

"Be a woman." But if I were male they would tell me to "grow a pair". We have to tackle the idea that a man seeking help and failing to be the rock upon whom everyone depends is shameful. That lies at the heart of the male suicide statistics.'

Leo is in his late forties and has worked for a bank in the City for the past twenty years. I arrange to meet him at his offices in Canary Wharf where I am ushered through a series of plush foyers and waiting rooms by smiling assistants, who offer coffee and mineral water at every turn. Ten years ago Leo was on the platform at Liverpool Street station, waiting for the train home, when the thought occurred to him that he might throw himself under it. The notion was fleeting but he remembers 'being in floods of tears on the platform, feeling like an idiot'. He can't recall if there was a particular trigger that day but 'there was all sorts of stuff going on at work. I wasn't doing well in my job at that point. I don't blame work for being stressful. But the experience of being a stressed and anxious male in the workplace is different from the female experience: there's this alpha male, jungle mentality among men, though you do meet women who adopt it. I was very lonely. There was no one to talk to.' I asked him if he had spoken to his wife about the pressure he was under: 'I started talking to my wife about it that night,' he tells me. 'My wife is my support network. The number of people I have an intimate conversation with are few and far between. I'm a member of a male book club, and part of a tennis four. Beyond that it's the husbands of my wife's bridge friends. I'm very friendly with one of them now. Sometimes I wish I'd kept up with my childhood friends more. But I've got a good friend from my schooldays who lives in New York. I was over there for work recently. And all week I thought to myself I must get in touch with my friend. But I didn't get round to it and by the end of the week I thought, Well it's a bit late now. So maybe I'm not that bothered about it. I think it's resignation, a sense of inevitability.' Over the past ten years Leo has been in therapy. 'My experience has not been: have a crisis, get help, move on. I'm not 100 per cent normal, get worse, get very bad, get help, seem okay, am not okay, get help, am okay, and so on. I continue with that to this day.' When I raise the issue of home life and the balance between time spent with his family and in the office he smiles: 'I think there's a point where the concept of work/life balance becomes absurd. I would find it very difficult to define myself other than by what I do in my career. So inevitably it is all consuming. It is not necessarily a bad thing. Despite the absolute madness I do love it.'

When I spoke to Jane Powell, she was just compiling the UK suicide statistics for 2014, which she gathers from the statistics agencies for the four nations. These show a slight dip in suicide among men from 4,858 suicides in 2013 to 4,623 in 2014.[50] Jane's hope is that the approach CALM takes in its work is beginning to have an effect among men. She firmly believes men will talk if they are approached and listened to in the right way: 'The demand for our helpline, which is confidential and anonymous, is bottomless. Men need to have a space where they can talk about what's happening to them without it affecting their status as men. It's easy to get guys to talk if you approach it in the right way.'

It was through researching CALM that I got in touch with James Harley, a twenty-seven-year-old Londoner, who founded REMEM-BER, a collective that puts on events and club nights, bringing people together to have fun and raise awareness of male suicide, as well as funds for CALM. James was moved to set up REMEMBER following the suicide of a friend. 'Ben was a good friend of mine, a huge character,' he tells me when we meet. 'He would be the life and soul but there was a sadness in him too. It's the people who are the most outgoing who are often the most troubled. You don't get the positive without the negative. He hanged himself just before Christmas in 2013. We were both part of the dance music scene in London. In the past four years, five people that I've known through that scene have committed suicide. It's a tight-knit community so each suicide affects a large number of people.' A year after Ben's death, James, along with some other friends, set up REMEMBER. 'We wanted to do something positive and take it away from such a dark place. REMEMBER incorporates all the things we love – urban culture, music, food – so that it appeals to the people we know and others of the same age. It's programmed around the passion. We host these great nights and then deliver a message under that. We say, "Remember the people we knew and remember there is someone to talk to."'

Just as Jane said, Ben and James' other friends who committed suicide were part of an active social group, but they couldn't open up to them. 'It is bollocks that suicidal people spend their time shut away in a room. That's a stigma in itself,' says James. 'You don't have to walk around deeply unhappy. You can go out and have a great time but still be locked into your own head. But you can't speak to anyone about it because it's not what men do. Talking isn't being a geezer, is it?' It is early days for REMEMBER but, as well as running events, James would eventually like to take its message into schools. 'Boys are culturally forced not to know who they are. We are pigeon-holed by our culture, home environment, schooling. That puts you on a path and you can't be yourself. I'd like to take what we do into schools, make it a bit cool to talk about. I'm cool and I look all right. I'm not a teacher. I'm not the Old Bill. You go in on their level and say to the boys, "It's all right if you are feeling shit. You can still be one of the lads. Mental health problems are something to be aware of but not to be ashamed about." They might laugh about it in front of their mates but they will think about it afterwards.'

The experience of boys being 'culturally forced not to know who they are' is strikingly illustrated by the experience of Rugby League player Keegan Hirst. Hirst came out as gay in 2015, shortly after splitting up from his wife and mother of his two children. His account for the *Sunday Mirror* newspaper of self-denial about his sexuality when growing up speaks volumes about the pressure to conform: 'I had girlfriends on and off, but at about fifteen I started feeling attracted to guys too. I was having conflicting feelings, but it was something I suppressed. It wasn't the done thing to admit it ... Society dictates that when you're a sixteen-year-old lad you have a girlfriend, you sleep with her and that's how it is ... You go out, go drinking, carrying on – that's what you do. I convinced myself, no way could I be gay, it was inconceivable.'[51] Struggling to come out and estrangement from family and peer groups are both risk factors for suicide attempts among young gay men.[52] Over a lifetime, gay and bisexual men are four times more likely to attempt suicide than straight men.[53] Hirst says that he did contemplate suicide but, tellingly, 'I have friends and family I love and was able to talk myself out of it.' Having told his wife (from whom he was already separated) about his sexuality and then publicly coming out as gay, Keegan says, 'I feel like I'm letting out a long breath that I've held in for a long time.'[54]

Despite the clear and significant problem of suicide among men, Jane Powell has spent much of her time at CALM fighting for the importance of gender to be recognised by others in the field. This echoes the struggle by feminist campaigners and researchers for crime to be accepted as largely man-made. Jane has had some recent success. Having historically barely acknowledged gender, the 2015 update to the Department of Health's Suicide Prevention Strategy for England notes the gap between male and female suicide rates, discusses male suicide prevention specifically and details the role of masculine stereotypes in determining male suicidal behaviour.[55] Jane says, 'It has been extraordinarily hard to get gender talked about in relation to suicide, but finally we do seem to be getting through. The Department of Health, like others, talks about "those at risk", such as prisoners, ex-service people, the LGBT community, the BME community, and those in certain professions. And in each case the majority of suicides within that group are men. Currently everyone in the mental health field is talking about the need to target *middle-aged* men. Why the fuck can't we simply talk about men? It is comic and tragic that talking about male suicide is so hard. Even men in the mental health industry are embarrassed to talk about gender, because it shows them as being potentially vulnerable and having needs.'

High unemployment rates and the squeeze on wages have played their part in the number of male suicides. The recent recession saw an increase in the male suicide rate.[56] Jane says, 'Experts tell me it's to do with economic issues, not gender nor the specific pressures men feel under to provide. So why aren't women who are in the same position taking their lives? Lots of women earn their own living, and face redundancy and job loss.' Men feel a particular obligation to bring money into a household. Just under a third believe their partner would see them as 'less of a man' if they lost their job.[57] Both men and women suffer from material disadvantage and mental health issues but only men are often brought up to believe that the breadwinner role rests on their shoulders and that showing vulnerability is shameful. There is a clear link between depression and unemployment in men.[58] Disadvantaged, middle-aged men are particularly vulnerable to suicide, and this is compounded by trends in mid-life relationship breakdown, when men lose the one confidante they might have relied on.[59] What are we doing wrong as a society to raise men whose sense of self is so dependent upon their earning power that – if they lose this foothold – the shame can, literally, kill them? Even at this point of crisis, men think that seeking help will only add to their shame. Talk? They would rather die.

At a conference I went to, which included a session on male suicide, many of the participants were anxious to point out that men were not the same as women, did not communicate in the same way and that they could not be expected to open up to each other or to those offering formal support in the manner that women may feel able to do. It is true that men have to be treated in a way that is likely to enable them to unburden themselves, exactly as CALM is doing.

But it is wrongheaded to argue that men are incapable of communicating in an open and emotionally honest manner. Many men may have learned to interact with each other in only a limited way, but they have the capacity for so much more. The way they communicate now has to change. The suicide rate is proof of that.

It is not just embarrassed men who resist what Jane is trying to do: 'I get an awful lot of criticism from feminists that we are running a service for guys. It comes down to a really deep-rooted assumption that men are in control and women aren't. Why should you look after the powerful? I am a militant feminist. It is stamped on my DNA. I was at Greenham Common. Women have fought to be who we want to be, so why wouldn't I want that for men? I don't want to practise sex discrimination. Why can't we give men and women space to define themselves free from assumptions around gender? We fought long and hard to change that for women, so why accept it for guys? At the heart of suicide is an inability just to be and to mess up and get help.' Jane is clear who the main detractors are, though: 'Women don't want to talk about men's issues because it's a man's world. And men in the mental health industry feel uncomfortable about talking about gender – I have more battles with senior male figures than anyone else.'

'It brings us all together'

As Jane indicates, some progress has been made in recent years. Beyond the Department of Health's explicit mention of male suicide, a broader range of interventions to reduce loneliness and depression among men has taken off. These include the Men's Shed initiative, which started in Australia and has since also been established in the UK. This brings together older men with an interest in making and mending and generally passing time on practical tasks. Walking Football targets the same demographic, by enabling the less agile to play sport in a group and so improve their physical and mental health. Harry is eighty-two and has been coming along to the Men's Shed in his part of London since it was established two years ago. His wife died eight years ago but he has tried to keep an active social life going ever since his retirement, volunteering for local community groups and even learning to sail. When I arrive he is playing pool with friends in the neighbouring community centre. He interrupts his game to show me round the shed. It is a big space with tool-boxes and wood stacked on shelves, photos of day trips on the walls, a computer on a side table and a kettle. Workbenches are a new addition. 'We got those cheap from Lidl,' Harry tells me. 'People need activities. Coming here allows me to get together with my friends and make something. Even if it's not perfect you are talking and getting along with each other.' As Carney's Community does with boxing, the Men's Shed harnesses stereotypically masculine interests to draw men in to a supportive, nurturing environment. 'I'm planning to make some birds' houses next,' says Harry. 'People say they get bored when they retire. How can they be bored? There is so much to do. I wasn't well when I was a young boy and I wasn't meant to live past sixteen, so I live life to the full.'

Men such as Harry are taking charge of their own emotional well-being, and being proactive in avoiding or overcoming loneliness. Josh, a university student in the north-east of England, has had a close group of friends since primary school. He was born with cerebral palsy, which was diagnosed when he was eighteen months old. 'I don't think about my disability. I just get on with my life. Some young people with the condition really struggle with loneliness, especially if they are in hospital a lot having operations. They can feel like an outcast. It's important for me to keep up a good social life while I have my health. If it gets worse I will have my close friends.' As well as studying and working for a local radio station, Josh volunteers as an ambassador for the organisation CP Teens UK, supporting other young people with the condition. Getting involved in the world around them – and on their doorstep – not only benefits men themselves but adds to the life of the community. Referring to the centre where he plays pool, Harry tells me, 'This place brings everyone in. It's all ages and races. Muslim women bring their kids here. You see dads with their children as well. School parties. It brings us all together.'

Beyond the positive and open outlook on life articulated by Harry, playing an active part in a neighbourhood can reap other rewards. Given the link between loneliness and poor physical health, some men who make a determined effort to forge connections not only stand to improve their mental well-being but perhaps their physical health too. Men's life expectancy is four years shorter than women's on average.[60] Men visit the doctor less frequently than women, are more likely to be overweight and to die from one of the major diseases that affect both sexes.[61] Good friends keep an eye on us, give us a prod to go to the doctor if we are not feeling well, and encourage us in our attempts to lead a more active life.

It is encouraging that Michael Kimmel, talking anecdotally, says he sees more mixed-sex friendships than he used to among the students he teaches.[62] This accords with many of my conversations with teenagers and their parents, although younger children tend to gravitate towards playmates of the same sex, especially within school. The encouragement of mixed-sex friendships from early childhood and beyond is an important way of breaking down the male rules that perpetuate and intensify in single-sex groups.

Even later in life, there are opportunities to change. Men need to see the rigid, destructive confines of masculinity for what they are, to take the decision to move beyond them and to reach out to others. Phil, a father of two, tells me, 'I used to be a very emotionally devoid individual. There wasn't much affection in the household when I was growing up. I didn't want to be emotionally close to people earlier in life because I didn't know any different. My wife made me realise I couldn't carry on that way. I'm trying to improve all the time, non-stop, especially now we have kids.' But rather than men facing this hurdle in the first place, it would be far better if they never lost the empathy and ability to make connections that they are born with. For this to happen, we need to make fundamental, systematic changes to the way that we treat boys and men.

CONCLUSION
Save the Male

In the months that I have been researching and writing this book, the films *Boyhood* and *45 Years* have both been released to critical acclaim. In a way, they act as bookends to the male life. *Boyhood* captures the early wonder and openness of male youth, an attitude that becomes bruised with wariness by the film's close as Mason, its protagonist, enters the adult world. He has witnessed drunkenness and violence, estrangement and loss, but also the joys of love and friendship, and a deepening of the bonds that tie him to his parents as their relationships grow and mature. In *45 Years*, the wilds of Texas are swapped for the flat lands of East Anglia, the backdrop to the long marriage between Geoff and Kate. Geoff struggles to express the depth of his love for, and dependence on, Kate. Speculating on whether he might break down and cry at his imminent forty-fifth wedding anniversary party, Kate's friend Lena says to her, 'It's always them that break first … We hold it together because we already know how important these things are.' Watching the film in the cinema, this line prompted amused grunts of recognition from the audience. Men's lack of emotional foresight is an accepted fact of life.

This scene and the reaction to it is an everyday and fleeting moment. Yet it captures a deeper truth. Many men and boys are regulated by a rigid set of rules that inform everything from the emotions they express to the interests they take up and the way they interact with each other and the opposite sex. This happens to varying degrees from one man to the next but every man is aware of the rules and of how they measure up to them, whether they actively embrace or steadfastly reject them. We need to free boys and men from these rules, so they can be happier and more fulfilled individuals. This will also benefit the girls and women in their lives, creating more harmonious and supportive relationships. Much of the debate about sex stereotyping and social pressure to conform in recent decades has, understandably, focused on girls and women. Now the stresses on boys and men need to be challenged in the same critical and compassionate way.

So how do we change life for the boys we know and also push for wider, social transformation? Throughout this book I have highlighted the inspirational work of people and organisations that are determinedly doing just this, from those making a profound difference in the lives of individual boys and men to those campaigning for social change. The work and advocacy from organisations such as CALM, the Domestic Violence Intervention Project, Carney's Community, the Young Dads Collective, the Fatherhood Institute, Let Toys Be Toys, Big Talk and Great Men, and from individual teachers and school leaders such as Stephen Drew and the staff at Gosforth Academy, is improving male life chances and sparking a wider debate about what society expects from boys and men. These organisations are continuing to gather momentum and to develop their activities. While still putting pressure on retailers and manufacturers, Let Toys Be Toys is now engaged in a debate with the television industry on stereotyping in children's programmes. It has also produced lesson plans on toys and gender stereotyping which it takes into classrooms. The Fatherhood Institute makes an ongoing and compelling case for policies to support men as fathers, while on a day-to-day basis doing valuable, practical work such as kick-starting a programme to encourage fathers to read to their children. The Great Men project has received funding to run longer, more intensive programmes in schools, working with boys from early secondary school over a number of years and developing a culture of peer mentoring. The urgent issue of male suicide is receiving much greater political and media attention, in large part because of the efforts of CALM and its supporters.

Other inspiring initiatives and organisations abound. The Eaton Foundation, founded by Alex Eaton, whose father had committed suicide, set up the first centre specialising in male mental health in the UK in 2015. Inclusive Minds campaigns and works with those in the book industry to improve diversity in children's books. There is a receptive audience for children's books, toys, apps and clothes that do not pander to stereotypes, with businesses springing up and winning plaudits. At the time of writing, Personal, Social, Health and Economic education (including sex and relationships education) remains non-statutory. But the calls for change are getting louder, with support from parents, teachers, politicians of all parties, children's charities and national newspapers.

It is clear that systemic, institutional change is needed. Within the classroom, given the strong evidence that teachers treat boys and girls differently – and often treat boys more harshly – it is vital that staff are taught to understand their unconscious bias. Behaviour management gets minimal attention during teacher training. Yet some teachers would say this is one of the most challenging parts of their job. There is a clear need for a greater emphasis on this area in training courses – including breaking down some of the myths about boys' behaviour and recognising the contribution teachers themselves can make to behaviour problems. But individual teachers can only do so much – a whole school approach is needed in order to halt stereotyping for both girls and boys.

Schools also have a vital role to play in enhancing male well-being. For boys from violent backgrounds or those with mental health issues, early intervention would save them and others from much trouble and heartache. Child and adolescent mental health services in England have suffered significant cuts since 2010, with early intervention programmes such as those in schools hardest hit.[1] This is a terrible place for the axe to fall, storing up grave problems for the future. In 2015, following sustained criticism, the government at Westminster pledged to boost mental health spending for young people, but concern remains about the damage already done, the waiting times for assessment and the high bar set for access to treatment.[2] A government with an eye to the future, and a sense of humanity, would ensure readily available, good quality mental health treatment for the young.

As I found in my research, the link between both mental health issues and exclusion at school and later criminality is disturbingly strong. For young people to be locked up is a sign of wider social failure. Among young offenders, a greater focus on therapy and rehabilitation is needed to avoid them becoming career criminals. This would not only benefit the young people involved, their families and those that might otherwise suffer because of their crime, but it would also benefit the taxpayer. In the United States, the Washington State Institute of Public Policy carries out ongoing evaluation of the state's 'functional family therapy program', which has been running since the late 1990s, with the aim of reducing youth re-offending. During the programme a therapist works intensively with a young offender and their family over a period of three months. Taking into account the fees for therapy, the Institute calculates that the money saved in reducing public costs associated with long-term criminality, and gained in tax paid by a person who is no longer offending and in work, is $30,500 per young person.[3] In the UK, funding therapy to clear the waiting list in young offender institutions and to pay for extra staff in order to enable offenders to attend their appointments would be money well spent.

Individuals can also work with institutions to improve the experience of growing up for boys. Indeed, individuals and institutions working in tandem are likely to produce more rapid and better results. Much of the work I have highlighted in this book comes from passionate individuals who want to break down the stereotypes that hamper children or intervene to improve the lives of boys and men. We can all join in that effort. This might be as ad hoc as challenging the ways that nurseries and schools often unthinkingly differentiate between girls and boys (separate rows when lining up in the playground or separate teams for classroom tasks). It might require more commitment, such as becoming a school or nursery governor, regularly volunteering for a youth group or a befriending service for the lonely. It may even require courage – becoming a prison visitor or training to work on a mental health phone line.

However we contribute, we can all help to make change. It is noticeable that much of the push-back against gender stereotypes comes from women. Men, too, should join this drive for change. This would not only broaden the support base but would also make clear to onlookers that stereotyping negatively affects boys and men as well as girls and women. And given that, the way things are, men are more likely than women to be running the businesses, media companies and other organisations that perpetuate stereotypes they might transform the culture from within as a result.

Men in power are in a good position to make an impact on the lives of boys and men. At its most basic this should entail modelling respectful interactions with others, demonstrating that jostling, bullying and prejudice will not be tolerated. More specifically, it might mean, as a manager and father, taking all the leave to which you are entitled after the birth of a baby, or switching to flexible working, to show colleagues that it is permitted and can be done. Recent parental leave reforms have prompted a renewed debate about enabling fathers to spend more time with their children: both male and female managers could proactively initiate conversations with fathers-to-be about considering changes to their working hours, rather than waiting for the odd determined man to broach the subject himself. Progressive economists in the UK argue for shorter working hours to share work out among more people – to both reduce unemployment and tackle the stress caused by the long-hours culture. This would also free up time for activities and friendships that often currently get squeezed out, enabling men to build up the interests and emotional support that are important to a good life. The New Economics Foundation, one of the proponents of this idea, has established a database of companies internationally that have introduced a shorter working week, from the USA to Sweden. These companies report greater motivation and energy among their staff and even a boost to profits.[4] Even those men at the top who are not inclined to cut staff working hours might encourage a better balance in the lives of all their male and female employees by allowing them to work flexibly.

These would all be hugely valuable interventions. Yet, although it can be done, changing the behaviour of adults is tough. It would be much easier, and rewarding, to get off on the right foot with boys. We need to take a broader and more fundamental approach to nurturing the boys among us now and in the generations to come. As adults interacting with children in all sorts of settings, we have a duty to treat boys with compassion and to accept them for who they are. Parents, most obviously, have the primary role here. From the books we read to our children, the language that we use, the pastimes we encourage and the clothes we dress them in we make a formative impression on children. Each of these should be done with a view to keeping their options and minds open. Above all, we need to be thoughtful in our interactions with our sons, trying to ensure – as much as it is ever possible – that we treat them gently and empathically. They deserve to live their early years free from outside pressures and judgement. Both come into their lives from beyond the family soon enough. Our time is best spent ensuring they are comfortable in themselves and have the confidence to negotiate the social dynamics of the outside world. We should talk openly with boys about the expectations that society will place upon them, so they are prepared, know we are on their side and can engage with these expectations thoughtfully and critically. Parents are sometimes quite mindful to treat their sons kindly and to give them emotional freedom in the very early years, but this falls away as the outside world impinges. Home should be a refuge rather than a try-out for the rigours beyond. Instead of encouraging our sons unquestioningly to fit in, we should fill them with confidence to be themselves and equip them to take a level-headed approach to the external pressures they will encounter. As Judy Chu – who has studied the group behaviour of boys – says, even if sometimes their behaviour digresses from their true beliefs, it is important that boys know at heart who they really are and strive to realise their true selves.

All this takes time and commitment. While writing this book I have realised the ways in which I treat my son and daughter differently (even though I have tried to avoid it) and how I am complicit in narratives that say they are different. Sometimes this is unconscious – it is only on reading the research that I have understood what I am doing. Sometimes it is because I don't want to make a fuss by launching into a discussion of nature vs. nurture with another parent when they make a brief, off-the-cuff remark about 'boys being boys'. At other times putting up a fight against my children's desire to conform with gendered peer behaviour seems too much trouble when there are ten other things to do and only half an hour to do it all in. But I have come to see that in the long run the rewards in keeping their minds questioning and receptive to a range of ways of being would be worth it. Writing this book has given me the resolve to redouble my efforts, encouraged by the example of those parents who have shown it can be done.

Fathers have a particularly crucial role to play in teaching their children – both their sons and their daughters – what it is to be a man. Every child is informed by the experience of being fathered, whether their father is a constant positive presence in their lives or rarely around. Involved fatherhood is good for children in the long term, having psychological, behavioural and educational benefits. It is also good for boys and girls in the here and now as they see their own fathers planning and delivering their care and grow to understand that men are able to provide nurture and love as much as women. Likewise in such families, children's first experience of women will not be as domestic doyennes but as equals in the home and the world out-side. Thus, as boys grow up and encounter girls and women at school, college and in the workplace, they are more likely to treat them as equals too. As we have seen, men who are more involved in home life tend to be more egalitarian in the treatment of their children, creating a virtuous cycle in which gender roles are broken down.

Aside from the important benefits to their children, fathers gain so much themselves from involvement in the day-to-day care of and planning for their children. Exhausting though it may sometimes feel in the moment, over the years it is a route to deeper, happier family relationships and a means of opening men up to emotions and ways of being that may have been closed to them since boyhood. As many of the fathers I spoke to have found, having children is a way of beginning again. Immersion in family life plugs parents into a series of networks, from neighbours who never before would have stopped to chat, to local shop owners, and other parents in parks and at the school gates. Some acquaintances are those of convenience but others produce a genuine and deep connection. Fathers who are actively involved in the daily lives of their children become knitted into their community and in turn show their neighbours that men can thrive in nurturing roles. Involved fatherhood has the potential to bring men the social ease and connection that many desire, itself a possible means of improving their own emotional and physical well-being. For individual fathers, making the commitment to be a loving, involved parent is perhaps the most important way they can support their sons and change themselves.

Many men and women are not parents but every adult interacts with boys at some level and can show acceptance of boys for who they are, rather than as society currently thinks they should be. Volunteers in community centres can lay on a range of activities for boys and girls to do together, from exercise classes to cooking to how to wire a plug. Coaches can encourage less able boys, as well as those who are confident sportsmen. They can show that good leadership involves treating others with dignity and respecting difference. Librarians can stock a diverse range of children's books and DVDs, depicting a variety of non-sex-stereotypical storylines and characters. Adults who run into children from time to time in the neighbourhood or at social events can come to conversations free of assumptions about a child's interests or abilities according to its sex.

In this way individuals can do so much, but people who come together to campaign for change are even more powerful. Perhaps the most successful social movement of the past one hundred years is feminism. Over that time, the feminist movement within the UK has secured votes for women, the equal pay act, reproductive rights and an increasing proportion of parliamentary seats. These gains were hard won and there is much more work to be done. But feminism has shown that women are limited by social and economic factors rather than by their bodies or emotions and that when they are free from these constraints the world opens up to them. Just as feminism continues to broaden horizons for girls and women, it can do the same for boys and men. This is the right thing to do: feminism is a humanitarian movement and it is humane to release men and boys from their bonds too. It is also the pragmatic thing to do. Women will not be free of patriarchal oppression until men stop oppressing women, and men will not stop oppressing women until they themselves are free from patriarchy. The anthropologist Margaret Mead is credited with declaring, 'Every time we liberate a woman, we liberate a man.' This is true, as is the reverse. In the past few years, I have come across some inspirational feminist women who are working to improve life for men. They know that men need feminism and feminism needs men. Men too are learning that patriarchy is harmful to both sexes. Indeed, men can both act in oppressive ways and feel oppressed themselves. Undoubtedly men will lose out in many respects in an equal world. For some men this may be too frightening to contemplate. But the wiser and braver among them recognise that a life half lived is too high a price to pay for male privilege. Adrienne Rich writes, 'If I could have one wish for my own sons, it is that they should have the courage of women.'[5] The feminist fight against male privilege is the only thing that can save men. This does not mean that feminist women will do all the work for men, rather that men must sign up to the collective effort in order to rescue themselves. Alongside the UN-backed campaign HeForShe, there should be room for SheForHe, not to mention the inelegant but preferable WeForUs.

I have had heartening conversations with a number of male feminists while writing this book, such as male volunteers and staff working at Great Men and male members of feminist societies within schools and colleges. All embrace the goals of feminism, are respectful of what the movement has achieved and thoughtful about their place within the feminist landscape. 'It's great if feminism helps men too but that's not really its core point or why it was created. It was set up for female liberation and that's personally what I care most about,' one of the members of City of London School's Feminist Society told me. It is understandable that boys and men who support feminism may feel wary of claiming it as the path to their own emancipation. Some female feminists are hostile to the idea of men joining and potentially 'taking up too much space' within the movement. But feminism is big enough to include men. Besides, we need them: not simply because they are men (although it always helps to have an inside job), but because they are 50 per cent of the population. As another boy at City of London School said, 'How can only half the world – women – be involved in something that is meant to change the whole world? If it is as revolutionary as defeating patriarchy and changing how society is structured, then the whole of society itself has to recognise its flaws.'

Rather than debating who feminism 'belongs' to, let us focus our collective energies on using feminism to change society. Men can learn much from the dynamism and achievements of feminism and they can contribute to the movement: securing greater justice for women and demonstrating by their own actions their wish to become better men. Male feminists can take the message to their more reluctant peers. Those who intervene when their college friends are descending into sexism, or root out pay inequalities at work, are valuable allies. Just before his retirement, the former Pro-Vice-Chancellor of Cambridge University, Professor Jeremy Sanders, wrote about how his feminism had informed his professional life. This included working flexibly so he and his wife could both spend the working week switching between childcare stints and time in the lab, setting up a university fund to help men and women returning to work after a career break and tackling 'unconscious bias' in the appointments process. Feminist men – often by dint of holding senior positions – are well placed to deliver social change. Thinking back to his childhood, Jeremy Sanders writes, 'I'm not sure when I first realised that I was a feminist, but I do remember that my father always ironed his own shirts … equality was something I took for granted.'[6] Decades later the effect of this egalitarian upbringing is being felt at a major academic institution, proving how important it is for fathers to teach their sons how to be good men from the beginning. Among the feminist boys and men I met, being raised by parents who advocate for equality was a common thread running through their stories. Others learned it from older siblings (usually sisters) or from relatives, family friends or people in the community. Boys absorb these messages from an early age and carry them into later life.

Every one of the boys and men I have spoken to has been thoughtful, insightful and intelligent. They have had so much to say about what it is to be a boy or man in our world. They have wanted to talk about emotions, relationships, fears and hopes: things boys and men supposedly are not interested in or do not want to discuss. Beyond policy proposals, project interventions and parenting approaches, one overarching message matters above all else: boys need love. In the broadest sense they need love at home, at school, among their family and within their friendship groups. We do not treat our boys with sufficient love: we discipline them more harshly than girls; we talk to them less; we encourage them to suppress their gentler feelings; we shrug off their exclusion from school and incarceration in young offender institutions; we assume they will commit most crime and account for most gang membership. That's what little toughies do. Boys want to be loved and they want to give love. They want to be loved for who they are and to look on others with the same acceptance. This is the 'love ethic' that bell hooks writes of so movingly in *The Will to Change*. It is not intangible hippy talk. Boys need to be treated with tenderness and compassion so that they grow up capable of doing the same. 'In patriarchal culture males are not allowed simply to be who they are ... Their value is always determined by what they do,' writes hooks. 'In an anti-patriarchal culture males do not have to prove their value and worth. They know from birth that simply being gives them value, the right to be cherished and loved.'[7]

It is in trying 'to prove their value and worth' that so much damage is done by boys and men. Social ills that we collectively deplore, such as gang activity, violence and other crime, mostly involve boys and men who have felt rejected and unloved as children and attempt validation in damaging ways. The misogynistic group mentality on campus is generated among young men who feel so insecure in their relationships with other men and women that this manifests itself in aggressive, macho displays. The same is true of workplace jostling and sexism. Patriarchy is built on gender and power hierarchies that offer a quick fix to men who feel a lack of love. Women sometimes support these hierarchies too: ridiculing men who don't conform to macho type or treating men as a class apart rather than as potential allies. Men who have experienced acceptance and love are best placed to feel secure enough in themselves to reject these hierarchies. Love has concrete, lasting effects.

When I set out to write this book, I envisaged ending with a call for a new masculinity, one that would overturn the dominant stereotypical masculinity in our culture and enable men to be their full selves. But, months later, I am through with masculinity. In the same way that I find femininity neither a relevant nor a useful guiding light in my own life, I do not see how masculinity is helpful to men. We are people, with a range of personality traits and abilities. None of the men I spoke to talked of masculinity in positive terms and many spoke of it as a negative pressure in their lives. But many men currently live according to male rules and we must engage with them on that basis, as organisations such as Carney's Community and CALM do. It is useful in the short to medium term to concentrate on aims such as reducing classroom and playground segregation among girls and boys, encouraging involved fatherhood, and tackling the stigma about male mental distress. But our ultimate aim must be for boys and girls to grow up free from assumptions about the types of people they are, to choose their interests, friendship groups and future goals as they please, to organise the roles within their relationships as they desire, and raise any children of their own to do the same. This is not about making men more like women: it is about doing away with such notions and letting people of both sexes be accepted for who they are and want to become.

Men's characters and desires are infinitely varied, just like those of women. If we enable boys and men to behave, think and feel more freely, then both sexes will enjoy the rewards. More boys and men will treat girls and women with greater respect. They will be true to themselves, have stronger friendships, be more present and loving fathers and live longer, healthier and happier lives. And they will be less tired: obeying the male rules takes up so much energy. This is what the men I spoke to want for themselves, for others and for future generations. We cannot assume that this will happen simply if we carry on as we are. Radical change requires radical action. Let us work together, men and women, to free boys. This will liberate us all.

NOTES

Introduction

1   David, D. S. and Brannon, R. (eds.) (1976) *The Forty-Nine Percent Majority: The Male Sex Role*. Reading, MA: Addison-Wesley.

2   Extract from 1973 epilogue to Betty Friedan's *The Feminine Mystique*, quoted in Kimmel, M. (2013) *Angry White Men: American Masculinity at the End of an Era*. New York: Nation Books.

3   'Gender and Education: The evidence on pupils in England', Department for Education and Skills, 2007.

4   'A profile of pupil exclusions in England', Department for Education, 2012.

5   Prison population bulletin: weekly 7 August 2015, Ministry of Justice (England and Wales).

6   2014 UK suicide statistics compiled by Campaign Against Living Miserably (CALM), based on separate data from the Office for National Statistics (England and Wales), National Records of Scotland and the Northern Ireland Statistics and Research Agency.

7   Bly, R. (2001 reissue) *Iron John: Men and Masculinity*. London: Rider.

8   'Return of the Male', Martin Amis, *London Review of Books*, December 1991. The books reviewed were: Bly, R. (1991) *Iron John: A Book about Men*, London: Element Books; Hudson, L. and Jacot, B. (1991) *The Way Men Think: Intellect, Intimacy and the Erotic Imagination*, New Haven and London: Yale University Press; *Utne Reader. Men, it's time to pull together: The Politics of Masculinity*, Minneapolis: Lens Publishing.

9   'General Election: results and reflections', Justice for Men and Boys website: https://j4mb.wordpress.com/2015/05/08/general-election-results-and-reflections/ (accessed 3 November 2015).

10   'The metrosexual is dead. Long live the "spornosexual"', Mark Simpson, *Daily Telegraph*, 10 June 2014: http://www.telegraph.co.uk/men/fashion-and-style/10881682/The-metrosexual-is-dead.-Long-live-the-spornosexual.html (accessed 3 August 2015).

11   Gap press release, 18 August 2015:http://www.gapinc.com/content/gapinc/html/media/pressrelease/2015/med_pr_GapxED.html (accessed 10 September 2015).

Chapter 1

1 Rothman, B. (1988) *The Tentative Pregnancy: Prenatal Diagnosis and the Future of Motherhood*. London: Pandora. Cited in Fine, C. (2012) *Delusions of Gender: The Real Science Behind Sex Differences*. London: Icon Books.

2 Lupton, D. (2013) *The Social Worlds of the Unborn*. Basingstoke: Palgrave Macmillan.

3 Kane, E. W. (2012) *The Gender Trap: Parents and the Pitfalls of Raising Boys and Girls*. New York: New York University Press.

4 See for example: 'Choosing Children's Sex is an Exercise in Sexism', Tereza Hendl, *The Conversation*, 23 August 2015: https://theconversation.com/choosing-childrens-sex-is-an-exercise-in-sexism-45836 (accessed 26 August 2015); 'Challenging Gender Selection', Tereza Hendl, TEDx Macquarie University: http://amara.org/en/videos/HBeswuVC4yMq/info/challenging-gender-selection-tereza-hendl-tedxmacquarieuniversity/ (accessed 23 August 2015); Mills, M. and Begall, K. (2009) 'The Impact of Gender Preferences on Third Births in Europe: A multilevel examination of men and women', University of Groningen. Also Andersson, G., Hank, K., Ronsen, M. and Vikat, A. (2006) 'Gendering Family Composition: Sex preferences for children and childbearing behaviour in the Nordic countries', *Demography*, 43 (2), 255–267.

5 'Men/Boys/Kissing', Rob Delaney, 26 December 2013: http://robdelaney.tumblr.com/post/71208713175/men-boys-kissing (accessed 21 July 2015).

6 Estimates for the percentage of people born with disorders of sex development range from 0.018 per cent to 1.7 per cent. See: Sax, L. (2002) 'How Common is Intersex? A response to Anne Fausto-Sterling', *Journal of Sex Research*, 39 (3), 174–178. Around 1 per cent is the figure that is frequently used.

7 Baron-Cohen, S. (2003) *The Essential Difference: Men, Women and the Extreme Male Brain*. London: Penguin.

8 Fine, C. (2012) *Delusions of Gender: The Real Science Behind Sex Differences*. London: Icon Books.

9 Eliot, L. (2012) *Pink Brain, Blue Brain: How Small Differences Grow into Troublesome Gaps – And What We Can Do About It*. Oxford: Oneworld Publications.

10 Connellan, J., Baron-Cohen, S., Wheelwright, S., Batki, A. and Ahluwalia, J. (2000) 'Sex Differences in Human Neonatal Social Perception', *Infant Behavior & Development* 23, 113–118.

11 Eliot, L. (2012) op. cit.; Fine, C. (2012) op. cit.

12 Connellan, J. et al. (2000) op. cit.

13 Eliot, L. (2012) op. cit.

14 Eliot, L. (2012) op. cit.; Fine, C. (2012) op. cit.

15 Escudero, P., Robbins, R. A. and Johnson, S. P. (2013) 'Sex-related Preferences for Real and Doll Faces Versus Real and Toy Objects in Young Infants and Adults', *Journal of Experimental Child Psychology*, 116, 367–379.

16 Eliot, L (2012) op. cit.

17 Ibid.

18 Fine, C. (2012) op. cit., citing Lawrence, P. A. (2006) 'Men, Women, and Ghosts in Science', *PLOS Biology*, 4(1), 13–15.

19 Jordan-Young, R. (2010) *Brainstorm: The Flaws in the Science of Sex Differences*. Cambridge, MA: Harvard University Press.

20 Rippon, G., Jordan-Young, R., Kaiser, A. and Fine, C. (2014) 'Recommendations for Sex/Gender Neuroimaging Research: Key principles and implications for research design, analysis, and interpretation', *Frontiers in Human Neuroscience*, 8, 650.

21 Ibid.

22 Joel, D. (2012) 'Genetic-gonadal-genitals sex (3G-sex) and the misconception of brain and gender, or, why 3G-males and 3G-females have intersex brain and intersex gender', *Biological Sex Differences*, 3, 27.

23 Rippon, G., Jordan-Young, R., Kaiser, A. and Fine, C. (2014) op. cit.

24 'Sex-trapolation in the Latest Brain Science', Lise Eliot, *Huffington Post*, 30 December 2013: http://www.huffingtonpost.com/lise-eliot/media-hype-and-the-scienc_b_4458458.html (accessed 2 October 2015).

25 Ingalhalikar, M., Smith, A., Parker, D., Satterthwaite, T. D., Elliott, M. A., Ruparel, K., Hakonarson, H., Gur, R. E., Gur, R. C. and Verma, R. (2013) 'Sex Differences in the Structural Connectome of the Human Brain', *Proceedings of the National Academy of Sciences of the United States of America*, 111 (2), 823–828.

26 'Brain Connectivity Study Reveals Striking Differences Between Men and Women', Penn Medicine News Release, 2 December 2013: http://www.uphs.upenn.edu/news/News_Releases/2013/12/verma/ (accessed 7 February 2015).

27 'The hard-wired difference between male and female brains could explain why men are "better at map reading"', *Independent*, 3 December 2013: http://www.independent.co.uk/life-style/the-hard-wired-difference-between-male-and-female-brains-could-explain-why-men-are-better-at-map-8978248.html (accessed 7 February 2015); 'Male and female brains wired differently scans reveal', *Guardian*, 2 December 2013: http://www.theguardian.com/science/2013/dec/02/men-women-brains-wired-differently (accessed 7 February 2015); 'Differences in how men and women think are hard-wired', *Wall Street Journal*, 9 December 2013: http://www.wsj.com/news/articles/SB10001424052702304744304579248151866594

232 (accessed 7 February 2015); 'Male, Female brains are wired very differently scans show', *Huffington Post*, 3 December 2013: http://www.huffingtonpost.com/2013/12/03/male-female-brains-wired-differently-scans_n_4374010.html (accessed 7 February 2015).

28 'Brain Connectivity Study Reveals Striking Differences Between Men and Women' op. cit.

29 Hänggi, J., Fövenyi, L., Liem, F., Meyer, M. and Jäncke, L. (2014) 'The Hypothesis of Neuronal Interconnectivity as a Function of Brain Size – A general organization principle of the human connectome', *Frontiers in Human Neuroscience*, 11 November 2014.

30 Rippon, G., Jordan-Young, R., Kaiser, A. and Fine, C. (2014) op. cit.

31 Blakemore, J. E. O., Berenbaum, S. A. and Liben, L. S. (2009) *Gender Development*. New York: Psychology Press.

32 For instance, a large-scale study of over 4,000 male and female participants aged from two to ninety found 'no sex difference was observed in overall estimates of general intellectual ability'. Camarata, S. and Woodcock, R. (2006) 'Sex Differences in Processing Speed: Developmental effects in males and females', *Intelligence*, 34 (3), 231–252.

33 Blakemore, J. E. O., et al. (2009) op. cit.

34 Biddulph, S. (2003) *Raising Boys: Why Boys are Different – and How to Help Them Become Happy and Well-balanced Men*. London: Thorsons.

35 Ball, R. and Millar, J. (2015) *The Gender Police: A Diary* (e-book).

36 See for review, Blakemore, J. E. O. et al. (2009) op. cit.

37 Mondschein, E. R., Adolph, K. E. and Tamis-LeMonda, C. S. (2000) 'Gender Bias in Mothers' Expectations about Infant Crawling', *Journal of Experimental Child Psychology*, 77, 304–16. Cited in Eliot, L. (2012) op. cit.

38 Reid, G. M. (1994) 'Maternal Sex-stereotyping of Newborns', *Psychological Reports*, 75, 1443–1450. Cited in Fausto-Sterling, A., Coll, C. G. and Lamarr, M. (2012) 'Sexing the baby: Part 1 – What do we really know about sex differentiation in the first three years of life?' *Social Science and Medicine*, 74 (11), 1684–1692.

39 Jacobs, J. E. and Eccles, J. S. (1992)' The Impact of Mothers' Gender-role Stereotypic Beliefs on Mothers' and Children's Ability Perceptions', *Journal of Personality and Social Psychology*, 63 (6), 932–944.

40 Fredricks, J. A. and Eccles, J. S. (2002) 'Children's Competence and Value Beliefs from Childhood Through Adolescence: Growth trajectories in two male-sex-typed domains', *Developmental Psychology*, 38 (4), 519–533.

41 Nash, A. and Krawczyk, R. (1994) 'Boys' and Girls' Rooms Revisited: The contents of boys' and girls' rooms in the 1990s', paper presented at the Conference on Human Development, Pittsburgh, Pennsylvania. Cited in Fine, C. (2012) op. cit.

42 See for review, Blakemore, J. E. O. et al. (2009) op. cit.

43 Fine, C. (2012) op. cit.

44 Langlois, J. H. and Downs, A. C. (1980) 'Mothers, Fathers and Peers as Socialisation Agents of Sex-Typed Play Behaviours in Young Children', *Child Development*, 51 (4), 1237–1247.

45 Zosuls, K. M., Ruble, D. N. and Tamis-LeMonda, C. S. (2014) 'Self-Socialization of Gender in African American, Dominican Immigrant, and Mexican Immigrant Toddlers', *Child Development*, 85 (6), 2202–2217.

46 'Even the Government can't force boys to play with girls' toys', *Daily Telegraph*, 14 January 2015: http://www.telegraph.co.uk/men/relationships/fatherhood/11344666/Even-the-Government-cant-force-boys-to-play-with-girls-toys.html (accessed 21 July 2015).

47 Zosuls, K. M. et al. (2014) op. cit.

48 Greever, E. A., Austrin, P. and Welhousen, K. (2000) 'William's Doll Revisited'. *Language Arts*, 77 (4), 324–330.

49 Friedman, C. K., Leaper, C. and Bigler, R. S. (2007) 'Do Mothers' Gender-Related Attitudes or Comments Predict Young Children's Gender Beliefs?' *Parenting, Science and Practice*, 7 (4), 357–366.

50 Ibid.

51 'The "Gendering" of Our Kids' Toys, and What We Can Do About It', *The Center for a New American Dream*. Elizabeth Sweet, 7 October 2011: https://www.newdream.org/blog/2011-10-gendering-of-kids-toys (accessed 27 August 2015).

52 Ibid.

53 'Gendered Horizons: Boys' and girls' perceptions of job and career choices', Chwarae Teg, August 2013.

54 Chu, J. Y. (2014) *When Boys Become Boys: Development, Relationships, and Masculinity*. New York: New York University Press; Trevarthan, C. (1998) 'The Concept and Foundations of Infant Intersubjectivity' in Braten, S. (1998) *Intersubjective Communication and Emotion in Early Ontogeny*. Cambridge: Cambridge University Press; Tronick, E. Z. (1989) 'Emotions and Emotional Communication in Infants', *American Psychologist*, 44 (2), 112–119; Weinberg, K. M, and Tronick, E. Z. (1996) 'Infant Affective Reactions to the Resumption of Maternal Interaction after the Still-Face', *Child Development*, 67 (3), 905–914.

55 See for review, Blakemore, J. E. O. et al. (2009) op. cit.

56 Doey, L., Coplan, R. J., and Kingsbury, M. (2014) 'Bashful Boys and Coy Girls: A review of gender differences in childhood shyness' *Sex Roles*, 70 (7–8), 255–266.

57 Chaplin, T. M., Cole, P. M., Zahn-Waxler, C. (2005) 'Parental Socialization of Emotion Expression: Gender differences and relations to child adjustment', *Emotion*, 5 (1), 80–8.

58 Fagot, B. I., Hagan, R., Driver Leinbach, M. and Kronsberg, S. (1985) 'Differential Reactions to Assertive and Communicative Acts of Toddler Boys and Girls', *Child Development*, 56, 1499–1505.

59 Fivush, R. (1989) 'Exploring Sex Differences in the Emotional Content of Mother-child Conversations about the Past', *Sex Roles*, 20 (11–12), 675–691.

60 Fivush, R. (1998) 'Gendered Narratives: Elaboration, structure, and emotion in parent-child reminiscing across the preschool years' in Thompson, C. P. and Herrmann, D. J. (eds.) *Autobiographical memory: Theoretical and applied perspectives*. Mahwah, NJ: Lawrence Erlbaum Associates. Cited in Blakemore, J. E. O. et al. (2009) op. cit.

61 See for review, Blakemore, J. E. O. et al. (2009) op. cit.

62 Ibid.

63 Eisenberg, N. and Lennon, R. (1983) 'Sex Differences in Empathy and Related Capacities', *Psychological Bulletin*, 94 (1), 100–131.

64 See for review, Lovas, G. (2010) 'Gender and Patterns of Language Development in Mother-toddler and Father-toddler Dyads', *First Language*, 31 (1), 83–108.

65 See for review, Blakemore, J. E. O. et al. (2009) op. cit.

66 Clearfield, M. W. and Nelson, N. M. (2006) 'Sex Differences in Mothers' Speech and Play Behavior with 6-, 9-, and 14-Month-Old Infants', *Sex Roles*, 54 (1/2), 127–137.

67 See for review, Blakemore, J. E. O. et al. (2009) op. cit.

68 Ibid.

69 Ibid.

70 Bezirganian, S. and Cohen, P. (1992) 'Sex Differences in the Interaction Between Temperament and Parenting', *Journal of American Academy of Child Adolescent Psychiatry*, 31 (5), 790–801.

71 Hsu, J. (2009) 'Marital Quality, Sex-Typed Parenting, and Girls' and Boys' Expression of Problem Behaviours' in Cowan, P. A. et al. (eds.) (2009) *The Family Context of Parenting in Children's Adaptation to Elementary School*. New Jersey: Lawrence Erlbaum Associates.

72 'Boy power! Watch these tweens reject the "be a man" stereotype', CNN.com, 19 March 2015, quoting a SheKnows Media survey of 1,200 men and women across the country.

73 McEwan, I. (1978) *The Cement Garden*. London: Jonathan Cape Ltd.

74 Kane, E. W. (2012) op. cit.

75 'Father of the Year Helps Dress-Wearing Son Feel Comfortable By Putting on a Skirt Himself', *The Gawker*, 28 August 2012:
http://gawker.com/5938676/father-of-the-year-helps-dress-wearing-son-feel-comfortable-by-putting-on-a-skirt-himself (accessed 22 July 2015).

76   Rust, J., Golombok, S., Hines, M., Johnston, K., Golding, J., ALSPAC study team (2000) 'The Role of Brothers and Sisters in the Gender Development of Preschool Children', *Journal of Experimental Child Psychology*, 77 (4), 292–303.

77   'Children and Parents: Media Use and Attitudes Report', Ofcom, November 2015.

78   Gots, M. et al. (2008) 'Gender in Children's Television: Worldwide results from a media analysis in 24 countries', *Televizion*, 21/2008/E.

79   See for review, Blakemore, J. E. O. et al. (2009) op. cit.

80   Gunter, B. and Harrison, J. (2006) 'Violence in Children's Programmes on British Television', *Children and Society*, 11 (3), 143–156.

81   'Toddlers mesmerised by surreal world of "unboxing" videos', *Daily Telegraph*, 22 September 2014: http://www.telegraph.co.uk/news/worldnews/northamerica/usa/11112511/Toddlers-mesmerised-by-surreal-world-of-unboxing-videos.html (accessed 20 July 2015).

Chapter 2

1   See for review, Rose, A. J. and Smith, R. L. (2011) 'Sex Differences in Peer Relationships' in Rubin, K. H., Bukowski, W. M. and Laursen, B. (eds.) (2011) *Handbook of Peer Interactions, Relationships, and Groups*. New York: Guildford Press.

2   Connolly, J., Craig, W., Goldberg, A. and Pepler, D. (2004) 'Mixed-Gender Groups, Dating, and Romantic Relationships in Early Adolescence', *Journal of Research on Adolescence*, 14 (2), 185–207.

3   Bigler, R. S. (1995) 'The Role of Classification Skill in Moderating Environmental Influences on Children's Gender Stereotyping: A study of the functional use of gender in the classroom', *Child Development*, 66 (4), 1072–1087.

4   Kane, E. W. (2012) op cit.

5   See for review, Blakemore, J. E. O. et al. (2009) op. cit.

6   Thorne, B. and Luria, Z. (1986) 'Sexuality and Gender in Children's Daily Worlds', *Social Problems*, 33, 176–190.

7   See for review, Blakemore, J. E. O. et al. (2009) op. cit.

8   See for review, Rose, A. J. and Smith, R. L. (2011) op. cit.

9   Leaper, C. (2014) 'Gender Similarities and Differences in Language' in Holtgraves, T. M. (2014) *The Oxford Handbook of Language and Social Psychology*. Oxford: Oxford University Press; Goodwin, M. H. (1990)

He-said-she-said: Talk as Social Organisation Among Black Children. Bloomington, IN: Indiana University Press.

10   Archer, J. (2004) 'Sex Differences in Aggression in Real-World Settings: A meta-analytic review', *Review of General Psychology*, 8 (4), 291–322.

11   Stroufe, L. A., Bennett, C., Englund, M., Urban, J. and Shulman, S. (1993) 'The Significance of Gender Boundaries in Preadolescence: Contemporary correlates and antecedents of boundary violation and maintenance', *Child Development*, 64 (2), 455–466.

12   See for review, Cook, J. L. and Cook, G. (2009) *Child Development Principles and Perspectives*. Boston, MA: Allyn and Bacon.

13   Martin, C. L. and Fabes, R. A. (2001) 'The Stability and Consequences of Young Children's S-sex Peer Interactions', *Developmental Psychology*, 37 (3), 431–446.

14   McHale, S. M., Kim, J-Y., Whiteman, S. and Crouter, A. C. (2004) 'Links Between Sex-Typed Time Use in Middle Childhood and Gender Development in Early Adolescence', *Developmental Psychology*, 40 (5), 868–881.

15   Chu, J. (2014) *When Boys Become Boys: Development, Relationships, and Masculinity*. New York: New York University Press.

16   Kimmel, M. (2009) *Guyland: The Perilous World Where Boys Become Men*. New York: Harper Perennial.

17   Chu, J. (2014) op. cit.

18   Ibid.

19   Adler, P. A. and Adler, P. (1998) *Peer Power: Preadolescent Culture and Identity*. New Jersey: Rutgers University Press; Rodkin, P. C., Farmer, T. W., Pearl, R. and Van Acker, R. (2000) 'Heterogeneity of popular boys: Antisocial and prosocial configurations'. *Developmental Psychology*, 36 (1), 14–24.

20   'Violence in the Everyday Lives of Our Boys', Smiler, A., *The Good Men Project*, 22 May 2014: http://goodmenproject.com/families/violence-everyday-lives-boys-hesaid/ (accessed 31 March 2015).

21   'Helping Boys to "Let it Go": How parents can enable boys to stay true to themselves', *Psychology Today*: https://www.psychologytoday.com/blog/when-boys-become-boys/201408/helping-boys-let-it-go (accessed 3 August 2015).

22   Tony Porter, co-founder of the American organisation A Call to Men: The National Association of Men and Women Committed to Ending Violence Against Women speaking at TEDWomen, December, 2010: http://www.ted.com/talks/tony_porter_a_call_to_men?language=en.

23   '1 in 2 young people say they are not 100% heterosexual,' YouGov, 16 August 2015: https://yougov.co.uk/news/2015/08/16/half-young-not-heterosexual/ (accessed 29 August 2015); Park, A., Bryson, C., Clery, E., Curtice, J. and Phillips, M. (2013) *British Social Attitudes 30: How and why*

Britain's attitudes and values are changing. London: National Centre for Social Research.

24 'The School Report: The experiences of gay young people in Britain's schools 2012', Stonewall and the University of Cambridge Centre for Family Research, 2012.

25 'Maybe "that's so gay" is actually OK for young people to say', Mark McCormack, Lecturer in Sociology at Durham University, *The Conversation*, 4 July 2014: http://theconversation.com/maybe-thats-so-gay-is-actually-ok-for-young-people-to-say-28687 (accessed 3 August 2015).

26 'Tackling Homophobic Language', Stonewall Education Guide, 2013.

27 Way, N. (2011) *Deep Secrets: Boys' Friendships and the Crisis of Connection.* Cambridge, MA: Harvard University Press.

28 Pascoe, C. J. (2012) *'Dude, You're a Fag': Masculinity and Sexuality in High School.* San Francisco, CA: University of California Press.

29 Harvey, Steven J. (1996) 'The Construction of Masculinity among Male Collegiate Volleyball Players', *Journal of Men's Studies*, 5 (2), 131.

30 Glen, F. and Hurrell, K. (2012) *Technical note: Measuring Gender Identity.* Manchester: Equality and Human Rights Commission: http://www.equalityhumanrights.com/sites/default/files/documents/technical_note_final.pdf (accessed 11 April 2015); 'About Transgender Children', Transkids: http://transkids.synthasite.com/about-transgendered-children.php (accessed 11 April 2015).

31 Glen, F. and Hurrell, K. (2012) op. cit.

32 'Children seeking gender identity advice sees 100% increase, says NHS', *Guardian*, 5 November 2015: http://www.theguardian.com/society/2015/nov/05/children-seeking-gender-identity-advice-sees-100-increase-nhs (accessed 12 November 2015).

33 Comparison of figures from 2014/15 and 2009/10. 'The story of two transgender children', BBC Online, 7 April 2015: http://www.bbc.co.uk/news/magazine-32037397 (accessed 12 April 2015).

34 'Gender Dysphoria, Overview', *NHS Choices.* http://www.nhs.uk/conditions/gender-dysphoria/Pages/Introduction.aspx (accessed 20 September 2015).

35 Evidence to Transgender Equality Inquiry, Women and Equalities Committee, 15 September 2015.

36 *Preventing Suicide Among Trans Young People: A toolkit for nurses,* Royal College of Nursing, 2015.

37 See for example, 'NHS Choices, Teenagers and Gender Identity': http://www.nhs.uk/Livewell/Transhealth/Pages/Transyoungpeople.aspx (accessed 11 April 2015).

38 Evidence to Transgender Equality Inquiry, Women and Equalities Committee, 15 September 2015.

39   Micali, N., Hagberg, K. W., Petersen, I. and Treasure, J. L. (2013) 'The Inci-
     dence of Eating Disorders in the UK in 2000–2009: Findings from the
     General Practice Research Database', *BMJ Open*, 3:e002646.
40   Micali, N., Ploubidis, G., De Stavola, B., Simonoff, E., & Treasure, J. (2014)
     'Frequency and Patterns of Eating Disorder Symptoms in Early Adoles-
     cence', *Journal of Adolescent Health*, 54 (5), 574–581.
41   Räisänen, U. and Hunt, K. (2014) 'The Role of Gendered Constructions of
     Eating Disorders in Delayed Help-seeking in Men: A qualitative interview
     study', *BMJ Open*, 4 (4).
42   National Centre for Eating Disorders – eating disorders in males:
     http://eating-disorders.org.uk/information/eating-disorders-in-males/
     (accessed 24 March 2015).
43   'Social media and TV Audiences', YouGov UK, 26 July 2012: https://
     yougov.co.uk/news/2012/07/26/social-media-tv-audiences/ (accessed
     29 July 2015); 'ITV to launch ITVBe', ITV press release, 12 February
     2014: http://www.itv.com/presscentre/press-releases/itv-launch-itvbe
     (accessed 30 July 2015).
44   'Paul Rudd on His Amazing *Ant-Man* Bod: I Quit Alcohol and Carbs
     for a Year', People.com, 15 July 2015: http://www.people.com/article/
     paul-rudd-ant-man-body-fitness-workout-diet (accessed 29 July 2015).
45   'Jurassic World's Chris Pratt: equality means objectifying men too',
     Guardian, 19 June 2015: http://www.theguardian.com/film/2015/jun/19/
     jurassic-worlds-chris-pratt-equality-means-objectifying-men-too
     (accessed 29 July 2015).
46   'Body-image Pressure Increasingly Affects Boys', *The Atlantic*, 10 March
     2014: http://www.theatlantic.com/health/archive/2014/03/body-image-
     pressure-increasingly-affects-boys/283897/ (accessed 24 March 2015).
47   See for example: 'GCSE results: biggest gap in 11 years between boys and
     girls A*–C pass rate', *Guardian*, 21 August 2014: http://www.theguardian.
     com/news/datablog/2014/aug/21/gcse-results-2014-biggest-gap-11-boys-
     and-girls-a-c-pass-rate (accessed 3 August 2015); 'GCSE results 2014:
     girls pulling further ahead of boys', *Daily Telegraph*, 21 August 2014:
     http://www.theguardian.com/news/datablog/2014/aug/21/gcse-results-
     2014-biggest-gap-11-boys-and-girls-a-c-pass-rate (accessed 3 August
     2014); 'Girls beat boys again in GCSE battle', *Independent*, 23 August 2012:
     http://www.independent.co.uk/news/education/education-news/girls-
     beat-boys-again-in-gcse-battle-8076438.html (accessed 3 August 2014);
     'March of the girls! GCSE days sees record results … but boys fall further
     behind as gender gap hits record level', *Daily Mail*, 25 August 2011: http://
     www.dailymail.co.uk/news/article-2029847/GCSE-results-2011-Record-
     results--boys-fall-girls.html (accessed 3 August 2015).

48 Revised GCSE and equivalent results in England, 2014 to 2015, Department for Education, 21 January 2016.

49 Brooks, V., Abbot, I. and Huddleston, P. (2012) *Preparing to Teach in Secondary Schools: A student teacher's guide to professional issues in secondary education.* Berkshire: Open University Press.

50 Revised GCSE and equivalent results in England, 2014 to 2015 op. cit.

51 Office for Standards in Education (Ofsted) (2013) 'Unseen Children: Educational access and achievement 20 years on', London: Ofsted.

52 'Is Britain Fairer? The state of equality and human rights 2015', Equality and Human Rights Commission (EHRC), 30 October 2015.

53 Department for Children, Schools and Families (DCSF) (2009) *Gender and Education – Mythbusters - Addressing Gender and Achievement: myths and realities.* Nottingham: DCSF.

54 Revised GCSE and equivalent results in England, 2014 to 2015 op. cit.

55 'Boys Reading Commission', The Report of the All Party Parliamentary Literacy Group Commission, compiled by the National Literacy Trust, 2012.

56 Ibid.

57 'The ABC of Gender Equality in Education: Aptitude, Behaviour, Confidence', Organisation for Economic Co-operation and Development (OECD), 2015.

58 Jin, W., Muriel, A. and Sibieta, L. (2010) 'Subject and Course Choices at Ages 14 and 16 Amongst Young People in England: Insights from behavioural economics', London: Institute for Fiscal Studies.

59 At Gosforth Academy, 77 per cent of boys gain 5A* to C GCSEs including English and maths, compared to 81 per cent of girls. Information supplied in email correspondence with Chris Duckett. This 4 per cent gap is less than half that of the England average (see Revised GCSE and equivalent results in England, 2014 to 2015 op. cit.).

60 See for review, Blakemore, J. E. O., et al. (2009) op. cit.

61 'A Profile of Pupil Exclusions in England', Department for Education, 2012.

62 Ibid.

63 4.46 per cent of pupils received a fixed-term exclusion in 2009/10, compared to 5.66 per cent in 2006/7. 0.08 per cent of pupils were permanently excluded in 2009/10, compared to 0.17 in 1995/6. In 2009/10, 4,460 boys received a permanent exclusion, compared to 1,270 girls. For fixed-period exclusions, these figures were 247,550 and 83,830 respectively. Boys represented 77.7 per cent of the total number of permanent exclusions and around 74.7 per cent of all fixed-period exclusions. 'A Profile of Pupil Exclusions in England' (2012) op. cit.

64   Evans, J. (2010) 'Not Present and Not Correct: Understanding and pre-venting school exclusions', London: Barnardos.

65   Excluded children are 37 per cent more likely to be unemployed than non-excluded peers; their predicted gap in earnings is £21, 175 over a lifetime; they are twice as likely to offend as other children. Brooks, M., Goodall, E. and Heady, L. (2007) *Misspent youth: The costs of truancy and exclusion*. London: New Philanthropy Capital.

66   Within the prison population for England and Wales, 63 per cent had been temporarily excluded and 42 per cent permanently excluded from school. Prison population statistics, House of Commons Library, 29 July 2013.

67   Hartley, B. L. and Sutton, R. M. (2013) 'A Stereotype Threat Account of Boys' Academic Underachievement', *Child Development*, 84, 1716–1733.

68   Fagot, B., Hagan, R., Leinbach, M. D. and Kronsberg, S. (1985) 'Differential Reactions to Assertive and Communicative Acts of Toddler Boys and Girls', *Child Development*, 56 (6), 1499–1505.

69   See for review, Blakemore, J. E. O., et al. (2009) op. cit.

70   Wilkins, D. and Kemple, M. (2011) 'Delivering Male: Effective practice in male mental health', London: Men's Health Forum and Mind.

71   'Boys Reading Commission', 2012, op. cit.

72   'The ABC of Gender Equality in Education: Aptitude, Behaviour, Confidence' (2015) op. cit.

73   See for review, 'Girls and women with autistic spectrum disorder', Autism Spectrum Australia, 2013.

74   'The ABC of Gender Equality in Education' (2015) op. cit.

75   Connell, R. W. (1996) 'Teaching the Boys: New research on masculinity, and gender strategies for schools', *Teachers College Record*, 98 (2).

76   Skelton, C., Francis, B. and Valkanova, Y. (2007) *Breaking Down the Stereotypes: Gender and achievement in schools*. Equal Opportunity Commission (EOC), Manchester.

77   Connell, R. W. (1996) op. cit.

78   Wilkins, D. and Kemple, M. (2011) op. cit.

79   'Gender and Education' (2007) op. cit.

80   Mental Health America – Conduct Disorder: http://www.mental-healthamerica.net/conditions/conduct-disorder (accessed 24 March 2015).

81   Brian Lightman quoted in: 'Boys Three Times More Likely to be Expelled Than Girls', *Huffington Post*, 21 March 2013. http://www.huffingtonpost.co.uk/2013/03/20/boys-three-times-expelled-school-girl_n_2918485.html (accessed 14 December 2015).

82   'Children with Special Educational Needs: An analysis – 2013', Department for Education, 2013.

83 'They Go The Extra Mile: Reducing Inequality in School Exclusions', Children's Commissioner, 20 March 2013: http://www.childrenscommissioner.gov.uk/info/schoolexclusions (accessed 15 March 2015).

84 Ibid.

85 See for review, Stamou, E., Edwards, A., Daniels, H. and Ferguson, L. (2014) *Young People At-Risk of Drop-out from Education: Recognising and Responding to their Needs*. Oxford: Oxford University.

86 Ibid.

87 Ofsted inspection report for Brentwood County High School, January 2014: http://www.bchs.essex.sch.uk/23/ofsted (accessed online 14 March 2015).

Chapter 3

1 McLaughlin, H., Uggen, C. and Blackstone, A. (2012) 'Sexual Harassment, Workplace authority, and the paradox of power', *American Sociological Review* 77 (4), 625–647; Welsh, S. (1999) 'Gender and Sexual Harassment', *Annual Review of Sociology* 25, 169–190; Phipps, A. and Young, I. (2015) '"Lad Culture" in Higher Education: Agency in the sexualisation debates', *Sexualities*. ISSN 1363–4607.

2 In comparison 14 per cent of teenage boys in England reported having suffered sexual violence and abuse and 12 per cent of them reported physical violence from a partner. Barter, C. (2015) Briefing Paper 2: 'Incidence, Rates and Impact of Experiencing Interpersonal Violence and Abuse in Young People's Relationships', Preston: Safeguarding Teenage Intimate Relationships (STIR). The countries surveyed were Bulgaria, Cyprus, Norway, England and Italy.

3 'Intimate Personal Violence and Partner Abuse', Office for National Statistics figures for England and Wales, February 2014. Figures for 2012/13.

4 'Changing the definition of domestic violence is just the start', *Guardian*, 20 September 2012: http://www.theguardian.com/comment-isfree/2012/sep/20/domestic-violence-young-people (accessed 30 April 2015).

5 Barter, C., McCarry, M., Berridge, D. and Evans, K. (2009) 'Partner Exploitation and Violence in Teenage Intimate Relationships'. London: NSPCC.

6 'He hit me but I really did deserve it', The Student Room, 9 December 2014: http://www.thestudentroom.co.uk/showthread.php?t=3017485 (accessed 28 April 2015).

7 Barter, C., McCarry, M., Berridge, D. and Evans, K. (2009) op. cit.

8   Burton, S., Kitzinger, J., Kelly, L. and Regan, L. (1998) *Young People's Attitudes Toward Violence*. Edinburgh: Zero Tolerance Trust; 'Gender Stereotypes Make Teenagers More Accepting of Violence', Dr Vanita Sundaram (Department of Education, University of York), *The Conversation*, 6 January 2015.

9   Barter, C. (2015) Briefing Paper 3: 'Risk and Protective (Predictive) Factors for IPVA Victimisation and Instigation', Preston: Safeguarding Teenage Intimate Relationships (STIR).

10   McCarry, M. (2010) 'Becoming a "Proper Man"': Young people's attitudes about interpersonal violence and perceptions of gender', *Gender and Education*, 22 (1).

11   Lacasse, A. and Mendelson, M. J. (2007) 'Sexual Coercion among Adolescents: Victims and Perpetrators', *Journal of Interpersonal Violence*, 22, 424–437.

12   Sundaram, V. (2014) *Preventing Youth Violence: Rethinking the Role of Gender in Schools*. Basingstoke: Palgrave Macmillan.

13   See for review, *Behind Closed Doors: The Impact of Domestic Violence on Children*. Unicef, 2006.

14   Barter, C., McCarry, M., Berridge, D. and Evans, K. (2009) op. cit.

15   See for review, Poon, B and Pittinskey, T. L. (2005)' Upward Advice Transmission in the Family: The role of gender in young adults giving advice to their parents', Faculty Research Working Paper Series, John F. Kennedy School of Government, Harvard University; Claes, M. (1998) 'Adolescents' Closeness with Parents, Siblings, and Friends in Three Countries: Canada, Belgium, and Italy', *Journal of Youth and Adolescence*, 27 (2), 165–184.

16   See for review, Blakemore, J. E. O. et al. (2009) op. cit.

17   Condry, R. and Miles, C. (2014) 'Adolescent to Parent Violence: Framing and mapping a hidden problem', *Criminology and Criminal Justice*, 14 (3), 257–275.

18   'Responding to Child to Parent Violence Project: Executive Summary', Joint report by University of Brighton, Brighton & Hove City Council, University of Valencia, National University of Ireland, Galway, National Association XXI Rhodopa Mountain Initiative and Åmåls Kommun, April 2015. Also Gallagher, E. (2008) 'Children's Violence to Parents: A critical literature review': Master's thesis written by a therapist and psychologist who works with families experiencing child-to-parent violence. Available here: Child Parent Violence Masters Thesis Gallagher 2008.pdfs (accessed 6 August 2015).

19   Gallagher, E. (2004) 'Parents Victimised by their Children', *Australian and New Zealand Journal of Family Therapy*, 25 (1), 1–12.

20   Ibid.

21 Facts and figures, Stop Porn Culture: http://stoppornculture.org/about/about-the-issue/facts-and-figures-2/ (accessed 3 May 2014).

22 Horvath, M. A. H., Alys, L., Massey, K., Pina, A., Scally, M. and Adler, J. R. (2013) '"Basically … Porn is Everywhere": A rapid evidence assessment on the effect that access and exposure to pornography has on children and young people', London: Children's Commissioner.

23 Between 4 and 66 per cent of children and young people reporting unwanted exposure. See for review, Horvath, M. A. H. et al. (2013) op. cit.

24 See for review, Horvath, M. A. H. et al. (2013) op. cit.

25 Interview for *Analysis* ('Pornography: What Do We Know?'), Radio 4, 30 June 2013.

26 Horvath, M. A. H. et al. (2013) op. cit.

27 Cumberbatch, G. (2011) 'Sexually Explicit Material and the Potential Harm to Minors: An independent review of the research evidence', London: Ofcom.

28 Provisional title: 'What Are Young People's Experiences of Consuming Sexually Explicit Material? An exploratory study'.

29 Buckingham, D. and Bragg, S. (2004) *Young People, Sex and the Media: The Facts of Life?* Basingstoke: Palgrave Macmillan, quoted in Wagg, S. and Pilcher, J. (eds.) (2014) *Thatcher's Grandchildren? Politics and Childhood in the Twenty-First Century*. Basingstoke: Palgrave Macmillan.

30 Malamuth, N. M. (1993) 'Pornography's Impact on Male Adolescents', *Adolescent Medicine: State of the Art Reviews*, 4, 563–576.

31 Interview for *Analysis*, BBC Radio 4 op. cit.

32 The figure is 11 per cent for 45 to 54 year olds, 6 per cent for 55 to 64 year olds and 3.5 per cent for 65 to 74 year olds. National Survey of Sexual Attitudes and Lifestyles, University College London, London School of Hygiene and Tropical Medicine and National Centre for Social Research, 2014; Marston, C. and Lewis, R. (2014) 'Anal Heterosex among Young People and Implications for Health Promotion: A qualitative study in the UK', *BMJ Open*, 4:e004996.

33 Marston, C. and Lewis, R. (2014) op. cit.

34 '"He's the stud and she's the slut": Young people's attitudes to pornography, sex and relationships', Zero Tolerance, 2014.

35 Kimmel, M. (2009) op. cit.

36 Student Opinion Survey, National Union of Students, November 2014.

37 Benn, M. (2014) *What Should We Tell Our Daughters? The Pleasures and Pressures of Growing Up Female*. London: Hodder.

38 'British Sex Survey 2014', *Observer*, 28 September 2014: http://www.theguardian.com/lifeandstyle/2014/sep/28/british-sex-survey-2014-nation-lost-sexual-swagger (accessed 5 August 2015).

39   Beckett, H., Brodie, I., Factor, F., Melrose, M., Pearce, J., Pitts, J., Shuker, L. and Warrington C. (2013) '"It's wrong ... but you get used to it": A qualitative study of gang-associated sexual violence towards, and exploitation of, young people in England'. London: Office of the Children's Commissioner's Inquiry into Child Sexual Exploitation in Gangs and Groups.

40   Interview with Carlene Firmin, *Evening Standard*, 3 December 2013.

41   Beckett, H. et al (2013) op. cit.

42   Kimmel, M. 'Men, Masculinity, and the Rape Culture' in Buchwald, E., Fletcher, P. R. and Roth, M. (eds.) (2005) *Transforming a Rape Culture*. Minneapolis: Milkweed Editions.

43   Stanton, J. (2014) 'Lad Culture & Sexism Survey: August–September 2014'. London: National Union of Students.

44   Krahe, B. and Berger, A. (2013) 'Men and Women as Perpetrators and Victims of Sexual Aggression in Heterosexual and Same-Sex Encounters: A study of first-year college students in Germany', *Aggressive Behavior*, 39, 391–404.

45   'Leaked frat minutes reveal shocking discussions of rape threats, sexual harassment, transphobia and hazing', *The Student*, 18 November 2014: http://www.studentnewspaper.org/leaked-frat-minutes-reveal-shocking-discussions-of-rape/ (accessed 7 August 2015); 'Edinburgh University investigates rape threats by "fraternity"', BBC News Online, 20 November 2014: http://www.bbc.co.uk/news/uk-scotland-edinburgh-east-fife-30128674 (accessed 5 May 2015).

46   'Outrage over London School of Economics Rugby Club leaflets calling women "slags, mingers and crumpets", *Evening Standard*, 6 October 2014: http://www.standard.co.uk/news/london/outrage-over-london-school-of-economics-rugby-club-leaflets-calling-women (accessed 5 May 2015).

47   '10 things female students shouldn't have to go through at university', *Guardian*, 10 October 2014: http://www.theguardian.com/lifeandstyle/womens-blog/2014/oct/10/10-things-female-students-face-university-misogyny-banter (accessed 5 May 2015).

48   National Union of Students (2013) '*That's* what she said: women students' experiences of "lad culture" in higher education'. London: National Union of Students.

49   Ibid.

50   Phipps, A. and Young, I. (2015) op. cit., 18 (4): 459–479.

51   Among sixteen to twenty-four year olds, in the week prior to being surveyed, 28 per cent of young women and 26 per cent of young men had drunk very heavily. Statistics on Alcohol, England, Health and Social Care Information Centre, 29 May 2014.

52 'Serious Case Review into Child Sexual Exploitation in Oxfordshire: from the experiences of Children A, B, C, D, E and F.' Approved by the Oxfordshire Safeguarding Children Board, 26 February 2015. Of the 373 children involved, fifty were boys. 'Oxfordshire grooming victims may have totalled 373 children', BBC News Online, 3 March 2015: http://www.bbc.co.uk/news/uk-england-oxfordshire-31643791 (accessed 23 September 2015).

53 'How we are fighting sexist laddism and abuse at Somerville College, Oxford', Alice Prochaska, *Guardian*, 15 May 2015: http://www.theguardian.com/commentisfree/2015/may/15/sexist-laddism-abuse-somerville-college-oxford (accessed 6 August 2015).

54 'Preparing young people for life in modern Britain', speech by the Rt Hon Nicky Morgan MP, Bright Blue think tank, 10 March 2015.

55 'Not Yet Good Enough: Personal, social, health and economic education in schools', Ofsted, 2013.

56 'A Curriculum for Life: The case for statutory PSHE education', PSHE Association, October 2015.

57 Parker, I. (2014) 'Young People, Sex and Relationships: The new norms', London: Institute of Public Policy Research.

58 Ibid.

59 Barter, C. (2015) op. cit.

60 'A grown-up's guide to sexting (or, why you should stop worrying about what your teenagers get up to online)', Rhiannon Lucy Cosslett, *Guardian*, 18 October 2013: http://www.theguardian.com/commentisfree/2013/oct/18/grown-ups-guide-to-sexting (accessed 6 August 2015).

61 Barter, C. (2015) op. cit.

62 Wiseman, R. (2013) *Ringleaders and Sidekicks: How to help your son cope with classroom politics, bullying, girls and growing up.* London: Piatkus.

Chapter 4

1 The median hourly earnings pay gap between men and women working full time is 9.4 per cent in the UK. Annual Survey of Hours and Earnings, 2014 Provisional Results, Office for National Statistics, 19 November 2014. Two-thirds of management positions in the UK workforce are occupied by men, and men are also more likely to be employed in higher skilled jobs. 'Women in the Labour Market', Office for National Statistics, 25 September 2013.

2   Lee, N., Sissons, P., Balaram, B., Jones, K. and Cominetti, N. (2012)' Short-term Crisis – Long-term Problem? Addressing the youth employment challenge', Lancaster: Work Foundation.

3   Crisis: 'Homelessness among Different Groups': http://www.crisis.org.uk/pages/homeless-diff-groups.html (accessed 11 August 2015).

4   Prison population bulletin: weekly 7 August 2015, op. cit.

5   See for review, Blakemore, J. E. O. et al. (2009) op. cit. ; also Smith, D. J. and Bradshaw, P. (2005) 'Gang Membership and Teenage Offending, The Edinburgh Study of Youth Transitions and Crime', University of Edinburgh.

6   Homicide statistics for England and Wales, Office for National Statistics, 13 February 2014.

7   'The cost of masculine crime', Ann Oakley and Cynthia Cockburn, *Open Democracy*, 8 March 2013: https://www.opendemocracy.net/5050/ann-oakley-cynthia-cockburn/cost-of-masculine-crime (accessed 20 May 2015).

8   Ibid.

9   Prison population statistics, House of Commons Library, op. cit.

10   Ibid.

11   Belfield, C., Cribb, J., Hood, A. and Joyce, R. (2014) 'Living Standards, Poverty and Inequality in the UK: 2014', London: Institute for Fiscal Studies.

12   'Recession and Recovery: Key Issues for the Next Parliament', House of Commons Library, 2010.

13   Based on data in: 'UK Labour Market', Office for National Statistics, November 2015 (statistics for July to September 2015).

14   Figures for 2010–2014 quoted in 'The UK's Youth Services: How cuts are removing opportunities for young people and damaging their lives', Unison, 2014.

15   'Scarred For Life: Creating a working future for young women', Young Women's Trust, 2015. There are 73,000 more young women aged sixteen to twenty-four who are NEET (497,000 young women compared to 424,000 young men). Figures for April to June 2015. 'Young People Not in Education, Employment or Training (NEET)', Office for National Statistics, 20 August 2015.

16   329,000 young women are economically inactive compared to 161,000 economically inactive young men. Figures for April to June 2015. 'Young People Not in Education, Employment or Training (NEET)' op. cit.

17   'Scarred For Life', 2015. op. cit.

18   'Smoking, Drinking and Drug Use among Young People in England: 2014', Health and Social Care Information Centre, 23 July 2015.

19   Youth Justice Statistics 2013/4 (England and Wales), Youth Board/Ministry of Justice Statistics Bulletin, 29 January 2015.

20 'Islamists, gangs, the EDL – all target alienated young men', David Lammy, *Guardian*, 24 May 2013: http://www.theguardian.com/uk/2013/may/24/islamists-gangs-edl-target-young-men (accessed 28 April 2015).

21 Ibid.

22 hooks, b. (2004) *We Real Cool: Black Men and Masculinity*. Abingdon: Routledge.

23 'Youth Unemployment and Ethnicity', TUC report, 2012.

24 'Moral Panics and the State' seminar, Stephen Crossley, 5 November 2013: https://moralpanicseminars.wordpress.com/seminars/programme/speaker-abstracts/ (accessed 30 May 2015).

25 'An Overview of Recorded Crimes and Arrests Resulting from Disorder Events in August 2011', Home Office, October 2011.

26 'Data journalism reading the riots: what we know. And what we don't', *Guardian*, 9 December 2011: http://www.theguardian.com/news/datablog/2011/dec/09/data-journalism-reading-riots (accessed 29 May 2015).

27 'The friendship crisis: Why are boys so lonely and violent?' Niobe Way, *Washington Post*, 13 June 2014: http://www.washingtonpost.com/posteverything/wp/2014/06/13/boys-are-bad-at-making-friends-and-its-at-the-heart-of-their-violent-behavior/ (accessed 31 March 2015).

28 Sarah-Jayne Blakemore, Professor of Cognitive Neuroscience, University College London, TED talk, June 2012.

29 Connell, R. W. (1995) *Masculinities*. Cambridge: Polity Press.

30 Prison population statistics, House of Commons Library, op. cit.

31 'Outcomes for Children Looked After by Local Authorities in England: 31 March 2012', Department for Education, 12 December 2012.

32 Robb, M., Featherstone, B., Ruxton, S. and Ward, M. (2015), 'Beyond Male Role Models: Gender identities and work with young men', Milton Keynes: The Open University.

33 Ibid.

34 Ibid.

35 Ibid.

36 Youth Justice briefing paper, Centre for Mental Health: http://www.centreformentalhealth.org.uk/youth-justice (accessed 2 June 2015).

37 'Youth justice facts and figures', Beyond Youth Custody: http://www.beyondyouthcustody.net/about/facts-and-stats/ (accessed 2 June 2015). Figures for England and Wales 2014.

38 Liaison and Diversion briefing paper, Centre for Mental Health: http://www.centreformentalhealth.org.uk/liaison-and-diversion (accessed 2 June 2015).

39 Wilkins, D. and Kemple, M. (2011) op. cit.

40 Liaison and Diversion briefing paper, op. cit.

41   Report on an announced inspection of HMYOI Feltham (Children and Young People) by HM Chief Inspector of Prisons, 11–15 August 2014. Published January 2015.

42   'Gang youths "suffer worse trauma that soldiers who fought Taliban"', *Evening Standard*, 12 January 2015.

43   Report on an announced inspection of HMYOI Feltham op. cit.

44   Ibid.

45   'Announcement of Review into Youth Justice', Written Statement to Parliament, 11 September 2015.

46   'Prison education must be "overhauled", Michael Gove says', BBC News Online, 17 July 2015: www.bbc.co.uk/news/uk-33554573 (accessed 13 August 2015).

47   'The Harris Review: Changing Prisons, Saving Lives. Report of the Independent Review into Self-inflicted Deaths in Custody of 18–24 year olds', July 2015.

48   'Suicide in Prison', Howard League for Penal Reform, Media Release, 22 January 2015: http://www.howardleague.org/suicide-in-prison/ (accessed 12 July 2015).

49   'How Chicago is using psychotherapy to fight crime – and winning', *Vox*, 1 May, 2014: http://www.vox.com/2014/5/1/5669578/how-chicago-is-using-psychotherapy-to-fight-crime-and-winning (accessed 2 June 2015).

50   'The cost of masculine crime', op. cit.

51   Ibid. Men account for 79 per cent, 76 per cent and 86 per cent of these crimes and incidents respectively.

52   Ibid.

53   Liaison and diversion briefing paper, op. cit.

54   Ibid.

55   'The cost of masculine crime', op. cit. Figure for 2012.

56   'Tories "confident" about £8bn NHS spending pledge', BBC News Online, 11 April 2015: http://www.bbc.co.uk/news/election-2015-32260220 (accessed 3 June 2015).

57   http://kareningalasmith.com/counting-dead-women/ (accessed 4 June 2015).

58   'We record all the killing of women by men. You see a pattern', *Guardian*, 8 February 2015: http://www.theguardian.com/society/2015/feb/08/killing-of-women-by-men-record-database-femicide (accessed 6 June 2015).

59   http://kareningalasmith.com/2015/05/18/femicide-mens-fatal-violence-against-women-goes-beyond-domestic-violence/ (accessed 6 June 2015). Official violent crime statistics have recently been questioned. See: Walby, S., Towers, J. and Francis, B. (2016) 'Is Violent Crime Increasing or Decreasing? A New Methodology to Measure Repeat Attacks Making Visible the Significance of Gender and Domestic Relations', *British Journal of Criminology*, 56 (1).

60 Women of the World event, Cambridge, UK, 8 March 2015.

61 'Alcohol and Distorted Views Implicated In Family Violence', Glenn Inquiry, 17 November 2014.

62 Hilman, B., Herbert, L. and Paul-Gera, N. (2014) 'The Making of Sexual Violence: How does a boy grow up to commit rape? Evidence from five IMAGES countries', Washington DC: International Centre for Research on Women & Promundo. The five countries in the study were Chile, Croatia, India, Mexico and Rwanda.

63 'Engaging Men and Boys: A brief summary of UNFPA experience and lessons learned', United Nations Population Fund, January 2013.

64 Statement by Rashida Manjoo, UN Special Rapporteur on Violence against Women, its causes and consequences, Office of the High Commissioner for Human Rights, 15 April 2014.

65 See for example, Moxon, S. (2008) *The Woman Racket: The new science explaining how the sexes relate at work, at play and in society*. Exeter: Imprint Academic; 'DV is not men only', *A Voice for Men*, 22 May 2013: http://www.avoiceformen.com/updates/news-updates/news-release-dv-is-not-men-only/ (accessed 24 September 2015); '"Feminists hate men": Meet Mike Buchanan the leader of Britain's new Justice for Men and Boys party', *Independent*, 14 January 2015: http://www.independent.co.uk/news/people/feminists-hate-men-meet-mike-buchanan-the-leader-of-britains-new-justice-for-men-and-boys-party-9977357.html (accessed 24 September 2015); Justice for Men and Boys Party, General Election Manifesto 2015, 28 December 2014.

66 Moxon, S. (2008) op. cit.

67 Justice for Men and Boys Party, General Election Manifesto 2015, op. cit.

68 Johnson, M. P. (2006) 'Conflict and Control: Gender symmetry and asymmetry in domestic violence', *Violence Against Women*, 12 (11), 1003–1018; Johnson, M. P. (2011) 'Gender and types of Intimate Partner Violence: A response to an anti-feminist literature review', *Aggression and Violent Behavior*, 16, 289–296.

69 Johnson, M. P. (2011) op. cit.

70 Johnson, M. P. (2005) 'Apples and Oranges in Child Custody Disputes: Intimate Terrorism vs. Situational Couple Violence', *Journal of Child Custody*, 2 (4), 43–52; Johnson, M. P. (2006) op. cit.; Johnson, M. P. (2011) op. cit. In this latter paper Johnson also notes a third type of violence – 'violent resistance'. This is a violent response to 'intimate terrorism' and is mainly enacted by a small number of women towards violent male partners.

71 See for example: 'Trouble 'n Strife for EastEnders Hardmen', *Mirror*, 4 November 2005: http://www.mirror.co.uk/3am/celebrity-news/trouble-n-strife-for-eastenders-hardmen-563994; 'Sun editor "assaults" TV hardman hubby', *Daily Mail*, 3 November 2005: http://www.dailymail.

co.uk/tvshowbiz/article-367490/Sun-editor-assaults-TV-hardman-hubby.html; 'EastEnder Hardman "Beaten Up by Wife"', *Evening Standard*, 3 November 2005.

72 'Jeremy Kyle defends male domestic abuse victim after audience laugh at him', *Independent*, 14 May 2015: http://www.independent.co.uk/arts-entertainment/tv/news/jeremy-kyle-defends-male-domestic-violence-victim-after-audience-laugh-at-him-10246296.html.

73 'Violence against Women and Girls Crime Report 2014–15', Crown Prosecution Service, June 2015. Includes statistics for England and Wales.

74 Letter to the *Guardian*, 2 July 2015: http://www.theguardian.com/society/2015/jul/02/anorexia-and-are-mens-problems-too (accessed 9 July 2015).

75 'Some violence is targeted at women and girls – we can't ignore that', Alison Saunders, *Guardian*, 28 July 2015: http://www.theguardian.com/commentisfree/2015/jul/28/violence-women-girls-male-victims-crimes-men (accessed 3 August 2015).

76 'The Use and Abuse of Honour-based Violence in the UK', Pragna Patel, *Open Democracy*, 6 June 2012: https://www.opendemocracy.net/5050/pragna-patel/use-and-abuse-of-honour-based-violence-in-uk (accessed 3 June 2015).

77 'Changing the Behaviour of Male Perpetrators of Domestic Violence', Angela Neustatter, *Open Democracy*, 28 November 2014: https://www.opendemocracy.net/5050/angela-neustatter/changing-behaviour-of-male-perpetrators-of-domestic-violence (accessed 14 April 2015).

78 Figure for England and Wales, End Violence Against Women coalition.

79 Kelly, L. and Westmarland, N. (2015) 'Domestic Violence Perpetrator Programmes: Steps Towards Change. Project Mirabal Final Report', London and Durham: London Metropolitan University and Durham University.

80 Ibid.

81 Ibid.

82 'Changing the Behaviour of Male Perpetrators of Domestic Violence', Angela Neustatter, op. cit.

Chapter 5

1 'Quality of life in Europe – facts and views – overall life satisfaction', *Eurostat*, March 2015.

2 'Annual Survey of Hours and Earnings, 2014 Provisional Results', Office for National Statistics, 19 November 2014.

3   'Female bosses work two hours a day for free as gender pay gap persists', *Guardian*, 25 August 2015: http://www.theguardian.com/business/2015/aug/25/female-bosses-work-free-gender-pay-gap-persists-uk-managers (accessed 25 August 2015).

4   Annual Survey of Hours and Earnings, 2014 Provisional Results, op. cit. Although mothers in Great Britain are now the main earners in one-third of working households, just under half of these women are lone mothers, rather than couple mothers out-earning male partners. Within this latter group, researchers suggest that the rise in the proportion of household income earned by women in recent years is likely to be linked to a sharp drop in male employment due to the 2008 recession, rather than a rise in female earnings. 'Who's Breadwinning in Europe? A comparative analysis of maternal breadwinning in Great Britain and Germany', Institute for Public Policy Research, October 2015.

5   Based on statistics in International Labour Office (2015) 'Women and the Future of Work - Beijing + 20 and Beyond: Briefing Note', ILO: Geneva.

6   Based on percentages from 'Stats and Facts on Women in Power', Fawcett Society, 28 February 2013.

7   74 per cent of teachers in England are women. 'School Workforce in England: November 2013', Office for National Statistics and Department for Education, 10 April 2014.

8   Based on percentages from 'Stats and Facts on Women in Power', op. cit.

9   Based on statistics in 'Women in the Labour Market', op. cit.

10   Ibid. UK statistics for those sixteen and over in work, 2013.

11   Rosin, H. (2012) *The End of Men and the Rise of Women*. London: Viking.

12   Men in Europe rate their life satisfaction at a mean average of 7.1 out of 10. For women it is 7.0. 'Quality of life in Europe' op. cit.

13   'What's the Better Life Index?', OECD, 2013.

14   'Gender Working Patterns: Labour Force Statistics', Office for National Statistics, June 2012. Cited in 'Women, men and part-time work', Equality and Human Rights Commission, January 2013.

15   Connolly, S., Aldrich, M., O'Brien, M., Speight, S. and Poole, E. (2013) 'Fathers, Work and Families in Twenty-first-century Britain: Beyond the breadwinner model?' NatCen, University of East Anglia & Thomas Coram Research Unit.

16   Kaufman, G. and Uhlenberg, P. (2000) 'The Influence of Parenthood on the Work Effort of Married Men and Women', *Social Forces*, 78 (3), 931–947.

17   Dermott, E. (2006) 'What's Parenthood Got to Do With It?: Men's hours of paid work', *British Journal of Sociology*, 57 (4), 619–634.

18   Burrows, G. (2013) *Men Can Do It: The real reason dads don't do childcare and what men and women should do about it.* NGO Media (e-book); 'I'd love to

read The Gruffalo for the 777th time but, alas, duty calls', Michael Gove, *The Times*, 13 May 2008.

19   Mothers report spending forty-nine hours per week on housework and looking after family members, for men it is twenty-four hours. Park, A. et al. (2013), op. cit.

20   Killewald, A. and Gough, M. (2010) 'Money Isn't Everything: Wives' earnings and housework time', *Social Science Research*, Nov 2010, 39 (6), 987–1003.

21   37 per cent of mothers with dependent children work part time rather than full time. 'Gender Working Patterns', op. cit.; Grant, L., Yeandle, S. and Buckner, L. (2005) 'Working Below Potential: Women and part-time work synthesis', Sheffield Hallam University & Equal Opportunities Commission. Also, 'Labour Force Survey 2004'. Cited in Hunt, S. A. (ed.) (2009) *Family Trends: British Families Since the 1950s*. London: Family and Parenting Institute.

22   Just under 40 per cent of single mothers and 30 per cent of couple mothers with primary-school-aged children do not have a paid job at all. 'Women in the Labour Market', op. cit.

23   UK Labour Market: Statistical Bulletin, Office for National Statistics, June 2015.

24   Burgess, A. (1997) *Fatherhood Reclaimed: The Making of the Modern Father*, London: Vermilion.

25   'Work and Care: A study of modern parents', Research Report 15, Equality and Human Rights Commission, 2009.

26   'For one week only, I'm allowed to say it: I get babies', *Guardian*, 1 April 2012: http://www.theguardian.com/commentisfree/2012/apr/01/can-say-i-get-babies (accessed 11 June 2015).

27   'Fatherhood Institute gives political parties Six Signposts to a better future for fatherhood', Fatherhood Institute press release, 20 April 2010.

28   Statistics for time spent with resident, dependent children. 'Parental Time in the UK: The Role of Parental Education', Cristina Borra, Department of Economics, University of Seville and Almudena Sevilla, School of Business Management, Queen Mary University of London, presentation of Economic and Social Research Council funded research, British Academy, London, 15 May 2014.

29   van der Gaag, N. (2014) *Feminism and Men*. London: Zed Books.

30   Connolly, S., Aldrich, M., O'Brien, M., Speight, S. and Poole, E. (2013) 'Fathers, Work and Families in Twenty-first-century Britain: Beyond the breadwinner model?' op. cit.

31   'The proof that we're winning the gender issues cultural battle', Joel Silberman, *Los Angeles Times*, 5 February 2015.

32 Kimmel, M. (2010) *Misframing Men: The Politics of Contemporary Masculinities*. New Jersey: Rutgers University Press.

33 See for review, Flouri, E. (2005) *Fathering and Child Outcomes*. Chichester: John Wiley and Sons; Lewis, C. and Lamb, M. E. (2007) 'Understanding Fatherhood: A review of recent research', York: Joseph Rowntree Foundation; Lamb, M. E. (ed.) (2010) *The Role of the Father in Child Development*, Fifth Edition. New Jersey: John Wiley and Sons.

34 Powdthavee, N., (2014) 'What Childhood Characteristics Predict Psychological Resilience to Economic Shocks in Adulthood?', *Journal of Economic Psychology*, 45, 84–101.

35 Saturn, S. R. (2014) 'Flexibility of the Father's Brain', *Proceedings of the National Council for Social Sciences*, 111(27), 9671–9672. Also, see for review, Lewis, C. and Warin, J. (2001) 'What Good Are Dads?' *Father Facts*, 1 (1), Fathers Direct; Feldman, R., Gordon, I., Schneiderman, I., Weisman, O. and Zagoory-Sharon, O. (2010) 'Natural Variations in Maternal and Paternal Care Are Associated with Systematic Changes in Oxytocin Following Parent-Infant Contact', *Psychoneuroendocrinology*, 35 (8): 1133–41.

36 See for review, Lamb, M. E. (ed.) (2010) op. cit. and 'Briefing on Paternity, Maternity and Parental Leave: Supporting families and relationships through parental leave', Fatherhood Institute, 2010.

37 Sigle-Rushton, W. (2010) 'Men's Unpaid Work and Divorce: Reassessing specialisation and trade in British families', *Feminist Economics*, 16 (2), 1–26.

38 See for review, Poole, E., Speight, S., O'Brien, M., Connolly, S., and Aldrich, M., (2013) 'Father involvement with Children and Couple Relationships', NatCen, University of East Anglia & Thomas Coram Research Unit.

39 Miller, T. (2005) *Making Sense of Motherhood. A Narrative Approach*. Cambridge: Cambridge University Press; Miller, T. (2010) *Making Sense of Fatherhood. Gender, Caring and Work*. Cambridge: Cambridge University Press.

40 'Reaching Out: Involving fathers in maternity care', 2011, Royal College of Midwives.

41 'Guidance urges fathers-to-be to get involved', Royal College of Midwives press release, 14 November 2011: https://www.rcm.org.uk/news-views-and-analysis/news/guidance-urges-fathers-to-be-to-get-involved (accessed 22 June 2015).

42 National Childbirth Trust Policy Briefing: Choice of Place of Birth, November 2011; Brocklehurst, P., Hardy, P., Hollowell, J., Linsell, L., Macfarlane, A., McCourt, C., Marlow, N., Miller, A., Newburn, M., Petrou, S., Puddicombe, D., Redshaw, M., Rowe, R., Sandall, J., Silverton, L. and Stewart, M. (2011) 'Perinatal and Maternal Outcomes by Planned Place of

Birth for Healthy Women with Low-risk Pregnancies: The birthplace in England national prospective cohort study', *BMJ*, 343 (7840).

43 'Maternity: Delivery Suite at Princess Anne Wing', Royal United Hospitals Bath: http://www.ruh.nhs.uk/patients/services/maternity/Delivery_Suite_Princess.asp?menu_id=5 (accessed 24 August 2015).

44 . 'First time fathers need more support', Oxford University press release, 18 May 2015.

45 La Valle, I., Clery, E., Carmen, M. C. (2008) 'Maternity Rights and Mothers' Employment Decisions', Department for Work and Pensions, Research Report No. 496. Cited in 'Shared Parental Leave Impact Assessment', Department for Business, Innovation and Skills, 29 January 2014.

46 Statistical briefing on fathers' leave and pay, Trades Union Congress (TUC), February 2015.

47 Guest post from Nick Clegg: 'This is a watershed moment in the fight for a family-friendly Britain', Mumsnet, 13 March 2014:. http://www.mumsnet.com/Talk/guest_posts/a2024446-Guest-post-from-Nick-Clegg-This-is-a-watershed-moment-in-the-fight-for-a-family-friendly-Britain (accessed 28 June 2015).

48 Ibid.

49 'Two in five fathers won't qualify for shared parental leave', Trades Union Congress (TUC) press release, 4 February 2015. The main reason for ineligibility is that a father's partner is not in paid work, and thus will not receive maternity leave and pay that can be converted into shared parental leave.

50 'Shared Parental Leave Impact Assessment' op. cit.

51 'Shared Parental Leave: Most fathers in the UK aren't taking up the chance', *Daily Telegraph*, 22 October 2015: http://www.telegraph.co.uk/women/womens-business/11946167/Shared-parental-leave-Most-fathers-in-the-UK-arent-taking-it-up.html (accessed 10 November 2015).

52 Nick Clegg speech at the launch of Cityfathers on shared parental leave, 23 April 2014; https://www.gov.uk/government/speeches/nick-clegg-at-the-launch-of-cityfathers-on-shared-parental-leave (accessed 22 June 2015).

53 'Shared Parental Leave Impact Assessment' op. cit. (see paragraphs 100–104).

54 In Sweden men took only 7 per cent of the total number of parental leave days by 1987: Chronholm, A. (2009) 'Sweden: Individualisation or Free Choice in parental Leave?' in Kamerman, S. B. and Moss, P. (eds.) (2009) *The Politics of Parental Leave Policies. Children, Parenting, Gender and the Labour Market.* Bristol: Policy Press. Only 4 per cent of fathers took parental leave in Norway by 1992. Kvande, E. 'Norway's Policy Approach to Fathering', presentation at Fathering and Work Life Balance: Challenges for Policy seminar, Gender Institute of the London School of Economics, London, 5 March 2010.

55   Kvande, E. 'Norway's Policy Approach to Fathering' op. cit.

56   Duvander, A.-Z., Ferrarini, T. and Thalberg, S. (2005) *Swedish Parental Leave and Gender Equality: Achievements and Reform Challenges in a European Perspective*. Stockholm: Institute for Futures Studies.

57   'Where new dads are encouraged to take months off work', BBC News Online, 6 January 2016: www.bbc.co.uk/news/magazine_35225982 (accessed 14 January 2016).

58   'Shared Parental Leave Impact Assessment' op. cit.; 'Beyond Bread-winners and Authority Figures – Dads enter the 21st century', Professor Margaret O'Brien, Director Thomas Coram Research Unit at University of London Institute of Education, *The Conversation*, 16 June 2015: http://theconversation.com/beyond-breadwinners-and-authority-figures-dads-enter-the-21st-century-43196 (accessed 16 June 2015).

59   Neilson, J. and Stanfors, M. (2014) 'It's About Time! Gender, Parenthood and Household Divisions of Labour Under Different Welfare Regimes', *Journal of Family Issues*, 35 (8) 1066–1088.

60   'In Sweden Men Can Have It All', *New York Times*, 9 June 2010: http://www.nytimes.com/2010/06/10/world/europe/10iht-sweden.html (accessed 24 June 2015).

61   Reich, N. (2010) 'Who Cares? Determinants of Fathers' Use of Parental Leave in Germany', Working Paper No. 1–31. Hamburg: Hamburg Institute of International Economics.

62   'A father's place', *The Economist*, 16 May 2015: http://www.economist.com/news/international/21651203-men-have-long-been-discouraged-playing-equal-role-home-last-starting (accessed 25 August 2015).

63   'Virgin Management Announces Shared Parental Leave Policy', Virgin News, 10 June 2015: http://www.virgin.com/news/virgin-management-announces-shared-parental-leave-policy (accessed 30 September 2015).

64   'What I learned on my (Swedish) paternity Leave', *Time*, 7 August 2015: http://time.com/3987742/paternity-leave-lessons/ (accessed 30 September 2015).

65   Huerta, M.C., Adema, W., Baxter, J., Han, W-J., Lausten, M., Lee, R. H. and Waldfogel, J. (2013) 'Fathers' leave, fathers' involvement and child development: are they related? Evidence from four OECD countries', OECD Social, Employment and Migration working papers, No. 140.

66   Rehel, E. M. (2014) 'When Dad Stays Home Too: Paternity leave, gender, and parenting', *Gender & Society*, February 2014, 28 (1), 110–132.

67   Kotsadam, A. and Finseraas, H. (2011) 'The State Intervenes in the Battle of the Sexes: Causal effects of paternity leave', *Social Science Research*, 40 (6), 1611–1622.

68 Olah, L. S., (2001) 'Policy Changes and Family Stability: The Swedish case', *International Journal of Law, Policy and the Family*, 15 (1), 118–134.

69 Duvander, A. and Jans, A. (2009) 'Consequences of Fathers' Parental Leave Use: Evidence from Sweden', *Finnish Yearbook of Population Research*, pp. 51–62 in the Special Issue of the 16th Nordic Demographic Symposium in Helsinki 5–7 June 2008. Cited in 'Fatherhood Institute Research Summary: Paternity Leave', 7 November 2014.

70 Eydal, G. B. (2009) op. cit.

71 Haas, L. and Hwang, P. (2008) 'The Impact of Taking Parental Leave on Fathers' Participation in Childcare and Relationships with Children: Lessons from Sweden', *Community, Work & Family*, 11 (4), 85–104. Cited in Fatherhood Institute Research Summary, op. cit.

72 OECD (2015), OECD Family Database, Paris: OECD. Also, OECD (2007) 'Babies and Bosses – Reconciling Work and Family Life: A Synthesis of Findings for OECD Countries', Paris: OECD.

73 Johannson, E-A. (2010) 'The Effect of Own and Spousal Parental Leave on Earnings', Working Paper 2010: 4. Uppsala: Institute of Labour Market Policy Evaluation.

74 McGinn, K. L., Castro, M. R., and Lingo, E. L. (2015) 'Mums the Word! Cross-national Effects of Maternal Employment on Gender Inequalities at Work and at Home', Working Paper 15–094.

75 Kotsadam, A. and Finseraas, H. (2013) 'Causal Effects of Paternity Leave', *Social Forces*, 92(1): 329–351.

76 The child poverty rate is significantly lower in countries with high maternal employment rates: e.g. Norway's child poverty rate is 2.9 per cent and Sweden's is 3.2 per cent, compared to the OECD average of 10.3 per cent. OECD (2007) op cit.

77 Goldberg, W. A., Lucas-Thompson, R. G. and Prause, J. (2010) 'Maternal Work Early in the Lives of Children and Its Distal Associations with Achievement and Behavior Problems: A meta-analysis', *Psychological Bulletin*, 136 (6), 915–942.

78 Dunne, G. A. (2005) *Balancing Acts: Lesbian Experience of Work and Family Life*. Swindon: Economic and Social Research Council (ESRC). Dunne, G. A. (2005) *The Different Dimensions of Gay Fatherhood*. Swindon: ESRC. Patterson, D. J., Sutfin, E. L. and Fulcher, M. (2004) 'Division of Labor Among Lesbian and Heterosexual Parenting Couples: Correlates of Specialized Versus Shared Patterns', *Journal of Adult Development*, 11 (3). Solomon, S. E., Rothblum, E. D. and Balsam, K. F. (2004) 'Pioneers in Partnership: Lesbian and Gay Male Couples in Civil Unions Compared with Those Not in Civil Unions, and Married Heterosexual Siblings', *Journal of Family Psychology*, 18 (2), 275–286.

79   Fagan, C., Hegewisch, A. and Pillenger, J. (2006) 'Out of Time: Why Britain needs a new approach to working-time flexibility', London: Trades Union Congress.

80   Equality and Human Rights Commission (2009) 'Working Better: Fathers, Family and Work – Contemporary Perspectives', Manchester: EHRC.

81   Plantenga, J. and Remery, C. (2009) 'The Netherlands: Bridging Labour and Care', in Kamerman, S. B. and Moss, P. (eds.) (2009) op. cit.

82   'Pink bus of Labour women on "kitchen table" tour to woo female voters', *Guardian*, 10 February 2015: www.theguardian.com/politics/2015/feb/10/pink-bus-labour-women-mps-kitchen-table-tour-female-voters (accessed 26 September 2015).

83   Saturn, S. R. (2014) 'Flexibility of the Father's Brain', *Proceedings of the National Council for Social Sciences*, 111 (27), 9671–9672. Also, see for review, Lewis, C. and Warin, J. (2001) 'What Good Are Dads?' op. cit.; Feldman, R. et al. (2010) op. cit.

84   Almost three-quarters of mothers still do some breastfeeding when their child is six months old in Sweden and 74 per cent do so in Iceland, compared with 29 per cent in the UK. See for review, O'Brien, M. (2009) 'Fathers, Parental Leave Policies and Infant Quality of Life. International Perspectives and Policy Impact', *The Annals of the American Academy of Political and Social Science*, 624, 190–213. Also, Eydal, G. B. (2009) 'Equal legal rights to paid parental leave – the case of Iceland'. Paper for ESPANET, The Network for European Social Policy Analysis. Fathers are known to have a strong influence on whether or not mothers start (and then continue) breastfeeding; see for review, 'Fathers and Breastfeeding', Fatherhood Institute Research Summary, 20 March 2007.

85   Women's Equality Party policy document, October 2015: https://d3n8a8pro7vhmx.cloudfront.net/womensequality/pages/405/attachments/original/1445332098/WE_Policy_Launch.pdf?1445332098 (accessed 10 November 2015).

86   'Majority of UK believe childcare should be shared equally between couples', Department for Business, Innovation & Skills press release, 13 January 2015: https://www.gov.uk/government/news/majority-of-uk-believe-childcare-should-be-shared-equally-between-couples (accessed 24 June 2015).

87   See for example: Allen, S. M. and Hawkins, A. J. (1999) 'Maternal Gatekeeping: Mothers' beliefs and behaviors that inhibit greater father involvement in family work', *Journal of Marriage and Family*, 61 (1), 199–212; Fagan, J. and Barnett, M. (2003) 'The Relationship between Maternal Gatekeeping, Paternal Competence, Mothers' Attitudes about the Father

Role, and Father Involvement', *Journal of Family Issues* 24 (8), 1020–1043; McBride, B. A., Brown, G. L., Bost, K. K., Shin, N., Vaughn, B. and Korth, B. (2005) 'Paternal Identity, Maternal Gatekeeping, and Father Involvement', *Family Relations* 54 (3), 360–372.

88 Campbell, B. (2013) *End of Equality: The Only Way Is Women's Liberation*. Calcutta: Seagull Books.

89 Craig, L. and Mullan, K (2013) 'Parental Leisure Time: A gender comparison in five countries', *Social Politics*, 20 (3), 329–357.

90 Calcagno, J. (2014) 'The "Mommy Tax" and "Daddy Bonus": Parenthood and income in New York City 1990–2010', City University of New York.

91 'Men as Change Agents for Gender Equality: Report on Policy Seminar July 2014', Government Equalities Office, 2015.

92 'Why Women Still Can't Have It All', Anne-Marie Slaughter, *The Atlantic*, June/July 2012: http://www.theatlantic.com/magazine/archive/2012/07/why-women-still-cant-have-it-all/309020/ (accessed 30 September 2015).

93 'Why I Put My Wife's Career First', Andrew Moravcsik, *The Atlantic*, October 2015: http://www.theatlantic.com/magazine/archive/2015/10/why-i-put-my-wifes-career-first/403240/ (accessed 30 September 2015).

94 Ibid.

95 Rich, A. (1976) *Of Woman Born: Motherhood as Experience and Institution*. New York: W. W. Norton & Company.

96 Park, A. et al. (2013) op. cit.

97 Ibid.

98 Anderson, D. and Hamilton, M. (2005) 'Gender Role Stereotyping of Parents in Children's Picture Books: The invisible father', *Sex Roles*, 52 (3/4).

99 'NBA Players' Sexist Hazing Ritual: Pushing Dolls in Strollers', Yahoo.com Parenting, 27 January 2015: https://www.yahoo.com/parenting/nba-players-sexist-hazing-ritual-pushing-dolls-109315381887.html (accessed 13 June 2015).

100 'Fighting for fatherhood, the other glass ceiling', Stephen S. Holden, Honorary Associate Professor, Macquarie Graduate School of Management, *The Conversation*, 17 July 2014: http://theconversation.com/fighting-for-fatherhood-the-other-glass-ceiling-29325 (accessed 11 June 2015).

101 Adoption 2013–14, Official Statistics Release, Ofsted, November 2014.

Chapter 6

1 'American Men's Hidden Crisis: They need more friends!', Professor Lisa Wade, *Salon.com*, 8 December 2013: http://www.salon.com/2013/12/08/

american_mens_hidden_crisis_they_need_more_friends/ (accessed 25 August 2015).

2   'Don't be fooled, loneliness affects men too', Roger Patulny, Lecturer in Sociology at University of Wollongong, Australia, *The Conversation*, 11 July 2013: http://theconversation.com/dont-be-fooled-loneliness-affects-men-too-15545 (accessed 12 July 2015).

3   'The Way We Are Now', Relate, 2014. Survey conducted among those aged sixteen and over.

4   Steptoe, A., Shankar, A., Demakakos, P. and Wardle, J. (2013) 'Social Isolation, Loneliness and All-cause Mortality in Older Men and Women', *Proceedings of the National Academy of Sciences of the United States of America*, 9 April 2013, 110 (15), 5797–5801.

5   'The Way We Are Now', op. cit.

6   Wylie, C., Platt, S., Brownlie, J., Chandler, A., Connolly, S., Evans, R., Kennelly, B., Kirtley, O., Moore, G., O'Connor, R. and Scourfield, J. (2012) 'Men, Suicide and Society: Why disadvantaged men in mid-life die by suicide', Ewell, Surrey: Samaritans.

7   Beach, B. and Bamford, S-M. (2014) 'Isolation: The emerging crisis for older men', London: Independent Age and the International Longevity Centre-UK.

8   Way, N. (2011) *Deep Secrets: Boys' Friendships and the Crisis of Connection*. Cambridge, MA: Harvard University Press.

9   'A manifesto for the new man: how the Great White Male can stay relevant', *New Statesman*, 8 October, 2014. http://www.newstatesman.com/culture/2014/10/manifesto-new-man-how-great-white-male-can-stay-relevant (accessed 14 December 2015).

10   'American Men's Hidden Crisis', op. cit.

11   Thornton, J. (2012) 'Men and Suicide': Why it's a social issue', Ewell, Surrey: Samaritans.

12   Ibid.

13   Wilkins, D. (2013) 'Try to See It My Way: Improving relationship support for men', London: Relate.

14   Vogel, D. L., Heimerdinger-Edwards, S. R., Hammer, J. H. and Hubbard, A. (2011) '"Boys Don't Cry": Examination of the links between endorsement of masculine norms, self-stigma, and help-seeking attitudes for men from diverse backgrounds', *Journal of Counseling Psychology* (2011), 58 (3), 368–382.

15   Thornton, J. (2012) op. cit.

16   Franklin, A. and Tranter, B. (2008) 'Loneliness in Australia'. Housing and Community Research Unit, Paper 13, School of Sociology and Social Work, University of Tasmania.

17 'Lone Parents with Dependent Children', Office for National Statistics, 19 January 2012.

18 Speight, S., Poole, E., O'Brien, M., Connolly, S. and Aldrich, M. (2013) 'Men and Fatherhood: Who are today's fathers?' London: National Centre for Social Research and Norwich: University of East Anglia.

19 In America pay for men with only a high-school certificate dropped 21 per cent in real terms between 1979 and 2013. For women with similar qualifications it increased by 3 per cent. Approximately one-fifth of working-age American men in this category have no job. 'The Weaker Sex', *The Economist*, 30 May–5 June 2015 (print edition). In the UK, the earnings of low-paid men dropped more sharply than that of low-paid women between 2009 and 2014 (a drop of -10.9 per cent for men, compared to -7.6 per cent for women). However, women continue to make up the majority of low-paid workers, at 61 per cent, although that percentage has fallen since the 1970s. Low Pay Britain 2015, Resolution Foundation, 5 October 2015.

20 78 per cent of never-married women regarded it as 'very important' that a potential spouse had a steady job, compared to 46 per cent for never-married men. 'Never-married women want a spouse with a steady job', Pew Research Center, 23 September 2014.

21 50 per cent of births to American women without college degrees are outside of marriage, compared to 6 per cent of births to college graduates. In Britain 90 per cent of professional couples marry before having children, compared with only half of those who earn the minimum wage. Southampton University research shows that the less educated a woman is, the more likely she is to have a baby outside of marriage. 'Men Adrift', *The Economist*, 30 May–5 June 2015 (print edition).

22 Faludi, S. (2011) *Stiffed: The Betrayal of Modern Man*. London: Chatto and Windus; Kimmel, M. (2013) *Angry White Men: American Masculinity at the End of an Era*. New York: Nation Books.

23 Beach, B. and Bamford, S-M. (2014) op. cit.

24 Beach, B. and Bamford, S-M. (2014) op. cit.

25 Beach, B. and Bamford, S-M. (2014) op. cit.

26 'Life without Fatherhood: A qualitative study of older involuntarily childless men', presentation by Robin Hadley to the UK Male Psychology Conference, London, 26 June 2015.

27 Guasp, A. (2013) *Lesbian, Gay and Bisexual People in Later Life*. London: Stonewall.

28 'Life without Fatherhood', presentation by Robin Hadley, 2015. Op. cit.

29 Tedstone Doherty, D. and Kartalova-O'Doherty, Y. (2010) 'Gender and Self-reported Mental Health Problems: Predictors of help-seeking from a general practitioner', *British Journal of Health Psychology* (2010): 15 (1), 213–228.

30 Williams, J., Stephenson, D. and Keating, K. (2014) 'A Tapestry of Oppression', *The Psychologist*, British Psychological Society, 27, 406–409: https://thepsychologist.bps.org.uk/volume-27/edition-6/tapestry-oppression.

31 Tedstone Doherty, D. and Kartalova-O'Doherty, Y. (2010) op. cit.

32 Wylie, C. et al. (2012) op. cit.

33 Wilkins, D. and Kemple, M. (2011) op. cit.

34 Mental Health Statistics: Prisons, Mental Health Foundation: http://www.mentalhealth.org.uk/help-information/mental-health-statistics/prisons/ (accessed 10 July 2015).

35 Ibid.

36 'A Manifesto for Better Mental Health', The Mental Health Policy Group, 2015.

37 'Mental health equality call gets high-profile backing', BBC News Online, 2 November 2015: http://www.bbc.co.uk/news/health-34676799 (accessed 11 November 2015); Equality for Mental Health UK: http://www.equality4mentalhealth.uk (accessed 11 November 2015).

38 'Two-thirds of Britons with depression get no treatment', *Guardian*, 13 August 2014: http://www.theguardian.com/society/2014/aug/13/two-thirds-britons-not-treated-depression (accessed 9 July 2015).

39 Thornton, J. (2012) op. cit.

40 Men accounted for 4,858 (78%) of suicides in 2013 (source: Suicides in the United Kingdom, 2013 Registrations, Office for National Statistics, 19 February 2015) and 4,623 (76%) of suicides in 2014 (source: UK suicide statistics compiled by CALM, based on separate data from the Office for National Statistics (England and Wales), National Records of Scotland and the Northern Ireland Statistics and Research Agency).

41 'What do people die of? Mortality rates and data for every cause of death in 2011 visualised', *Guardian*, 6 November 2012: http://www.theguardian.com/news/datablog/2012/nov/06/deaths-mortality-rates-cause-death-2011 (accessed 1 October 2015).

42 'A Crisis in Modern Masculinity: Understanding the causes of male suicide', Campaign Against Living Miserably (CALM), 2014.

43 Suicides in the United Kingdom, 2013 Registrations, Office for National Statistics, 19 February 2015.

44 Statistics for 2012, age-standardised suicide rates (per 100,000). Suicide rates data by country, Global Health Observatory Data Repository, World Health Organisation.

45 50 per cent of men have experienced depression at some time, compared to 59 per cent of women. 'A Crisis in Modern Masculinity', CALM, op. cit.

46 28 per cent of women have had suicidal thoughts, compared to 22 per cent of men. YouGov research for the Campaign Against Living Miserably, 2012.

47   56 per cent of men commit suicide by hanging, strangulation and suffocation compared to 40 per cent of women. Suicides in the United Kingdom, 2013 Registrations op. cit.

48   'A Crisis in Modern Masculinity', CALM, op. cit.

49   'Suicide', Mental Health Foundation: http://www.mentalhealth.org.uk/help-information/mental-health-a-z/S/suicide/ (accessed 12 July 2015).

50   UK suicide statistics compiled by CALM, based on separate data from the Office for National Statistics (England and Wales), National Records of Scotland and the Northern Ireland Statistics and Research Agency. The statistics compiled by CALM show, worryingly, there has also been a small rise in suicide among women, from 1,375 in 2013 to 1,486 in 2014.

51   'Rugby League star Keegan Hirst becomes first Brit player to come out as gay', *Sunday Mirror*, 15 August 2015: http://www.mirror.co.uk/sport/rugby-league/rugby-league-star-keegan-hirst-6260707 (accessed 30 August 2015).

52   'The RaRE Research Report, LGB&T Mental Health – Risk and Resilience Explored', Project for Advocacy Counselling and Education (PACE), 2015.

53   'Mental Disorders, Suicide, and Deliberate Self-harm in Lesbian, Gay and Bisexual People. A systematic review', National Institute for Mental Health in England, 2007.

54   Sunday *Mirror*, 15 August 2015, op. cit.

55   'Preventing suicide in England: Two years on', second annual report on the cross-government outcomes strategy to save lives, Department of Health, February 2015.

56   Statistics for 1981–2013, 'A Crisis in Modern Masculinity' op. cit. Also, Suicides in the United Kingdom, 2013 Registrations, op. cit.

57   'A Crisis in Modern Masculinity' op. cit.

58   McKee-Ryan, F., Song, Z., Wanberg, C.R. and Kinicki, A. J. (2005) 'Psychological and Physical Well-being During Unemployment: A meta-analytic study', *Journal of Applied Psychology*, 90 (1). Cited in Poole, E. et al. (2013) op. cit.

59   Wylie, C. et al. (2012) op. cit.

60   'Understanding Men and Health: Musings on contradictory masculinities', Professor Steve Robertson, Inaugural lecture, Leeds Metropolitan University, 23 April 2013: http://www.fightlikeamaninternational.org/webdocuments/steve-robertsons-selected-publications.pdf (accessed 26 August 2015).

61   See for review, Gough, G. (2013) 'The Psychology of Men's Health: Maximising masculine capital', *Health Psychology*, 32 (1), 1–4.

62   'Men and Masculinities: Leveling Up With Michael Kimmel', Porter Anderson, *Thought Catalog*, 16 September 2014: http://thoughtcatalog.com/porter-anderson/2014/09/men-and-masculinities-leveling-up-with-michael-kimmel/ (accessed 12 July 2015).

Conclusion

1   'Children and young people's mental health – policy, CAMHS ser-
    vices, funding and education', House of Commons Library Briefing
    Paper, 29 October 2015; 'Cuts to UK mental health services are
    destroying young lives and families', *Guardian*, 27 July 2015: http://
    www.theguardian.com/commentisfree/2015/jul/27/uk-child-men-
    tal-health-services-destroying-lives-families (accessed 5 October
    2015); 'Children and young peoples mental health services slashed by
    funding', Young Minds, 28 July 2011: http://www.youngminds.org.
    uk/news/blog/2611-children-and-young-peoples--mental-health-ser-
    vices-slashed-by-funding (accessed 12 November 2015); 'Education
    Secretary to Pledge £8.5m for Early Intervention Funding', Young Minds:
    http://www.youngminds.org.uk/news/blog/2453educationsecre-
    tary-to-pledge-8-5m-for-early-intervention-funding (accessed 12
    November 2015); 'Is Britain Fairer?' Equality and Human Rights Commis-
    sion, October 2015, op. cit.
2   'Mental health "time-bomb" looming as children denied support',
    Children & Young People Now, 12 October 2015: http://www.cypnow.
    co.uk/cyp/news/1154194/mental-health-time-bomb-looming-as-chil-
    dren-denied-support (accessed 12 November 2015); 'Children face
    six-month wait for mental health assessments', *Children & Young People
    Now*, 12 November 2015: http://www.cypnow.co.uk/cyp/news/1154745/
    children-face-six-month-wait-for-mental-health-assessments
    (accessed 12 November 2015).
3   Functional Family Therapy (youth in state institutions), Washington
    State Institute of Public Policy Benefit-Cost results (Benefit-cost estimates
    updated July 2015. Literature review updated December 2014): http://
    www.wsipp.wa.gov/BenefitCost/ProgramPdf/40/Functional-Family-
    Therapy-youth-in-state-institutions (accessed 5 October 2015).
4   'Around the world in a shorter working week', New Economics Foundation,
    3 September 2014: http://www.neweconomics.org/blog/entry/around-
    the-world-in-a-shorter-working-week (accessed 16 November 2015).
5   Rich, A. (1976) op. cit.
6   'Professor Jeremy Sanders on men and feminism at Cambridge Women
    of the World Festival', *Cambridge News*, 23 February 2015.
7   hooks, b. (2004) *The Will to Change: Men, Masculinity, and Love*. New York:
    Washington Square Press.

ACKNOWLEDGEMENTS

Many people have been generous with their time and their thoughts while I've been writing *Man Up*. My agent, Zoë Waldie, and Elizabeth Foley, publishing director at Harvill Secker, were enthusiastic supporters from the beginning. Ellie Steel has been the most intelligent and rigorous of editors, and Kate Bland and Mari Yamazaki the smartest of publicists. Rachel Dykins' research at the start of the project helped me to see the wood, when I felt overwhelmed by the trees. Cordelia Fine was kind enough to read and advise me on chapter 1: her comments were invaluable and any errors that remain are, of course, mine alone. Ian Emerson opened a series of school doors. My early conversations with Reg Bailey, Phil Beadle, Paula Calderwood, Ben Hine, Nikki van der Gaag, Glen Poole, Martin Robb and Sandy Ruxton helped to frame and refine my thinking. I was lucky enough to meet Melissa Benn, Adrienne Burgess, Olivia Dickinson and Tina Miller when writing my first book, *Shattered*: these excellent women continue to be sources of sound advice and good laughs. David Brockway and Sarah Perry at Great Men, Chris Duckett at Gosforth Academy, Ben Jamal and Phil Price at DVIP, Lindsey Hinds in David Lammy's office, Miranda Horvath and Lucy Neville at Middlesex University, Andrew McBroom at City of London School, Charlie Rice at the Fatherhood Institute, Emma Rule at 24 Hour PR People and George Turner at Carney's Community all went out of their way to help me. Fran O'Brien kept me solvent while Elaine Lester kept me sane. Catherine Carr kindly let me use her idea for a chapter title. Kate Barker, Kim Barnes, Richard Beecham, Sara Beecham, Emma Bell, Leanne Buckle, Clare Burleigh, Rob Burley, Nicky Busch, Rachel Charmant, Anna Darnell Bradley, Holly Dustin, Victoria Finney, Alex Gardiner,

Eliane Glaser, Jo Kavenna, Anna Lucas, Azra Onur, Lizz Pearson, Jo Riordan, Chris Rybczynski, Sharmini Selvarajah, Sue Thompson and Olivia Trench lent me their ears and suggested people or angles. I am grateful to everyone who agreed to be interviewed for the book, all of whom undoubtedly had more important or enticing calls on their time. Every interviewee threw new light on the subject. Likewise, I've enjoyed my conversations with my children, Hal and Erica, as they negotiate and question a gendered world. Their experiences are as much an education for me as for them. Sometimes, though, you need the space to think and write. Coin Street Children's Centre and Archbishop Sumner Primary School have provided stellar care for my son and daughter; so too have my in-laws, Lynda Pearce and Guy Schofield, and my parents, Pat and John Asher. As in every other aspect of my life, I could not have done without my husband, Nick Pearce: my first reader and the brightest and kindest of men.

INDEX

A

Aaron, 60, 63, 110, 112, 205
Abel, 57–8
absent fathers, 136–7, 169, 193
Achilles Heel, 7
Adams, John, 174, 177
adoption, 196
advertising, 12, 31, 43, 100, 170, 178
aggression, 6, 9, 19, 22, 34–5, 38, 43,
    52, 53, 58, 59, 76–7, 89, 131, 146,
    151, 158, 214
alcohol, 7, 10, 109–10, 112, 127, 140,
    141, 205, 206, 214, 229
Alda, Alan, 30
All Party Parliamentary Literacy
    Group Commission, 72
Amis, Martin, 7
anal sex, 101, 103
Angry White Men (Kimmel), 211
Ant-Man, 70
antisocial behaviour, 9, 98, 141, 145
Ark, The, 131
assertiveness, 15, 18, 27, 34–5, 76–7, 89
Association of School and College
    Leaders, 80
Atkinson, Dr Maggie, 80
Australia, 94, 181, 201–2, 209, 215, 222
autism, 78

B

bad behaviour, 75–85, 231
Ball, Ros, 27, 32, 34, 44, 46
banter, 109
Barnard College, 21
'Barnledig Pappa!', 178, 195
Baron-Cohen, Simon, 18–21

'Basically … Porn is everywhere', 100
basketball, 194–5
Beckham, David, 68
'Being a Man' programme, 144
Ben & Holly's Little Kingdom, 43
Benn, Melissa, 106
Berenbaum, Sheri A., 23
'Beyond Male Role Models' research
    project, 137
Biddulph, Steve, 25
Bieber, Justin, 68
Big Talk Education, 116, 230
'big-build', 215
biological determinism, 5–6, 15–25,
    45–6
Blair, Tony, 73–4
'Blurred Lines' (Thicke), 95
Bly, Robert, 6
body image, 67–70, 104
body sculpture, 60
Boer War (1899–1902), 7
bonding, 6, 10, 55
books, children's, 30–1, 33, 194, 231,
    234, 237
boxing, 69, 127, 156–61
boyhood
    aggression, 19, 34–5, 43, 53, 58, 59,
        76–7, 89, 148
    assertiveness, 27, 34–5, 76–7
    bad behaviour, 75–85, 231
    body image, 67–70, 104
    clothing, 40–1, 42, 49, 63, 234
    competitiveness, 53, 54
    conformity, 38, 54, 56, 62–3, 75,
        103, 196, 220, 235
    discipline, 37–9, 240

dominance, 45, 89, 104, 107, 108, 114
eating disorders, 68, 70
educational achievement, 71–5, 77,
   89, 90, 132, 133, 135, 165
emotional education, 34–6, 45, 59,
   63, 201, 204, 219, 234, 236, 240
exclusion from school, 5, 7, 75–85,
   145, 232, 240
friendships, 49–55, 134, 138,
   205, 241
hierarchy, 52–3, 59, 63, 89, 94, 114
homosexuality, 33, 39–40, 42,
   61–7, 103
language development, 21, 24, 36
literacy, 72–5, 230
machismo, 55, 59, 135
media, 42–5, 67–70
mental health, 68, 70, 77, 79, 231–2
peer groups, 49–60, 89–90, 91, 95,
   107–14, 134, 205
physicality, 3, 16, 21, 37, 49, 51, 53
pornography, 95–106
risk taking behaviour, 27
school, 49–85, 89, 96, 100, 105–6,
   108, 111, 113–21, 128
segregation, 31–3, 44–5, 49–55, 89,
   114, 147, 224, 230–3, 241
siblings, 41–2, 138, 239
sports, 16, 25, 26, 27, 39, 49, 56–8,
   65, 69, 80
status, 49–60, 89–90, 91, 95, 107–8
stoicism, 4, 54, 89, 114
toy choices, 20–1, 25, 28–34, 44, 46,
   50, 55, 58, 194
violence, 53, 59, 90–5
Boyhood, 229
Boys from the Blackstuff, 10
brain organisation theory, 18–25,
   45–6
brain size, 23, 24
Brainstorm (Jordan-Young), 21
Branson, Richard, 180
Brentwood County High School,
   Essex, 82

Bristol Dads, 30, 46, 166, 173
Bristol University, 91–3
British Broadcasting Corporation
   (BBC), 43, 101, 131, 194
British Folk Art, 9–10
British National Surveys of Sexual
   Attitudes and Lifestyles, 102
British Social Attitudes, 193
Brooker, Charlie, 168
Brooks, Gwendolyn, 132
Brooks, Mel, 30
Brooks, Rebekah, 149
Bullet Boy, 160
bullying, 41, 52–3, 58–9, 62, 64, 66, 89,
   114, 233
Burgess, Adrienne, 168

C
Calvinism, 130
Cambridge University, 18, 239
Cameron, David, 143
Campaign Against Living Miserably
   (CALM), 141, 216, 218, 220–2,
   230, 241
Campbell, Beatrix, 188
camping, 6, 16, 206, 209
Canada, 170, 181
Canterbury Christ Church Univer-
   sity, 99
care homes, 135
career progression, 6
Carney, Mick, 156–61
Carney's Community, 139, 157–61,
   169, 230, 241
CBeebies, 43, 194
Cement Garden, The (McEwan), 39
Centre for Mental Health, 140,
   141, 145
cerebral palsy, 223–4
Changing Men Publishing
   Collective, 7
Charlie and Lola, 43
Cheerios, 170
Chicago, Illinois, 144

child abuse, 113, 148
childcare, 184–5, 195
childlessness, 212–13
children's books, 30–1, 33, 194, 231, 234, 237
Children's Commissioner, 80, 81, 96, 98, 100, 107
Chippendales, 68
Christianity, 130
Chu, Judy, 54–5, 59, 235
City of London School, 64–5, 69–70, 74–5, 238
class, *see* social class
Clegg, Nick, 176–7
Clinton, Hillary, 190
clothing, 12, 40–1, 42, 49, 63, 234
co-rumination, 51
Coalition Government, 137, 176–7, 214
Cockburn, Cynthia, 145–6
Cognitive Behavioural Therapy (CBT), 144
colour-coding, 32–3, 184
community, 6, 9, 11, 12, 138, 158, 173, 201, 203, 236–7
competitiveness, 21, 53, 54, 207
computer games, 42, 95
Condou, Charlie, 42, 49, 63–4, 183, 187–8, 196, 197
conformity, 35, 38, 54, 56, 62–3, 75, 77, 103, 196, 207, 220, 229, 235
Connell, Raewyn, 78, 135
Connexions, 126
consent, *see* sexual consent
conservatism, 6, 29, 115, 193–4
Conservative Party, 115, 119, 137, 143, 146, 184, 214
'coolness', 58, 78–9, 128–30, 142, 157, 219
Cosslett, Rhiannon Lucy, 117
Counting Dead Women, 146
CP Teens UK, 224
Crimean War (1853–6), 10
Criminal Justice Act (1991), 146

criminality, 7, 9, 12, 107–8, 125, 127–48, 155–6, 159–60, 169, 214, 232, 240
  and education, 133, 135, 232
  gangs, 7, 12, 107–8, 125, 127–32, 139, 142, 155–6, 169, 240
  as male problem, 144–8, 220
  and marginalisation, 125, 131–2, 134
  and mental health, 140–4
  prison, 125, 130, 135, 139–40, 169, 214, 233
  and role models, 136–9, 153
  and sexual violence, 107–8
  and status, 107–8, 127, 131, 135, 142, 156
'Crisis in Modern Masculinity, A' (CALM), 216
crisis of masculinity, 7, 111, 216
Crown Prosecution Service, 150
curriculum for life, 114

D
Dadly Arts, The, 166–7
Dahlgren, Lennart, 178
Daily Telegraph, 29
dangerous driving, 7, 125, 141, 145, 214
DeGeneres, Ellen, 12
Delaney, Rob, 17
Delusions of Gender (Fine), 19
Denmark, 181
Department for Education, 80
Department of Business, Innovation and Skills, 187
Department of Health, 220, 222
depression, 141, 171, 176, 214–22
determinism, *see* biological determinism
Dines, Gail, 101–3
disablism, 115
discipline, 37–9, 240
divorce, 209–10
Doc McStuffins, 43

dog analogy, 3–4
dolls, 20, 25, 28, 29, 30–1, 33, 36, 46,
  50, 55, 194–5
domestic inequalities, 6, 28, 36, 126,
  165–98, 236
domestic violence, 90–5, 115, 139,
  146–55
  against men, 148–51
  gender-neutral approach, 145–8
  intimate terrorism, 149
  self-blaming, 91–2, 154
  situational couple violence, 149
  treatment of perpetrators, 151–5
Domestic Violence Intervention Project, 94, 150, 152, 230
dominance, 8, 45, 46, 89, 104, 107,
  108, 114, 153, 155
Drew, Stephen, 81–5, 230
driving, 7, 125, 141, 145, 214
drugs, 127, 131, 141, 201, 206, 214
Duckett, Chris, 74
Dude, You're a Fag (Pascoe), 63
Duggan, Mark, 129

E
Eastwood, Clint, 201
eating disorders, 6, 68, 70
Eaton Foundation, 230–1
Edinburgh University, 109
Educating Essex, 81
education, 71–85, 89, 90, 105–6,
  113–21, 128, 129, 132, 133, 135,
  231–3, 241
  bad behaviour, 75–85, 231
  and class/ethnicity, 71–2,
    80–1, 132
  and coolness, 78–9, 128, 129
  and criminality, 133, 135, 232
  emotional, 34–6, 45, 59, 63, 201,
    219, 234, 236, 240
  exclusion from, 5, 7, 75–85, 145,
    232, 240
  and gender, 71–2
  literacy, 72–5, 230

Personal, Social, Health and
  Economic education (PSHE),
  114–19, 231
  school isolation, 83
  segregation, 50, 73, 75, 147, 231,
    232–3, 241
  sex education, 105–6, 113–21, 231
  special educational needs (SEN),
    80, 85
  university lad culture, 109–14, 121
Educational Maintenance
  Allowance, 126
Eliot, Lise, 19–20
emotion, 4, 5, 9, 11, 24, 34–6, 45,
  58–9, 61, 63, 160, 197, 201, 204–9,
  213–15, 221–2, 224–5, 229, 233,
  234, 236, 240
emotional education, 34–6, 45, 59, 63,
  201, 204, 219, 234, 236, 240
empathising–systemising (ES) theory,
  19–20
empathy, 11, 18–19, 35, 61, 112
employment, 4, 6, 10, 11, 75, 125–6,
  132, 137, 155, 165–70, 176–85,
  186, 188–94, 201, 208, 211, 217,
  221, 233–6, 239, 240
  and criminality, 132
  and parenting, 126, 137, 165–70,
    176–85, 186, 188–94, 233–6, 239
  pay gap, 6, 165–6, 211, 239
  sexism, 239
  and suicide, 221
  unemployment, 75, 125–6, 132, 155,
    171, 221, 233
  working hours, 137, 167–70, 183–4,
    189, 191–2, 233–4
  workplace stress, 6, 217, 233–4
End of Equality (Campbell), 188
End of Men, The (Rosin), 166
End Violence Against Women, 152
England riots (2011), 129, 132–4
English Defence League (EDL),
  129, 130
English Literature, 73–4

English Longitudinal Study of
Ageing, 212
entitlement, 94, 113, 147, 148, 153, 211
Equalities Office, 29, 190
Equality and Human Rights Commission, 72
Equality for Mental Health, 215
Essential Difference, The (Baron-Cohen), 18–19
European Union (EU), 184
Everyday Sexism (website), 107
exclusion from education, 5, 7, 75–85, 145, 232, 240

F
Facebook, 112
'fag discourse', 63, 103
Faludi, Susan, 211
family life, 6, 9, 11, 12, 16–17, 126–7, 136–9, 153, 165–98, 208–10, 235–6
Fatherhood Institute, 169, 230
Fatherhood Reclaimed (Burgess), 168
fatherhood revolution, 170
fatherhood, fathering, 11, 17, 29–30, 34–41, 46, 127, 136–7, 166–98, 209–10, 233–6, 239, 241
   absence, 136–7, 169, 193
   discipline, 38–9
   divorce, 209–10
   emotional education, 34–6
   employment, 137, 167–70, 176–85, 186, 188–94, 233–6, 239
   hands-on, 11, 172
   homophobia, 33, 39–40
   maternity services, 173–6
   paternity leave, 176–82, 186, 188, 195, 233
   role specialisation, 165–98
   rough-and-tumble play, 37
   social pretend play, 36
   toy choices, 29, 46, 58
Feltham Young Offender Institution, 141–3

female genital mutilation (FGM), 151
Femicide Census: Profiles of Women Killed by Men, 147
Feminine Mystique, The (Friedan), 5
femininity, 4, 5, 6, 16, 18, 22, 29, 36, 38, 39, 43, 49, 58, 78, 79, 89, 92, 152, 195, 203
feminism, 8, 12, 25, 132, 151, 154, 187, 193, 220, 222, 237–41
Feminism and Men (van der Gaag), 170
Feminist Society, 64, 238
Fine, Cordelia, 19–21, 24
Firmin, Carlene, 107
Fitzroy Lodge, London, 127, 156–61
Foden, Ben, 195
Fogg, Ally, 150
football, 3, 4, 16, 25, 26, 38, 42, 50, 56–7, 111, 129, 130, 135, 137, 202, 206, 209, 210, 223
Force Majeure, 179
forced marriage, 151
45 Years, 229
France, 215
Free to Be … You and Me (Thomas), 30
Freshers' Week, 110, 112
Friedan, Betty, 5
friendships, 6, 7, 9, 11, 26, 49–55, 134, 138, 201–13, 214, 222–4, 229, 236, 239, 241
Fryer, Mark, 74
Full Monty, The, 68
'functional family therapy program', 232
Future Jobs Fund, 126

G
gambling, 10
gaming, 42, 95
gangs, 7, 12, 107–8, 125, 127–32, 139, 142, 155–6, 169, 240
Gap, 12
gay people, *see under* homosexuality
geekiness, 11, 39
gender, 17–18, 146

gender binary, 18, 21, 65–6
gender identity disorder, 66
gender neutral childhood, 5,
    30–1, 237
gender stereotypes, 5–16, 24–5,
    29–31, 33–4, 36, 38, 41, 44, 46, 50,
    53–6, 60, 74–8, 84, 89, 104–5, 111,
    136, 148–9, 157, 159, 182, 220,
    223, 229, 230–3, 237, 241
Gender Diary, 27, 32, 34, 44, 190
Gender Police, The (Ball and Millar), 27
Gender Trap, The (Kane), 16
Geordie Shore, 69
Germany, 109, 112, 179, 183, 215
Glenn Inquiry into Child Abuse and
    Domestic Violence, 148
global financial crisis (2007–8), 125,
    126, 221
Good Lad workshops, 113
Gosforth Academy, Newcastle upon
    Tyne, 69, 73, 230
Gove, Michael, 143
Grand Theft Auto V, 95
Gray, John, 19
Grayling, Chris, 143
Great Men, 56, 60, 65, 67, 96, 100, 104,
    230, 238
Green, Susie, 65–6
Greenham Common Women's Peace
    Camp (1981–2000), 222
greetings cards, 3
Grylls, Bear, 137
Guardian, 23, 133, 196
Guyland (Kimmel), 103
gyms, 69, 206

H
Hadley, Robin, 212–13
hands-on fatherhood, 11, 172
Harley, James, 218–19
Harris, Toby, 143–4
Harvard Business School, 182
health

mental, 68, 70, 77, 79, 140–4, 176,
    213–22, 223, 231–2, 233, 241
physical, 6, 7, 203, 223, 224
HeForShe campaign, 238
Hegedus, Nathan, 178
hierarchy, 4, 52–3, 59, 63, 89, 94, 114,
    127, 233, 240
Hine, Ben, 28
Hirst, Keegan, 219–20
Holden, Stephen S., 195
homelessness, 125
homosexuality, 11, 33, 39–40, 42,
    61–7, 103, 115–16, 150, 170, 182–
    3, 195–6, 207, 212, 213, 219–20
and bullying, 62–4
and domestic violence, 150
fag discourse, 63, 103
and friendship, 207
homophobia, 33, 39–40, 115–16,
    195, 219–20
and old age, 212, 213
parenting, 42, 49–50, 182–3,
    170, 196
and play/toy choices, 33, 39–40
and suicide, 219–20
honour killings, 151
hooks, bell, 132, 240
Horvath, Miranda, 99, 104, 115, 117
hostels, 139, 140
housework, 28, 36, 168, 182
housing benefit, 126
Howard League for Penal Reform, 144

I
IBM, 180
Iceland, 181, 182
Inclusive Minds, 231
Independent, 23
Independent Age, 212
Indigo, 36, 49, 77, 97
Ingala Smith, Karen, 146–7, 153
Intensive Supervision and Surveillance
    Project, 157

Internet, 11, 27, 42, 43–4, 116–17, 119, 120–1
  censorship, 119
  pornography, 11, 95–106, 114, 116, 117, 119, 120–1
  social media, 11, 112
intimate terrorism, 149
involuntarily childlessness, 212–13
iRights campaign, 120
Iron John (Bly), 6
Is Britain Fairer?, 72
Islam, 130, 224

J

Jackman, Hugh, 68
Jakobsson, Hampus, 180
Jamal, Ben, 94–5, 150, 152, 154, 155
Jay Z, 137
Joel, Daphna, 22
Johnson, Michael, 149
Jordan-Young, Rebecca, 21
Justice for Men and Boys Party, 8, 149

K

Kane, Emily, 16, 39
Kanter, Catherine, 42
Keele University, 213
Kelly, Liz, 152, 154
Kemp, Ross, 149
Kimmel, Michael, 55, 103, 108, 171, 211, 224
Knausgaard, Karl Ove, 179
Knight, Glenn, 141
Kyle, Jeremy, 149

L

Labour Party, 73, 129, 137, 174, 184
lad culture, 109–14, 121
lads' mags, 67–8, 96
Lambeth and Wandsworth Youth Offending teams, 157
Lammy, David, 129–30, 133, 136–7, 138, 156, 174, 188, 196, 197

language development, 21, 24, 36
Laux, Cameron, 42
Lee, Josh, 29–30, 46, 166, 173, 174, 195
Lego, 16, 31, 50
Lemberg, Raymond, 70
Let Toys Be Toys, 33, 230
LGBT (lesbian, gay, bisexual, and transgender), 11, 33, 39–40, 42, 61, 62–7, 103, 113, 115–16, 150, 170, 182–3, 195, 196, 207, 212, 213, 219–20
Liben, Lynn S., 23
Liberal Democrats, 137, 176–7, 214
life expectancy, 224
Lightman, Brian, 80
literacy, 72–5, 230
literature, 73–4
London Metropolitan University, 152
London Review of Books, 7
London School of Economics, 109, 133
London 7/7 bombings (2005), 129
loneliness, 201–24
  low-income, 210–11
Los Angeles Lakers, 194–5
love ethic, 240
low-income loneliness, 210–11
Lumbersexuals, 10–11
Lunn, Alex, 69, 74

M

machismo, 4, 55, 59, 135, 158, 159, 179, 240
Made in Chelsea, 69
magazines, 67–8, 96, 179
Magic Mike XXL, 68
Malamuth, Neil, 98, 100, 101
male bonding, 6, 10, 55
Manjoo, Rashida, 148
marginalisation, 125, 131–2, 134
marriage, 209–11
masculinity, *see* men, masculinity
Massey, Kristina, 99

maternal gatekeeping, 187
maternity leave, 176; *see also* parental
    leave
maternity services, 173–6
McBroom, Andrew, 64, 74
McEwan, Ian, 39
Mead, Margaret, 237
Mean Girls, 53
media, 22–4, 27, 42–4, 67–70, 113,
    170, 178, 179, 194, 233
    advertising, 12, 31, 43, 100, 170, 178
    children's books, 30–1, 33, 194, 231,
        234, 237
    computer games, 42, 95
    Internet, 11, 27, 42, 43–4, 116–17,
        119, 120–1
    magazines, 67–8, 96, 179
    television, 27, 30, 42–4, 69, 101,
        131, 194
men, masculinity
    aggression, 6, 9, 19, 22, 34–5, 38,
        43, 52, 53, 58, 59, 76–7, 89, 131,
        146, 158, 214
    assertiveness, 15, 18, 27, 34–5,
        76–7, 89
    body image, 67–70, 104
    bonding, 6, 10, 55
    childlessness, 212–13
    community, 6, 9, 11, 12, 138, 158,
        173, 201, 203, 236–7
    competitiveness, 21, 53, 54, 207
    conformity, 38, 54, 56, 62–3, 75,
        103, 196, 207, 220, 229, 235
    criminality, 7, 9, 12, 107–8, 125,
        127–36, 139–48, 155–6, 159–60,
        169, 214, 240
    crisis of masculinity, 7, 111, 216
    dominance, 8, 45, 46, 89, 104, 107,
        108, 114, 153, 155
    eating disorders, 68, 70
    educational achievement, 71–5, 77,
        89, 90, 132, 133, 135, 165
    emotion, 4, 5, 9, 11, 24, 34–6, 45,
        58–9, 61, 63, 160, 197, 201, 204–9,

    213–15, 221–2, 224–5, 229, 233,
        234, 236, 240
    employment, 4, 6, 10, 11, 75,
        125–6, 132, 137, 155, 165–70,
        201, 208, 211, 217, 221, 233–4,
        239, 240
    entitlement, 94, 113, 147, 148,
        153, 211
    family life, 6, 9, 11, 12, 127, 136–9,
        153, 165–98, 208–10, 235–6
    fatherhood, fathering, 11, 17, 29–30,
        34–41, 46, 127, 136–7, 166–98,
        209–10, 233–6, 239, 241
    friendships, 6, 7, 9, 11, 26, 49–55,
        134, 138, 201–13, 214, 222–4, 229,
        236, 239, 241
    health 6, 7, 203, 223, 224
    hierarchy, 4, 52–3, 59, 89, 94, 114,
        233, 240
    homosexuality, 33, 39–40, 42, 61–7,
        103, 113, 195
    lad culture, 109–14, 121
    loneliness, 201–24
    machismo, 4, 55, 59, 135, 158, 159,
        179, 240
    marginalisation, 125, 131–2, 134
    media, 42–5, 67–70
    mental health, 140–4, 176, 213–22,
        223, 231–2, 233, 241
    navigation, 22–3
    old age, 211–13
    peer groups, 49–60, 89–90, 91, 95,
        107–14, 134, 153, 205, 239
    policing of behaviour, 38, 51, 55, 59,
        63, 64, 109–10
    privilege, 94, 95, 125, 148, 165,
        167, 238
    role models, 136–9, 153
    spatial visualisation, 22
    sports, 3, 4, 16, 25, 26, 27, 39, 49,
        56–8, 65, 69, 80, 109, 110–12,
        127–8, 129, 130, 135, 137,
        156–61, 194–5, 202, 206, 209, 210,
        219–20, 223

status, 4, 9, 52–3, 56, 60, 89–90, 92,
  107–8, 110, 127, 131, 135, 156
stoicism, 4, 54, 89, 114
suicide, 5, 7, 144, 215–22, 231
systems, understanding of, 19
violence, 6, 9, 22, 43, 53, 59, 90–104,
  107–8, 115, 116, 125, 129, 132–4,
  139, 144, 145, 146–55, 229, 240
violence against, 148–51
women, treatment of, 6, 9, 11, 39,
  45, 60, 78, 89–121, 146–55, 241
*Men Are from Mars, Women Are from
  Venus* (Gray), 19, 121
Men's Health, 68
men's rights, 8, 11–12, 133, 148–9, 151
Men's Shed initiative, 222–3
mental health, 68, 70, 77, 79, 140–4,
  176, 213–22, 223, 231–2, 233, 241
Mental Health America, 79
Mermaids, 65
Metrosexuals, 10
middle-class, 74, 78, 111, 113
midwives, 173–5
Millar, James, 27, 34, 46, 190–1
Miller, Tina, 172
Mind, 77
misogyny, 11, 32, 90, 95, 109, 114, 121,
  147, 149
Montenegro, 109
mood board, 67
Moravcsik, Andrew, 190–1
Morgan, Nicky, 114
Morocco, 131
motherhood, mothering, 3, 6, 9,
  15–17, 25–32, 34–8, 126–7,
  165–6, 168, 170, 173–6, 181–2,
  185–90, 193–4
  community, 203
  discipline, 37–8
  emotional education, 34–6
  employment, 6, 126, 165–6, 168,
    170, 181–2, 186, 189–90, 193–4,
    239
  expectations, 15–17, 25–8

maternity leave, 176
pregnancy, 15, 173–6
role specialisation, 165–98
social pretend play, 36
toy choices, 29, 31, 58
Moxon, Steve, 149
Mr Drew's School for Boys, 81
MsUnderstood, 107
multitasking, 22–3
murder, 108, 125, 145–6, 151–2
mythopoetic men's movement, 6

N

National Health Service (NHS), 65–6,
  146, 175, 214
National Society for the Prevention of
  Cruelty to Children (NSPCC), 91–3
National Union of Students (NUS),
  105, 109, 112, 115
navigation, 22–3
NEETs (not in education, employment
  or training), 126, 155
Netflix, 179
Netherlands, 183–4
neurology, 19–25, 45–6, 134
neuromotor skills, 24
Neverland, 43
New Deal for Schools, 73
New Economics Foundation, 234
New Lads and Men, 10
New York Times, 6
New York University, 63, 134
New Zealand, 148
newspapers, 67
Nia Project, 146
Nick Jr., 43
Nina and the Neurons, 43
Norway, 177, 179, 181, 182
Nottingham University, 109

O

Oakley, Ann, 145–6
Obama, Barack, 170
Of Woman Born (Rich), 192

Ofcom, 99
Office for National Statistics (ONS), 91, 165
Ofsted, 71, 85, 115
Ohlsson, Birgitta, 179
old age, 211–13
Oliver, Jamie, 170
Open University, 137, 153
Organisation for Economic Co-operation and Development (OECD), 73, 77, 167, 184
outdoorsmanship, 6, 16, 206, 209
Owen Blakemore, Judith E., 23

P

paedophilia, 213
parenthood, parenting, 3, 6, 9, 11, 15–17, 25–32, 34–41, 46, 126–7, 136–7, 165–98, 233–6, 239
  adoption, 196
  childcare, 184–5, 195
  community, 203
  discipline, 37–9, 240
  divorce, 209–10
  emotional education, 34–6, 45, 59, 63, 201, 219, 234, 236, 240
  employment, 126, 137, 165–70, 176–85, 186, 188–94, 233–6, 239
  expectations, 15–17, 25–8
  homophobia, 33, 39–40
  parental leave, 176–82, 186, 188, 195, 233
  role specialisation, 165–98
  rough-and-tumble play, 37, 49
  same sex, 42, 49–50, 170, 182–3, 196
  sex education, 105–6, 115–17, 119–21
  social pretend play, 36
  toy choices, 29, 31, 58
parental leave, 176–82, 186, 188, 195, 233
'Parental Leave Dad!', 178, 195

part-time work, 168, 170, 183–4, 190, 193
Pascoe, C. J., 63
Patel, Pragna, 151
paternity leave, 176–82, 186, 188, 195, 233
patriarchy, 8, 18, 25, 39, 90, 132, 147, 148, 151, 237, 238, 240
Paw Patrol, 43
pay gap, 6, 165–6, 211, 239
Peckham, London, 136, 139
pecking orders, 52–3, 59, 63, 89, 94, 114, 233
peer groups, 49–60, 89–90, 91, 95, 107–14, 134, 153, 205, 239
Perry, Grayson, 11
Perry, Sarah, 56, 100
Personal, Social, Health and Economic education (PSHE), 114–19, 231
Pew Research Center, 211
physicality, 3, 16, 21, 37, 49, 51, 53
Pickert, Nils, 40–1
Pink Brain, Blue Brain (Eliot), 19
pink bus tour, 184
'Playing for Success', 137
policing of behaviour, 38, 51, 55, 59, 63, 64, 109–10
polygamy, 151
Pornhub, 96
pornography, 11, 95–106, 114, 116, 117, 119, 120–1
Porter, Tony, 61
poverty, 125, 182, 210–11, 212
Powell, Jane, 141, 216, 218, 220–2
Pratt, Chris, 68, 70
pregnancy, 15–17, 173–6
'premature self-congratulation', 171
Princeton University, 190
prison, 5, 75, 125, 130, 135, 139–40, 169, 214, 233
private schools, 111, 159
privilege, 94, 95, 125, 148, 165, 167, 238
Project Mirabal, 152–4

Q

Queen Bees and Wannabes (Wiseman), 53
quilt-making, 10

R

race, racism, 71–2, 80–1, 111, 113,
    129, 130, 132, 133, 157, 167, 220
Raising Boys (Biddulph), 25
rape, 101, 108, 109, 116, 148
Reading the Riots project, 133
recession, 125, 126, 221
Reflection and Intervention Zone, 84
Relate, 202, 208
REMEMBER, 218–19
revenge porn, 114
Rich, Adrienne, 192, 238
Rigby, Lee, 129
'right to wipe' campaign, 120
Ringleaders and Sidekicks
    (Wiseman), 119
riots, 129, 132–4
risk-taking behaviour, 27
role models, 136–9, 153
role specialisation, 165–98
Rosin, Hanna, 166
Ross, Diana, 30
rough-and-tumble play, 16, 37, 49, 53
Royal College of Midwives, 174
Royal College of Psychiatrists, 215
Royal United Hospital, Bath, 175
Rudd, Paul, 70
Rugby League, 219–20
rugby, 25, 57, 65, 69, 109, 110, 112,
    195, 219–20
Ryan, Shane, 125, 126

S

Samaritans, 203, 207, 215
Sanders, Jeremy, 239
Saunders, Alison, 150
Saunt, Katherine 74–5
schizophrenia, 141
schools, *see under* education
Scott, Byron, 194–5

segregation, 31–3, 44–5, 49–55, 89,
    114, 147, 224, 230–3, 241
    in classroom, 50, 73, 75, 147, 231,
        232–3, 241
    of peer groups, 49–55, 89, 114,
        147, 224
    of play and toys, 31–3, 37, 44–5, 49,
        194, 230, 231
separation, 209–10
sex, 17–18
sex education, 105–6, 113–21, 231
sexism, 6, 7, 9, 15, 25, 31, 43, 89, 148,
    170, 239, 240
    and biological determinism, 6,
        15, 25
    and employment, 239
    and lad culture, 109–14, 121
    in media, 43, 170, 194, 233
    and misogyny, 11, 32, 90, 95, 109,
        114, 121, 147, 149
    and power, 89–90, 95, 104, 114, 153,
        155, 240
sexting, 114, 118–19
sexual consent, 95, 105, 113, 114,
    115, 117
sexual exploitation, 113, 115
sexual harassment, 6, 90, 109–14, 119
sexual panic, 112
sexual violence, 95–104, 107–8, 115,
    116, 145–8
    and dominance, 89, 90–1, 94–5, 104,
        107–8
    and gangs, 107
    and pornography, 95–104, 114, 116
    victim blaming, 107
'shoulder to shoulder' friendships,
    201–2
siblings, 41–2, 138, 239
Silicon Valley, 180
Simpson, Mark, 10
'sissy', 4, 6, 39, 41
situational couple violence, 149
Slaughter, Anne-Marie, 190
Smith, Lynnette, 116

So Solid Crew, 131
social class, 63, 71–2, 74, 105, 111,
    113, 126, 133, 134, 210–11
social hierarchy, 4, 52–3, 59, 63, 89, 94,
    114, 127, 233, 240
social isolation, 203, 205, 210, 212
social media, 11, 112
social networks, 158, 173, 203–13,
    222–4, 236
social pretend play, 36
socialisation, 4, 23, 26–46, 49,
    141, 215
Southall Black Sisters, 151
Spain, 31, 215
spatial visualisation, 22
special educational needs (SEN),
    80, 85
spiking drinks, 110
Spornosexuals, 10–11
sports, 3, 4, 16, 25, 26, 27, 38, 39, 42,
    49, 50, 53, 56–8, 65, 69, 80, 109,
    110–12, 127–8, 129, 130, 135, 137,
    156–61, 194–5, 202, 206, 209, 210,
    219–20, 223
status, 4, 9, 49–60, 52–3, 56, 60, 89–90,
    91–2, 95, 107–8, 110, 127, 131,
    135, 156
stereotypes, 5–16, 24–5, 29–31, 33–4,
    36, 38, 41, 44, 46, 50, 53–6, 60,
    74–8, 84, 89, 104–5, 111, 136,
    148–9, 157, 159, 182, 220, 223,
    229, 230–3, 237, 241
Stewart, Jay, 66–7
Stiffed (Faludi), 211
stoicism, 4, 54, 89, 114
Stonewall, 62, 212
Stony Brook University, 55
Stop Porn Culture organisation, 95
strong man myth, 213–15
Student Room, The (website), 92
suicide, 5, 7, 144, 215–22, 231
Suicide Prevention Strategy for
    England, 220
Sun, 149

Sunday Mirror, 219–20
Super Bowl, 171
superheroes, 44, 46, 50
Swashbuckle, 43
Sweden, 97, 178–9, 180, 181, 182,
    183, 234
Sweet, Elizabeth, 31
Swinson, Jo, 29–30

T
Tate Britain, 9–10
Tavistock and Portman NHS
    Trust, 65
TED (Technology, Entertainment,
    Design), 61
television, 27, 30, 42–4, 69, 101,
    131, 194
terrorism, 129
testosterone, 19, 20, 77
'They Go the Extra Mile' report, 81
Thicke, Robin, 95
Thomas, Marlo, 30
Threlfall, David, 131
tomboys, 39, 41, 113
Topsy and Tim, 194
Torremolinos, Spain, 31
Tottenham, London, 129–30
TOWIE, 69
toys, 20–1, 25, 28–34, 44, 46, 50, 55,
    58, 194, 230
transgender people, 65–7
Tree Fu Tom, 43
'Troops to Teachers' initiative, 137
Turner, George, 139–40, 142,
    157–61
Twitter, 27, 82, 190

U
'unboxing' videos, 43
Unconditional Positive Regard, 82
unconscious bias, 231, 239
unemployment, 75, 125–6, 132, 155,
    171, 221, 233
United Nations (UN), 148, 238

United States, 179, 181, 190, 215, 232, 234
universities, 109–14
University of Bedfordshire, 107
University of California, 98
University of Kent, 76
University of Oregon, 63
University of Pennsylvania, 22

V

van der Gaag, Nikki, 170
'Velvet Dads', 178
Verma, Ragini, 22–3
violence, 6, 9, 22, 43, 53, 59, 90–104, 107–8, 115, 116, 125, 129, 132–4, 139, 144, 145, 146–55, 229, 240
  bullying, 53, 59, 94
  crime, 107–8, 125, 129, 132–4, 139, 144, 145, 146, 240
  domestic, 90–5, 115, 139, 146–55
  honour-based, 151
  intimate terrorism, 149
  pornography, 95–104, 114
  riots, 129, 132–4
  sexual, 95–104, 107–8, 115, 116, 145–8
  situational couple violence, 149
Violence against Women and Girls Crime Report, 150
Virgin Management, 180

W

Wade, Lisa, 201, 207
Wade, Rebekah, 149
Walking Football, 223
Walters, Ashley, 130–1, 133, 136, 160, 196–7, 206
Wandsworth, London, 134
Washington State Institute of Public Policy, 232
Way, Niobe, 63, 134
'We Real Cool' (Brooks), 132
We Real Cool: Black Men and Masculinity (hooks), 132

Wessely, Simon, 215
Westmarland, Nicole, 154
Westminster, 29, 66, 72, 73, 80, 81, 91, 96, 98, 100, 107, 113, 114–15, 119, 137, 143, 145, 146, 147, 174, 176–7, 184, 190, 195, 214, 220, 222, 231
What Should We Tell Our Daughters? (Benn), 106
When Boys Become Boys (Chu), 54
'Why Women Still Can't Have It All' (Slaughter), 190
widowers, 209, 212
Will to Change, The (hooks), 240
William's Doll (Zolotow), 30–1
Williams, Rowan, 207
Wiseman, Rosalind, 53, 119–20
Woman Racket, The (Moxon), 149
women, femininity, 4, 5, 6, 18, 22, 29, 36, 38, 39, 43, 49, 58, 78, 79, 89, 92, 152, 195, 203
  aggression, 53, 76
  behaviour at school, 76–7
  co-rumination, 51
  domestic responsibilities, 126
  educational achievement, 71–2, 77–8, 90, 166
  empathy, 18–19, 35
  employment, 6, 126, 137, 165–6, 168, 170, 181–2, 186, 189–90, 193
  family life, 16–17, 126, 165, 167, 170, 173–6, 181–2, 185–8, 189, 193
  friendships, 49–51, 203, 207
  language development, 24, 36
  literacy, 72–5
  media, 42–4
  motherhood, mothering, 3, 6, 9, 15–17, 25–32, 34–8, 126–7, 165–6, 168, 170, 173–6, 181–2, 185–90, 193–4
  multitasking, 22–3
  pay gap, 6, 165–6, 211, 239

physicality, 37, 49
segregation, 31–3, 44–5, 49–55, 89,
    114, 147, 224, 230–3, 241
suicide, 215
toy choices, 20–1, 28–34, 44,
    55, 194
violence against, 90–104, 107–8,
    115, 116, 139, 146–55
violence against men, 148–51
Women's Aid, 147
Women's Equality Party, 187
work, *see under* employment

Working With Men, 125
working-class, 63, 71, 105, 111, 126,
    133, 134, 210–11

Y
YouGov, 216
Young Dads Collective, 79, 230
Young Women's Trust, 126
YouTube, 43

Z
'Zeus energy', 6

Rebecca Asher has worked in television news and current affairs and as the Deputy Editor of *Woman's Hour* and an executive producer at BBC Radio 4. Her first book was *Shattered: Modern Motherhood and the Illusion of Equality*. Her experiences as a mother of both a boy and a girl inspired her to write this book.